Are Southern Baptists "Evangelicals"?

213

Are Southern Baptists "Evangelicals"?

by James Leo Garrett, Jr.
E. Glenn Hinson
James E. Tull

Mercer University Press
Macon, Ga. 31207

ISBN 0-86554-033-0

All books published by Mercer University Press are produced
on acid-free paper that exceeds the minimum standards set by the
National Historical Publications and Records Commission.

Library of Congress Cataloging in Publication Data

Garrett, James Leo.
    Are Southern Baptists "Evangelicals"?

    Bibliography: p. 233.
    Includes index of persons.
    1. Southern Baptist Convention.   2. Evangelicalism—
United States.   I. Hinson, E. Glenn.   II. Tull,
James E.   III. Title.
BX6462.7.G37   1983   286'.132   82-18870
ISBN 0-86554-033-0

Table of Contents

Preface

This book is a historical-theological study of the question as to whether Southern Baptists are and ought to be reckoned as "Evangelicals." It has been written amid the publication of numerous books and articles about Evangelical Christians in the United States during the 1970s and early 1980s. It reflects a growing awareness among Southern Baptists that questions about their identities with, differences from, and relations with Evangelical Christians ought to be explored and clarified. It does not address directly the political involvements of Evangelicals and/or Southern Baptists during recent years.

These pages consist of a fraternal debate which has as its purpose the clarification of who Southern Baptists have been, are, and ought to be. Its purpose is not to divide or disrupt but to enlighten and strengthen.

Garrett's three basic chapters grew out of the Carver-Barnes Lectures which he delivered at Southeastern Baptist Theological Seminary, Wake Forest, North Carolina, in November 1979. Chapters one and two were essentially delivered on that lectureship, whereas chapter three has been expanded beyond the somewhat sketchy form in which it was presented in Wake Forest.

Garrett wishes to express his gratitude to the faculty of Southeastern Baptist Theological Seminary for the invitation to deliver the Carver-Barnes Lectures, so fittingly named for two distinguished Southern Baptist educators. Especially are thanks due to Dr. T. Furman Hewitt, chairman of the faculty's committee on convocations, special lectures, and missionary days. To Baylor University and to Southwestern Baptist Theological Seminary for jointly providing a sabbatical leave during which this research was undertaken Garrett is also grateful.

Hinson's four basic chapters are an outgrowth of lectures given in November 1980 to the Historical Society of the South Carolina Baptist

State Convention in Columbia, the Wilkinson Lectures for 1980 at Northern Baptist Theological Seminary in Chicago, and four lectures delivered to the Pastors' School of the University of Richmond in July 1981. All four lectures have undergone revision as a consequence of interaction with these audiences.

Hinson wishes to thank each of those responsible for extending invitations to do the kind of brainstorming represented in this book. Numerous letters in response to the published paper (now one of these four chapters) "Baptists and Evangelicals: What Is the Difference?" have helped to sharpen the argument at several points. Some comments on this presentation by Professor Eric H. Ohlmann of Northern Baptist Theological Seminary were especially helpful in clarifying use of the term "evangelical."

Appreciation is also due to four of Garrett's faculty colleagues at Southwestern Baptist Theological Seminary, each of whom has read critically a chapter or more of this book and offered important comments and suggestions: Dr. H. Leon McBeth, Dr. Ebbie C. Smith, Dr. W. Boyd Hunt, and Dr. John P. Newport. Gratitude is expressed to Mrs. Carol M. Simpson, Mrs. Dora Etta Bridgford, Mrs. Sheri Kuenzle, and Miss Jacquelyn Madon for the preparation of the typescript.

We are indebted to Mr. Paul A. Basden and Mr. Mark E. Matheson, Ph.D. students and teaching fellows in theology at Southwestern Baptist Theological Seminary, for the preparation of the index of persons.

We are deeply grateful to Professor James E. Tull of Southeastern Baptist Theological Seminary for providing the insightful introduction and conclusion to the volume. Mercer University Press requested that Professor Tull write his introduction *before* examining any of our chapters, and write his conclusion *after* examining all that we had written.

James Leo Garrett, Jr.   E. Glenn Hinson
Fort Worth, Texas   Louisville, Kentucky
                              27 January 1982

Introduction

"Evangelicals" and Baptists
—the Shape of the Question

by James E. Tull

In his book entitled *The Emerging Order,* Jeremy Rifkin advances the thesis that the Christian world may be in the dawning hours of a second Protestant reformation. The moving force which has the potential for bringing this about, he says, is Evangelicalism. In what he calls the "Evangelical-Charismatic" movement, there is a possibility that millions of frightened Americans may find sanctuary, while on the other hand there is also the possibility that the same movement may furnish a recruiting ground for the development of a repressive religious fascism. "Certainly," Rifkin claims, "in terms of structure and outreach, ... there is no other single cultural force in American life today that has as much potential as the evangelical community to influence the future direction of this country."[1]

If Rifkin and other intelligent observers of like mind are near to an accurate assessment of the importance of the growing evangelical movement, it is timely to ask what the relationship is between Baptists and this

[1]Jeremy Rifkin with Ted Howard, *The Emerging Order* (New York: G. P. Putnam's Sons, 1979), p. xi.

significant movement. The question is therefore posed and debated in this volume by two distinguished Southern Baptist scholars.

The purpose of this introduction is to furnish the nonspecialist reader enough information and interpretation to enable him or her better to understand the subject under discussion. An agreement between the publisher of the book and the writer of this chapter stipulated that, in the interest of objectivity, this writer would not see or read the text contributed by the principal authors until after the introductory chapter was written. After reading their materials, I shall write a concluding chapter in which I shall attempt to summarize the discussion.

Evangelicalism in Historical Perspective

Traditionally, the term, "Evangelicalism" has had a much wider application than it receives in the movement to which Jeremy Rifkin refers. Cullen Murphy, in an article which appears in the Autumn 1981 issue of *The Wilson Quarterly*, gives the following definition, which comports with this broader usage.

> The word *evangelical* (from the Greek *evangelion*, or "good news") referred in the 18th century, and refers now, to Christians of whatever denomination who are determined to rest their faith and religious practice on the authority of the Bible; who believe that the New Testament promises eternal life through a morally transforming experience of the Holy Spirit that Jesus described to Nicodemus as being "born again", and who are, for these reasons, intensely committed to missionary work ("evangelism"), both in their own towns and neighborhoods and around the world.[2]

The more restricted use of the term, as it is applied by contemporary "Evangelicals," will be clarified in subsequent discussion. At this point, it is important to remember that "Evangelicalism" is an old term. For example, during the Reformation, Protestants used the term to distinguish themselves from Roman Catholics, because they believed that in the newly rediscovered doctrine of justification by faith alone they had recovered the essence of the Gospel. The union of the Lutheran and Reformed churches in Prussia was termed the Evangelical Church. Today

---

[2]Cullen Murphy, "Protestantism and the Evangelicals," *The Wilson Quarterly* 5:4 (Autumn 1981): 105.

the Protestant Church of Germany is called the Evangelical Church of Germany. In different parts of Europe, the term "evangelical" serves to distinguish Lutheran from Reformed (Calvinist) churches. The Wesleyan revivals of the eighteenth century in England were given the appellation "evangelical" revivals. Perhaps largely as a result of their influence a "Low-Church" party emerged in the Church of England which ever since has been called the "evangelical" branch of Anglicanism.[3]

In America, the Evangelical Revival of England had its counterpart in a great burst of revivalism known to history as the Great Awakening, the central figure of which was George Whitefield, an English Anglican. In his book on the Great Awakening, Joseph Tracy noted in 1840 that the doctrine of the "new birth," as an *ascertainable* change, was hardly held in any church group in New England prior to the beginning of the Whitefield revivals in 1740. Under the leadership of the revivalists, however, the conversion experience became the central emphasis of the Awakening.[4]

No religious group profited more from the outburst of revivals than did the Baptists. In Massachusetts, for example, there were five Baptist churches before Whitefield's first appearance there in 1740; fifty years later there were 136. Comparable multiplications of Baptist churches occurred in Connecticut, Vermont, New Hampshire, and Rhode Island.[5] As a result of the revivals, a new denomination of Baptists came into being called the Separate Baptists. With their most striking successes in the South, their intense and wide-ranging evangelistic efforts left a heritage which has indelibly impressed itself upon the life of Southern Baptists.

It should be remembered that the Baptist movement, as far as clear historical evidence is concerned, emerged from among the English Puritans of the seventeenth century. Their separation was based upon the conviction that the church should be composed of believers only. Founding their churches upon the principle of a regenerate church membership, with believer's baptism as a corollary tenet and practice, Baptists from the first took their stand upon a central principle of Evangelicalism.

---

[3] *Encyclopedic Dictionary of Religion* (Washington, DC: Corpus Publications, 1979), p. 1268.

[4] Joseph Tracy, *The Great Awakening* (Worcester: Spooner and Howland, 1840), pp. vii-ix.

[5] Edwin Scott Gaustad, *The Great Awakening* (New York: Harper and Brothers, 1957), pp. 120-21.

Since their beginnings, Baptists have avowed this principle. Therefore, if Evangelicalism is defined in accordance with its original significance, there would seem to be little doubt that Baptists historically have been Evangelicals. But the story of Evangelicalism and the story of the Baptists have been, as we shall see, much more complex than is indicated here.

William G. McLoughlin, in a penetrating discussion of American Evangelicalism during the nineteenth century, says that the history of Evangelicalism for that period must be told on three levels—as a philosophy, as a theology, and as a *social* history.[6]

As a *philosophy*, this account must reckon with the permeation of the religious thought of the early part of the century with the ideas of the Scottish Common Sense School. During this period, college texts on Moral Philosophy, as well as the teachers of this subject, were set to oppose the infidelity which had been spawned by the Age of Reason.

> The American college presidents, most of them ordained evangelical ministers, who taught these compulsory courses of Moral Philosophy found the Scottish philosophers useful because they provided irrefutable proof of the existence of God against the claims of skeptics and because in answering these skeptics they provided equally sound evidence for the truths of evangelical religion as found in Scripture.[7]

As a *theology*, McLoughlin contends, Evangelicalism was involved with the decline of Calvinism on the American continent. In its successful fight against infidelity, deism, and Unitarianism, the Calvinists used many of the arguments of the Scottish school. However, the Calvinist victory was costly to traditional Calvinist views, many of which were modified by concessions to the logic of the rationalists.

> They had, for example, to concede that God was benevolent and not wrathful, merciful not stern, reasonable not mysterious; that he worked by means and not by miracles, that man was active not passive in his salvation, that grace was not arbitrarily or capriciously dispensed like the royal prerogative of a sovereign but offered freely to all men as the gift of a loving Father to his children.[8]

---

[6]William G. McLoughlin, *The American Evangelicals 1800-1900* (New York: Harper and Row, 1968), pp. 1-28.

[7]Ibid., p. 2.

[8]Ibid., p. 4.

This reorientation of Calvinism in the direction of Arminianism took place in the period which historians call the Second Great Awakening, which lasted from 1800 to 1835. The chief proponents of the change were Nathaniel W. Taylor, Lyman Beecher, Albert Barnes, and Charles Grandison Finney.

Nathaniel Taylor (1786-1858) was a great theologian who was in the Calvinist tradition. Perhaps his most important contribution to the evangelical cause was an emphasis upon a freedom of the will—an emphasis which greatly modified traditional Calvinism. While Taylor thought that conversion is, in an ultimate sense, the work of God, not man, a person is free to repent, believe, and cast himself upon the unfailing mercy of God.

As *social history*, says McLoughlin, Evangelicalism embraced a complex of components, of which we shall mention here what was perhaps only the most important one. This was evangelism. A result of the Arminianized Calvinism which Taylor espoused was a renewed emphasis upon revivalistic preaching, and the most distinguished practitioner of such preaching was Charles G. Finney (1792-1875).

Finney made an enduring impression upon American Evangelicalism. He was the greatest revivalist of his time. He believed that "measures" and "protracted meetings" were divinely chosen means for bringing salvation to multitudes. Though originally a Presbyterian, he emphasized a "Christian perfection," a belief in which had been advocated by John Wesley. Beyond the experience of being "born again," Wesley, and Finney also, held that there was the possibility of a "second moment" or "higher blessing" of grace which erased the taint of sin in the Christian's life. While this belief never became central to Evangelicalism, it has been held by many Evangelicals. Finney also voiced a millennial hope which has characterized much of Evangelicalism.

Unlike many Evangelicals of the twentieth century, Finney was a champion of social reform. He was a leader in evangelical efforts to reform gamblers, drunkards, prostitutes, and opium addicts, and in efforts to aid the blind, the dumb, the deaf, the criminals in jail, and the tramps on the streets.[9] In distinction from much of what was later called the "social gospel," however, Finney believed that reform was a direct result of saving individually the souls of these unfortunate people.

---

[9]Ibid., p. 13.

Before the Civil War, Evangelicalism had become the "religious mainstream" of the United States. But before the beginning of the new century, the evangelical consensus had begun to disintegrate.[10] A sweeping intellectual, cultural, and theological change was underway in America which was destined to affect the direction, mood, and character of Evangelicalism profoundly. To this change, and to some of its effects, we turn our attention now.

The Fundamentalist-Modernist Controversy

Evangelicalism came under serious challenge during the latter part of the nineteenth century. Charles Darwin's *The Origin of Species* (1859) did not have much impact upon American intellectual life until some years after the Civil War. By 1870 it was receiving much attention. In 1871 Darwin published *The Descent of Man*, in which he applied the hypothesis of evolution to the origin and development of mankind.

By the 1870s Christian evolutionists were beginning to proclaim publicly that evolution was compatible with the tenets of Christianity. Prominent churchmen, like Henry Drummond of Scotland, President James McCosh of Princeton University, Henry Ward Beecher, and Lyman Abbott all embraced evolutionist views.

By the turn of the century, scientists, theologians, and noted ministers were proclaiming that a belief in evolution had strengthened their faith. By no means, however, were all Christians friendly towards evolutionist thought. Indeed, the theory was felt to be inimical to the Christian faith by the rank and file of clergy and laity. This attitude was especially intense in the South.

Besides evolution, biblical higher criticism began to exert a strong influence in America during the post-Civil War era. Higher criticism brought the Bible and the whole history of the church under critical examination, in which the disciplines of geology, genetics, philology, paleography, comparative religion, and other approaches were freely employed.

> Because the Old Testament was more complex and less sensitive on doctrinal grounds, it was attacked first, but the New Testament was soon involved. Authorship questions arose:

---

[10]William W. Wells, *Welcome to the Family* (Downers Grove, IL: Inter-varsity Press, 1979), p. 38.

Did Moses write the Pentateuch? Did John write the Fourth Gospel? Did Paul write Ephesians? In their train were much larger questions of interpretation: Was the Creation story derived from Babylonian myth? Did St. Paul transform and distort "the religion of Jesus"? Could the historical Jesus be recovered? And beneath all of these searchings lay the real, the basic question: Was the Bible inspired? Could something so historically conditioned truly bear a revelation, and if so, how and in what sense?[11]

Other developments became profoundly disturbing to orthodox evangelicals. After the Civil War, the influence of the great German theologian, Friedrich Schleiermacher (1768-1834) began to be felt in Christian intellectual circles in America. Schleiermacher's thought shifted the principal locus of authority from the Bible to religious experience. Philosophical idealism, an optimistic philosophy which held that the universe is essentially rational and that irrational elements will eventually be overcome by reason, attained a strong, if unobtrusive influence upon much of Christian thought in America. Ritschlianism, whose founder and principal exponent was Albrecht Ritschl (1822-1899), contributed to the shaping of the theological views of many American theologians in the late nineteenth and early twentieth centuries. Ritschlianism's concern for a practical Christianity and its profound interest in the Jesus of history gave it a strong appeal to many American minds of a liberal bent. Evangelical thinkers, however, viewed Ritschlianism with distrust, believing that it exalted Jesus as leader and example rather than as Savior and Lord.

The Liberals. The emergence of a new intellectual environment, some features of which have been sketched above, posed a sharp challenge to convictions held by the conservative Evangelicals, who represented traditional orthodoxy. Out of the intellectual climate of the time, an alignment emerged which came to be known as "Liberalism." Liberal Christians were Christians who drank deeply from the fountain of modern thought. Deane William Ferm says:

The term Protestant liberalism is generally used to refer to that Protestant school of thought which believed that a rein-

---

[11]James Ward Smith and A. Leland Jamison, eds., *The Shaping of American Religion,* vol. 1, *Religion in American Life* (Princeton, NJ: Princeton University Press, 1961), pp. 290-91.

terpretation of the Christian message in accordance with the modern world view was necessary. Liberals claimed that Christianity must harmonize with the contemporary ways of thinking if it were to be relevant to the modern believer.[12]

Two groups of liberals should be distinguished. One group may be called "modernistic" Liberals and the other "evangelical" Liberals. The "Modernists" were never a large group. Robert T. Handy says of the "Modernists" that

> they were less interested in preserving the Christocentric heritage than the evangelical liberals, and found many theological traditions not worth preserving in the light of fresh knowledge about the universe and in view of increased awareness of the relativities of historical religions and their doctrines.[13]

The evangelical Liberals, on the other hand, believed that Christianity in its essence could and must be preserved, while at the same time being reinterpreted in the light of modern knowledge and culture. While modernistic thought sometimes verged towards humanism, the Liberals were concerned to preserve the complete integrity of the Christian faith. It is significant that, when the liberal embroilment with orthodox Evangelicals developed, the latter almost invariably called the Liberals "Modernists."

Although the Liberals were a varied group, they quite generally adhered to the following positions: They

> (1) accepted the principle of organic evolution; (2) employed the historical-critical method in their study of the Bible; (3) appropriated the insights of modern philosophy, and especially those of philosophical idealism; (5) recognized vital moral values in a fully socialized democracy.[14]

---

[12]Deane William Ferm, *Contemporary American Theologies* (New York: The Seabury Press, 1981), p. 3.

[13]Robert T. Handy, *A History of the Churches in the United States and Canada* (New York: Oxford University Press, 1977), p. 289.

[14]H. Shelton Smith, Robert T. Handy, and Lefferts A. Loetscher, eds., *American Christianity* (New York: Charles Scribner's Sons, 1963), 2:256.

Many Liberals believed that, despite weaknesses and failures, mankind has a natural tendency to progress towards a noble spiritual destiny. Common views of sin among them equated sin with a social contamination, a failure of human beings to moralize their inherited animal instincts, or ignorance. These opinions posed a direct challenge to the orthodox view of Original Sin, which view claimed that somehow all of mankind had fallen in Adam.

While evangelical Liberals professed a reverence for Christ, their usual emphasis was upon Christ's humanity rather than upon his "deity." Liberals thought of God in terms of his "immanence" in the world process, more than of his "transcendence" over it. Since God indwells the cosmos and the human spirit, the world was believed to be a rationally ordered system capable of being understood by human reason.

The liberal synthesis of Christian faith and modern thought exercised a strong influence within American Protestantism for several generations. Liberal parties arose in mainline denominations, among which the Congregationalists and Methodists were most deeply affected. Liberal views particularly invaded many Northern universities, seminaries, and pulpits. Woodbridge, Noll, and Hatch call attention to the acute loss which the conservatives felt as they "watched Modernists in theology dismantle orthodoxy from within. One after another the major Protestant seminaries—Congregational, Methodist, Baptist, Presbyterian, Episcopal—began to tolerate, if not champion, religious liberalism."[15]

Not many of the rank and file of Baptists became enamored of liberal views. Liberalism domiciled itself much more readily in Northern Baptist pulpits, universities, and seminaries. As early as 1906, Baptist historian A. H. Newman estimated that in the Northeast and Middle States not one Baptist in ten was "conscious of any important change in theology or departure from the old Baptist orthodoxy." In the Eastern and Southeastern states he thought the ratio would be hardly one in twenty; in the South, not one in a hundred.[16]

Newman noted that in varying degrees liberal influence had infiltrated the Divinity School of the University of Chicago, some of the

---

[15]John D. Woodbridge, Mark A. Noll, and Nathan O. Hatch, *The Gospel in America* (Grand Rapids: Zondervan Publishing House, 1979), p. 155.

[16]Albert H. Newman, "Recent Changes in the Theology of Baptists," *American Journal of Theology* 10:4 (October 1906): 608.

Baptist schools of the east, of which Brown University was a conspicuous example, Rochester Theological Seminary, Hamilton Theological School, and Newton Theological Institution. The Southern Baptist Theological Seminary at Louisville remained conservative, though as early as 1879 Crawford H. Toy, a professor of Old Testament, left the seminary because he was under pressure for teaching Wellhausen views.

Newman observed that, perhaps most important of all, Baptist lay students by the thousands, and a considerable number of theological students, had graduated from non-denominational or non-Baptist universities and seminaries which were noted for their adherence to liberal thought. Many of these students had naturally been deeply affected by this exposure, and had taken their liberal outlook into their church relations.

An important feature of Liberalism was the development of what came to be called the "Social Gospel," whose most brilliant exponent in the early part of the twentieth century was a Baptist, Walter Rauschenbusch (1861-1918). It was noted above that a social application of Christianity was a strong ingredient of nineteenth century Evangelicalism. The social gospel of the Liberals, however, had a new tone. Influenced by English, German, and Swiss socialism, the industrial revolution, urban development, burgeoning immigration, and a racing technological advance, many Liberals took to heart the necessity of an informed social application of Christianity.

Liberals began to explore the implications and applications for a new time of the ethical teachings of the Old Testament prophets, and of the New Testament. For many Liberals, Jesus' concept of the Kingdom of God became the central focus of the social gospel. This kingdom, they believed, could be established on earth by God's purpose for the world as that purpose moved through the cooperative dedication of Christian men and women.

Orthodox Evangelicals feared the liberal approach, because they believed that it verged towards humanism, that it was more social than gospel, and that it therefore left out the most crucial factor—personal redemption.

The Fundamentalists. Fundamentalism appeared in the early twentieth century in response to the challenge of Liberalism. As a movement, it was in progress for some years before it received its name. Its adherents were not called "Fundamentalists" until Curtis Lee Laws, the editor of *The Watchman-Examiner*, used this designation for them in 1920. Laws used the term for Evangelicals who opposed "Modernism"—that is, who defended orthodox beliefs in biblical infallibility and who therefore controverted the use of the historical-critical method of Bible study.

Concern for the doctrinal integrity of the Christian message began to be expressed by conservative Evangelicals even before the turn of the century, but it should be remembered that many conservatives were never drawn actively into the Fundamentalist—Modernist Controversy. Winthrop Hudson sets the conflict in a proper perspective:

> While party alignments did take place in every denomination during the years which bridged the turn of the century, the centering of attention on the theological debates between conservatives and liberals can be misleading. Few of the rank-and-file members of the churches were caught up in the controversy. To the extent that they were theologically self-conscious, the great body of American Protestants were undoubtedly conservative and traditional in their basic beliefs, but they were not rigidly so.[17]

Between 1910 and 1915 *The Fundamentals*, a series of twelve small volumes, were sent to clergymen and theological students across the nation as a gift from two wealthy California brothers, Milton and Lyman Stewart. Counting copies received by other persons also, it is reported that a total of 3,000,000 pieces of literature comprising *The Fundamentals* were distributed. *The Fundamentals* contained articles over a broad spectrum of subjects, but the aim envisioned was to affirm the central realities of the Christian faith. Significantly, about a third of the articles were devoted to the defence of the authority and verbal inspiration of the Scriptures. Other articles dealt with the deity of Christ, the virgin birth, the substitutionary atonement, the bodily resurrection of Christ, and Christ's imminent and visible return. It was apparent from these articles that Fundamentalism had not coalesced into a coherent movement, although the fundamentalist concerns were expressed.

Also in 1910, the Presbyterian General Assembly, in reply to questions about the orthodoxy of some Union Theological Seminary graduates, adopted a five-point declaration of what they considered to be essential Christian doctrines. These points were: (1) the inerrancy of the Bible; (2) the virgin birth of Christ; (3) Christ's substitutionary atone-

---

[17]Winthrop S. Hudson, *Religion in America* (New York: Charles Scribner's Sons, 1965), p. 283.

ment; (4) Christ's bodily resurrection; and (5) the authenticity of miracles.

These five points were not intended to be a definitive statement or creed. However, in the 1920s they came to be known as "the five points of fundamentalism," except that for point five enumerated above there was substituted the statement of a belief in Christ's bodily return to earth.[18] Soon the five points were being used polemically by the larger community of Fundamentalists.

Obviously, the five points were intended to be a sharp rebuttal to what were considered to be crucial liberal aberrations in doctrine, and to outline, in brief, positive form a perimeter of defence by which essential Christianity was to be guarded. While the aim of Fundamentalism was to affirm and defend the whole "body of divinity" as understood by Protestant orthodoxy, the polemics of the fundamentalist movement tended to narrow around the five points, until these points became a virtual creed to the movement's devotees.

This rallying center of concentration, Carl F. H. Henry declares,

> often displaced doctrinal responsibilities of the Church in the wider dimensions of historic creeds and confessions of faith. Evangelical pulpits resounded almost exclusively with "the fundamentals" supplemented periodically with "the case against evolution." The importance of other indispensables became tragically marginal.[19]

The first of the five points, the inerrancy of the Scriptures, further narrowed the outlook of many Fundamentalists. This doctrine assumed a position of first importance because it was conceived to be the sentinel on guard against the violation of all other Scriptural doctrines. "When this tenet is granted the other doctrines of the evangelical faith follow as a matter of course," said Fundamentalist Loraine Boettner.[20]

For their uncompromising stand upon inerrancy, the indebtedness of the Fundamentalists to the Princeton school of theology was incalculable. During a large part of the nineteenth century, Princeton Theological

---

[18]George M. Marsden, *Fundamentalism and American Culture* (New York: Oxford University Press, 1980), p. 117.

[19]Carl F. H. Henry, *Evangelical Responsibility in Contemporary Theology* (Grand Rapids: Eerdmans, 1957), p. 32.

[20]*Baker's Dictionary of Theology* (Grand Rapids: Baker, 1960), p. 200.

Seminary was a major theological fortress which opposed the growing influence of liberal theology. The Princeton school made no concessions to higher criticism. Their principal contribution to Fundamentalism was a formidable, intellectually impressive defense of the doctrine of the plenary, verbal inspiration of the Bible. Charles Hodge (1797-1878), the most imposing figure of the Princeton school, not only affirmed that the Scriptures are infallible with respect to doctrine, but also with respect to historical and scientific fact.

In 1881 B. B. Warfield and A. A. Hodge, two conservative stalwarts of the Princeton school, published what became a famous defense of inerrancy. This defence was true to the thought of the older Hodge. Warfield claimed, however, that inerrancy applies only to the original "autographs" of the Bible, and this claim has been for many years an important feature of the fundamentalist defense of biblical inspiration. "The learned, scholastic arguments of the Princeton theologians," Robert T. Handy observes, "greatly comforted those who believed in an infallible bible, and provided much ammunition for those who set themselves against historical criticism."[21]

In the early part of the twentieth century, an enthusiastic subscription to a premillennial eschatology became a prominent feature of Fundamentalism. Towards the close of the nineteenth century, a growing number of Christians became advocates of premillennialism. Although this position had been held to some degree throughout Christian history, seldom if ever had it been conceived to be a central feature of Christian doctrine. Some Christians in the late nineteenth and early twentieth centuries had advocated a postmillennial position, but this view lost ground with the coming of World War I, and was not held with the intensity which premillennialism came to receive.

Out of premillennialism sprang dispensationalism, a development to which a bit of historical notation should be give here. Near the middle of the nineteenth century, John N. Darby (1800-1882), who broke with the Church of Ireland and became the leader of the Plymouth Brethren, developed a dispensational interpretation of history. He brought his peculiar interpretations to the United States and propagandized them with singular effectiveness during the last third of the century, especially among Presbyterians and Baptists in the northern areas of the United States.

---

[21]Handy, *History of the Churches*, p. 290.

Darby divided history into a number of periods, or dispensations, which he claimed to find in the Bible. Each dispensational era, he believed, has been very different from the other eras, for the rules and strategies which God used to deal with the human race in one dispensation were not applicable to other eras. A great asset to the dispensational theology was the publication of the *Scofield Reference Bible* (first published in 1909), an annotated edition of the King James Version. To this day the "Scofield Bible" is the text to which most Fundamentalists are devoted. The dispensational doctrine was popularized by itinerant evangelists, by "prophetic" Bible conferences which convened annually after 1876, and by a growing number of "Bible schools." Dispensationalism made significant inroads into virtually all Protestant denominations.

During the second decade of this century, dispensationalism allied itself with the Princeton theology and the union comprised one of the most popular and effective weapons for combatting liberalism. This alliance could hardly have been anticipated, for the Princeton school members were not premillennialists or dispensationalists. However, even today, dispensationalism is held with great tenacity among large segments of Fundamentalists. Within liberal circles it has had little if any support.

Two other doctrinal features frequently associated with Fundamentalism should be mentioned here, although they are separable from the fundamentalist doctrinal system and therefore should be considered peripheral to it. One is the doctrine of Christian perfection.

The quest for perfect sanctification is as old as the Christian movement. But in the eighteenth century John Wesley gave it a powerful impetus by promoting it among his followers. It received a strong allegiance in Methodism, and it became a part of much late nineteenth century American revivalism. The holiness movement penetrated most of the Protestant denominations, both before and after the Civil War. In the twentieth century, Christian perfectionism has been especially prominent in the various Holiness churches, in the Church of God, the Church of the Nazarene, and the Salvation Army. While perhaps most of the believers in Christian perfection would accept the theology of Fundamentalism, the larger part of Fundamentalists do not subscribe to the doctrine of Christian perfection.

A similar judgment can be made about the charismatic movement, which has enjoyed an astonishing resurgence in recent years. Many charismatics are Fundamentalists, yet a growing number are not. Many

Fundamentalists, in fact, vigorously oppose the charismatic emphasis. In no sense, therefore, can it be considered an organic part of Fundamentalism.

A succinct summary of the course of the fundamentalist movement as a whole has been made by William W. Wells, whose personal orientation is towards "new Evangelicalism." As a result of continuing controversy, Wells says,

> some of the fundamentalists became more and more defensive
> . . . after about 1920. Many of them fastened on the theory of
> evolution as a particularly insidious manifestation of secular-
> ism and naturalism. . . . During the next ten years the funda-
> mentalist movement retreated slowly and defensively from
> the Protestant mainstream. The battle for control of the
> denominations was bitter, and a few groups split as a direct
> result of the controversy. The majority of conservatives
> remained in their denominations, but limited their involve-
> ment. Some fundamentalist leaders became militant separa-
> tists. Their perception of a growing attack on the gospel
> impelled them to separate from liberalism totally and com-
> pletely. Furthermore, some leaders insisted that fundamental-
> ists should separate themselves not only from the liberals but
> also from conservatives who compromised the gospel by asso-
> ciating with liberals.[22]

While the controversy caused serious disturbances in many of the leading Protestant denominations, including the Northern Baptist Convention, only a few minor schisms resulted. The Fundamentalists failed in their efforts to impose upon any denomination their sharply defined theological points of controversy. By the end of the 1920s the conflict had definitely waned in intensity.

The dispute sparked intense repercussions in the Southern Baptist Convention also, but these were sporadic outbreaks which did not extend over the whole range of issues. A student of the controversy has put the reason for this limitation with fine precision: "Of primary importance," he says, "in their [Southern Baptists'] avoidance of dispute was the orthodox nature of their church, where no group, or even minister, arose to challenge the basic doctrines held by all."[23]

---

[22]Wells, *Welcome to the Family*, pp. 147-48.

[23]Norman F. Furniss, *The Fundamentalist Controversy, 1918-1931* (New Haven, CT: Yale University Press, 1954), p. 118.

While by no means all Southern Baptists were Fundamentalists, the deep conservatism of the great body of that denomination, including its ministers, furnished little occasion for a widespread conflagration upon the issues which Fundamentalism raised. The agitation which did arise was fomented over the question of evolution. W. L. Poteat, the president of Wake Forest College, and a distinguished biologist, came under fire in the 1920s in his own state (North Carolina) because of his avowed evolutionist beliefs. Poteat retained his post—and his reputation— probably due to the fact that many Wake Forest alumni courageously defended him.

In 1925 the evolution issue was brought to the floor of the Southern Baptist Convention, which was in session at Memphis. Adroit diplomacy by President E. Y. Mullins of Southern Baptist Theological Seminary, and by George White McDaniel, president of the convention, prevented what threatened to become a fractious controversy. By 1929 the matter was hardly a live issue in the convention.

The dissipation of controversy in mainline Protestantism did not indicate that Fundamentalism was dead. Subsequent years demonstrated that it was still very much alive, as we shall see. In the meantime, we should take notice of a dynamic new movement which sprang from Fundamentalism.

The New Evangelicals

As early as the mid-thirties, some of the more moderate Fundamentalists began to sense a growing cleavage between themselves and their more militant brethren. About 1940, these disenchanted Fundamentalists began to call themselves by the more historic term, "Evangelicals."

Because of the divisiveness of Fundamentalism, one of the earliest concerns of Evangelicalism was that of promoting evangelical unity. A leading theologian among the new Evangelicals was Edward J. Carnell, who wrote the following in 1958 concerning Fundamentalism: "Its tests for Christian fellowship become so severe that divisions in the Church are considered a sign of virtue. And when there are no modernists from which to withdraw, fundamentalists compensate by withdrawing from one another."[24]

---

[24]Marvin Halverson and Arthur A. Cohen, eds., *Handbook of Christian Theology* (New York: Meredian Books, 1958), p. 143.

The Federal Council of Churches of Christ (later named The National Council of Churches) was organized in 1908 and was believed by conservatives to be based upon liberal theology and motivation. In 1940 a group of right-wing extremists organized itself into the American Council of Christian Churches. It was reactionary in spirit and directed a great deal of polemic against the Federal Council.[25]

In 1942 a small group of moderate Evangelicals, finding that the Federal Council was dominated by Liberals, and that the spirit of the American Council was too negative, organized the National Association of Evangelicals. One of the prime objectives of this organization was to promote the cause of evangelical unity. It stressed the doctrines which Evangelicals held in common, such as the deity of Christ and the infallibility of the Scriptures, but its members stressed also evangelism, education, publication, radio broadcasting, missions, and social action.[26]

While no one who belonged to the American Council was permitted to join the Federal Council, the National Association was not so restrictive. They remained aloof from the Federal Council, but they permitted membership in that body if one continued to adhere to the doctrinal principles of the National Association.

Although the origin of the National Association of Evangelicals preceded the coalescence of the group which today call themselves the "New Evangelicals," the spirit of the latter permeated the National Association, and some of their leaders were the same. Harold Ockenga, for example, became the first president of the Association. In an article published some years later (1960) in *Christianity Today*, Ockenga claimed that the fundamentalist defeat on the ecclesiastical scene was due in part to its mistaken doctrine of the church, which equated the church with believers who were orthodox in their theology and separatist in their ethics. Of the new Evangelicals, however, Ockenga claimed that

> the younger orthodox scholars are repudiating the separatist position, . . . have expressed a willingness to reexamine the problems facing the theological world, have sought to return to the theological dialogue and have recognized the honesty and Christianity of some who hold views different from their

---

[25]Millard Erickson, *The New Evangelical Theology* (Westwood, NJ: Fleming H. Revell Company, 1968), pp. 41-42.

[26]Ibid., p. 42.

own in some particulars.[27]

It appears to have been Ockenga himself who contributed the term "new Evangelicalism" to the movement which sprang from Fundamentalism. In 1954, Dr. Ockenga spoke at the inauguration of Dr. Edward J. Carnell to the presidency of Fuller Theological Seminary. In his address, Ockenga said, "The 'new Evangelicalism' embraces the full orthodoxy of fundamentalism but manifests a social consciousness and responsibility which was strangely absent from fundamentalism."[28]

Ockenga's affirmation that new Evangelicalism embraced "the full orthodoxy of fundamentalism" indicated a notable feature of the new movement. This was the large area of doctrinal kinship which it shared with Fundamentalism. A statement by Millard Erickson is even more enlightening:

> It was not an abandonment of the fundamentalist message that was called for. . . . All of the fundamentals could be unreservedly subscribed to by the new evangelicals. . . . They saw themselves as in no sense a departure from classical orthodoxy, but rather a reinstitution of it.[29]

While new Evangelicals found themselves in agreement with the "five points," Evangelicals of Carl Henry's probity saw that "interest in the isolated fundamentals often concealed the organic sweep of biblical theology and minimized the comprehensive exhibition of Christianity as a world-life view."[30] He accused Fundamentalism of narrowing the gospel to a kind of pietistic religious experience in which the role of the intellect was disparaged, and which virtually made cliches, rather than deeply reasoned doctrines, of the great theological verities.[31]

New Evangelicalism emphasized an intelligent recommitment to the larger evangelical heritage which Fundamentalism had lost by a too narrow theological understanding. Therefore a prominent note in the new Evangelicalism became a strong accent upon education. As liberal

---

[27]Victor M. Matthews, *Neo-Evangelicalism* (Des Plains, IL: Regular Baptist Press, 1971), p. 11.

[28]Ibid., p. 2.

[29]Erickson, *New Evangelical Theology*, p. 32.

[30]Henry, *Evangelical Responsibility*, p. 46.

[31]Ibid.

thought had increasingly infiltrated colleges and theological seminaries, the Fundamentalists had drawn more and more of their pastoral leadership from their Bible schools. When the educational level of the public rose, especially after World War II, new Evangelicals discerned that they must raise the quality of the education of their ministers.

Fuller Theological Seminary, organized in 1954, was a product of this determination. The founders dedicated themselves to the task of developing a seminary of high academic excellence, and at the same time of grounding the school firmly upon orthodox Christian principles. Other seminaries and colleges raised their educational standards and received accreditation from reputable accreditation agencies. The National Association of Evangelicals appointed a Commission on Education which promoted cooperation between evangelical schools and sought to upgrade evangelical education at its various levels. Evangelical scholars were encouraged to take a part of their academic training in secular graduate universities and liberal seminaries in order to broaden their intellectual outlooks.

By their emphasis upon education the new Evangelicals, also, addressed themselves to the task of rebuilding an evangelical apologetic of high quality. They believed that the Fundamentalists had lost their apologetic battles with the liberals because they were not prepared academically to speak with authority to the burning issues of their time. A new generation of Evangelicals, they thought, should be ready to challenge the optimism and secular presuppositions of liberal thought.

Like Fundamentalism, new Evangelicalism placed a supreme value upon the authority of the Scriptures. In his book entitled *The Case for Biblical Christianity*, the late Edward Carnell described Evangelicalism as "that branch of Christendom which limits the ground of religious authority to the Bible."[32] In defining the meaning of Evangelicalism, Bernard Ramm declares, "In the most general sense, evangelical Christianity refers to that version of Christianity which places the priority of the Word and Act of God over faith, response, or experiences of men."[33] Ramm blames Schleiermacher for the reversal in which faith is exalted

---

[32]Cited in Richard Quebedeaux, *The Young Evangelicals* (New York: Harper and Row, 1974), p. 4.

[33]Bernard L. Ramm, *The Evangelical Heritage* (Waco, TX: Word Books, 1973), p. 13.

above truth, and subjective response above objective reality. This reversal, Ramm says, is a "fatal reconstruction of the Christian faith."[34]

A major interest of some of the leaders of the new Evangelicalism has been for its proponents to make an intelligent recommitment to the larger evangelical heritage which Fundamentalism lost by a too narrow theological understanding. In his book entitled *The Evangelical Heritage*, Bernard Ramm calls the Evangelicals to the task of reclaiming by diligent study what he considers to be their rightful literary and doctrinal heritage.

The "fountainhead" of orthodox Protestant thought, Ramm feels, is "the writings of the Reformers themselves."[35] The great creedal statements of the Reformation and post-Reformation periods should also be studied. Ramm finds especially valuable the Augsburg Confession (1530), the Formula of Concord (1580), the Second Helvetic Confession (1566), and the Heidelberg Catechism (1563).

Ramm is acutely interested in the literature and theology of the Protestant scholastics of the seventeenth century. Evangelicals ought to familiarize themselves with these writings, Ramm believes, for the scholastic theologians are closer to the Reformers than is any other school of theology, and because in the scholastic writings are to be found some of the basic roots of evangelical theology.[36]

Ramm notes that all of the major theological movements of the Reformation accepted either implicitly or explicitly the great creeds of the patristic period of church history. Special consideration should be given to the creeds of Nicaea-Constantinople, Chalcedon, and Athanasius. While these creeds are, of course, not infallible, they are important because they deal authoritatively with the same great realities which were the concerns of the New Testament writers—realities pertaining to the incarnation, the person and work of Christ, and the meaning of a trinitarian faith. Much of the patristic theology was absorbed into medieval theology, and was thus passed on to the Reformers. "Evangelical theology," Ramm says, "has its roots deep in patristic, medieval, and Reformation thought."[37]

---

[34]Ibid., p. 14.

[35]Ibid., p. 50.

[36]Ibid., p. 55.

[37]Ibid., p. 58.

The supreme evangelical authority, Dr. Ramm believes, is the Scriptures themselves. Indeed, the whole of the evangelical literary heritage must be critically examined and evaluated in the light of the Scriptures. Also, Evangelicalism, like Protestant orthodoxy of former centuries, does not forget that the Christian faith is learned and taken to heart under the tutelage of the Holy Spirit. Protestant orthodoxy bequeathed to contemporary Evangelicalism the "password" of the Reformers—the Word and the Spirit. Evangelicalism "wants to put side by side with the divine inspiration of Scripture the divine witness of the Spirit."[38]

From the time of their emergence from fundamentalist ranks, one of the points which differentiated the new Evangelicals from the Fundamentalists was their assignment of a high priority to a social expression of Christianity. The new Evangelicals, in the words of Dr. Ockenga, found this emphasis to be "strangely absent" from Fundamentalism. The new Evangelicals' concept of social Christianity was more in the pattern of Charles G. Finney than in that of the liberal social gospel, but they believed that to abandon a Christian social ethic was to depart from an essential dimension of Christian responsibility.

New Evangelicalism also determined to employ a positive program devoted to a world evangelistic outreach. For this task they found a most able leader in Billy Graham. While Graham began his ministry as a strict Fundamentalist, in the course of years he gave up some of his biblical literalism. The appeal of his preaching has been due, not only to the attractiveness of his personality and the skilful organization of his campaigns, but also to the old orthodoxy which he proclaims. He has spoken out on social issues, particularly upon race relations, and has insisted upon integrating his revival assemblies. He practices also something of an ecumenical outreach in winning hearty cooperation across many segments of theological opinion and denominational affiliation. Of Graham, Harold Ockenga remarked in 1965:

> In him we have seen the phenomenon of an evangelical who crossed all theological lines in his work while maintaining a strictly orthodox position. His work has not been disregarded by those of other theological positions and has compelled them to rethink the basis of their approach.[39]

---

[38]Ibid., p. 61.

[39]Cited in Matthews, *Neo-Evangelicalism*, p. 12.

In 1956 *Christianity Today*, edited by Carl F. H. Henry, began its surprising career. At first it was sent free of charge to ministers and students of various denominations and theological persuasions, and thus built up a large circulation which soon eclipsed that of its liberal rival, *The Christian Century*. The purpose of the paper, the editor stated in the first issue, was to mediate historical Christianity to a new generation. Promotion of the doctrine of the plenary inspiration of the Bible was candidly acknowledged to be one of the aims of the paper. Another stated aim was to present the gospel message in its bearing upon social issues. At the present time the circulation of the paper totals about 185,000 copies. It has given Evangelicalism a national voice, and has become probably the most influential Christian journal in the world.

The Current Scene

The present status of Evangelicalism is as complex as it is dynamic.* Fundamentalism and new Evangelicalism, sharing much of the same theological ground, yet differing widely in many respects, have experienced a vigorous growth in the last three decades. There are other, large alignments of conservatives who were never engaged directly in the Fundamentalist-Modernist Controversy, and who therefore do not think of themselves as either Fundamentalists or new Evangelicals.

The last of the three groups mentioned in the paragraph above is discussed at some depth in an article by Cullen Murphy in the Autumn 1981 issue of *The Wilson Quarterly*.[40] On the basis of a rather broad use of the term "evangelical," a use cited early in this chapter, Murphy thinks that the following groups are Evangelicals: a half-million "peace-church" conservatives, comprised of Mennonites, Quakers, and Brethren; about two million Arminian conservatives who derive from Alexander Campbell's nineteenth-century Disciples of Christ; a group whose members are rooted in the immigrant experience, numbering more than three million persons, in the Missouri Synod Lutheran Church; almost half a million Dutch Calvinists in the Christian Reformed Church; and a variety of both free-church and Lutheran Scandinavians and Finns, plus Italian, Romanian, Ukranian, and German Baptists.

---

*For an *insiders' view* of the complex and dynamic state of fundamentalism in the 1980s, see *The Fundamentalism Phenomenon: The Resurgence of Conservative Christianity*, by Ed Dobson and Ed Hindson, edited by Jerry Falwell (Garden City: Doubleday & Co., 1981). —Ed.

[40]Murphy, "Protestantism and the Evangelicals," pp. 105-20.

Another group are the black Pentecostals, comprising perhaps as many as one quarter of the sixteen million Christian blacks in this nation. Murphy describes many Baptist groups as Evangelicals, including the fourteen-million-member Southern Baptist Convention, which he considers to be "America's strongest evangelical movement."[41] Murphy thinks that both black Baptists and Methodists are Evangelicals. They, with black Pentecostals, Murphy says, comprise one-fourth of the Evangelical Christians in this country. Black and white Pentecostals share many of the beliefs of other Evangelicals, but add a distinctive element— "speaking in tongues." Other evangelical groups are the Seventh-Day Adventists, Wesleyans, and conservative Calvinists.

None of these groups, Murphy thinks, fits the fundamentalist mold, which emerged in the public battles of the early 1920s in the fight against Darwinism and the historical criticism of the Bible. He argues that the preoccupation of the media with the Evangelical Right "diverts attention from the great majority in the middle."[42] Evangelicals are a diverse lot, and belong to many different denominations, but they are tied together, Murphy suggests,

> by webs of nondenominational "para-church" organizations, Christian liberal arts and Bible colleges, publishing houses, radio and television ministries, family vacation camps, women's fellowships, businessmen's associations, and so on. Evangelical associations are resilient, comfortable with diversity, and successful in maintaining loyalties over long periods of time.[43]

Although Fundamentalism at one time appeared to be on the wane after losing so many of its battles to the Liberals, the appearance was deceiving. William Hordern, who has been neither a Fundamentalist nor a new Evangelical, observed in 1966 that to those who were "writing the obituaries of fundamentalism," there were some disturbing signs. Fundamentalists generally were drawn from low-income segments of society, but they raised more money per capita than did liberal congregations. Moreover, fundamentalist churches were furnishing far more than their share of candidates for the ministry and for mission work in foreign

---

[41]Ibid., p. 111.

[42]Ibid., p. 116.

[43]Ibid., p. 113.

fields. During the 1950s, when American church membership was growing in record numbers, a disproportionate share of the growth was in fundamentalist or other conservative churches.[44]

Moody Bible Institute, established in Chicago in the 1880s, became by the turn of the century a very strong center of Fundamentalism. A network of other fundamentalist institutions, such as Philadelphia College of the Bible, Dallas Theological Seminary, the Bible Institute of Los Angeles, and Northwestern Bible Institute in Minneapolis, have been centers of Fundamentalism whose influence has radiated throughout every section of the nation.[45] The fundamentalist movement also extended its influence by forming independent churches, by capturing smaller church bodies, and by founding numerous Bible schools. "Christian" schools, evangelical alternatives to public schools, have enrolled hundreds of thousands of children and young people.[46]

A striking feature of contemporary Fundamentalism is its astonishing hold on radio and television broadcasting. More than any other Christian group in America, Fundamentalists have made expert use of these media. Fundamentalists today dominate what has been called "televangelism." Oral Roberts appears to be the most popular television preacher, while Robert Schuller, Rex Humbard, Jimmy Swaggert, Jerry Falwell, Jim Bakker, Pat Robertson, and James Robison hold impressively large numbers of viewers and auditors.[47] Jerry Falwell, the founder of the "Moral Majority," has led many of his followers into an influential but very controversial involvement in radical right political and social activity.

Much of the preaching of the "televangelists" expounds a traditional fundamentalist gospel. The five points are basic assumptions, it would seem, though much of the preaching is geared to the limitations of time on the air, and to an element of sedate but lively entertainment, calculated to hold the attention of the viewers. Hadden and Swann, the authors of *Prime Time Preachers*, observe that the stock-in-trade of the televangelists

---

[44]William Hordern, *New Directions in Theology Today*, vol. 1, *Introduction* (Philadelphia: The Westminster Press, 1966), p. 75.

[45]Cf. Murphy, "Protestantism and the Evangelicals," p. 112.

[46]Cf. Quedebeaux, *Young Evangelicals*, p. 46.

[47]Murphy, "Protestantism and the Evangelicals," p. 112.

is an endless stream of easy answers to difficult questions. The most difficult human problems are brought to satisfactory resolution in one hour. Many require only a half hour. Many more are handled in just thirty seconds, the length of most television commercials.[48]

The fundamentalist resurgence has brought to the fore once again the doctrine of scriptural inerrancy. The principal denominations in which this issue has been particularly agitated have been the Missouri Synod Lutheran Church and the Southern Baptist Convention. In the Missiouri Synod the bitter dispute led to a damaging division. Among Southern Baptists, the debate is still in progress. The two most recent presidents of the Southern Baptist Convention have been avowed inerrantists, and their election to their high office has shown the large support which their doctrinal position and political power have enjoyed in the denomination. It has appeared to many Southern Baptist observers that a strong group of radical Fundamentalists is determined to obtain control of the convention's organizational machinery.

The intellectual leader of the radical inerrantists among Southern Baptists is Harold Lindsell. Lindsell, now a Southern Baptist, has a rather broad background in interdenominational circles. He has taught at Fuller Theological Seminary, Columbia Bible College, and Northern Baptist Seminary in Chicago. He has been editor of *Christianity Today*, and on 12 June 1978, was elected president of the Baptist Faith and Message Fellowship. Two of his books have been very influential in the current inerrancy dispute. These are entitled *The Battle for the Bible* (1976), and *The Bible in the Balance* (1979). The militant inerrantists in the convention appear to see the doctrinal issues more or less as Dr. Lindsell views them. The doctrinal substance of the inerrantists' message is based upon what may be called classical Fundamentalism. Not surprisingly, this stand has seized upon inerrancy as its main point.

In a recent reversal in the use of terminology, however, the inerrantists do not call themselves "Fundamentalists," but "Evangelicals." Lindsell denies the designation "Evangelical" even to such conservative scholars and theologians as Daniel Fuller, David Hubbard, G. C. Berkouwer, F. F. Bruce, Bernard Ramm, Carl F. H. Henry, and Clark Pinnock.

---

[48]Jeffrey K. Hadden and Charles E. Swann, *Prime Time Preachers* (Reading, MA: Addison-Wesley, 1981), p. 100.

They are not Evangelicals, Lindsell believes, because they concede that there may have been some factual errors, if not doctrinal errors, in the original autographs of the Bible. Only those who believe in complete inerrancy, Lindsell holds, deserve to be called "Evangelicals."

As far as Southern Baptists are concerned, the inerrantists appear intent upon using the Baptist Faith and Message confession of 1963 as a polemical weapon against employees of the agencies of the Southern Baptist Convention. The focus of their attack at present seems to be directed towards teachers in the denomination's seminaries, who are suspected of not subscribing to the confession's statement that the Bible is the word of God "without any mixture of error."

Today there is a marked contrast between the Fundamentalists and many of the new Evangelicals. While the positions of self-conscious Fundamentalists seem to be hardening, those of a sizable contingent of the new Evangelicals are becoming more tolerant and more flexible. In his recent book entitled *Contemporary American Theologies*, Deane William Ferm has included a chapter on evangelical theology.[49] Ferm's principal interest in this chapter is not to assess the present state of Fundamentalism, but to examine recent trends in the theology and practice of the new Evangelicals. Ferm notes that the new Evangelicals seem less interested in forming separate denominations or splinter groups than were their fundamentalist forebears. Increasingly, they are content to exercise their witness in churches and denominations to which they already belong. They have a growing interest in the application of Christianity to social problems. They are showing a cautious receptivity to some of the findings of historical criticism.

Many of the younger Evangelicals, Ferm thinks, are moving away from a belief in total inerrancy to a belief in "partial" inerrancy. This change means that they will still hold to the authority and completeness of biblical doctrine but concede that the Bible may have some errors in it pertaining to historical and scientific fact. There is a trend, Ferm believes, towards a "relational" theology, in which God's commandment to love one's neighbor is stressed more avidly than are specific doctrines. Many new evangelical theologians are giving searching study to the works of outstanding "neo-orthodox" theologians such as Barth, Brunner, Bonhoeffer, and Reinhold Niebuhr. Ferm quotes Robert S. Ellwood, who

---

[49]Ferm, *Contemporary American Theologies*, pp. 95-112.

wonders whether the left wing of the new Evangelicalism "is really something new *within* evangelicalism, or is (it) the shaky, searching first steps of a reborn liberalism?"[50]

The new Evangelicals of the 1970s embraced a wide spectrum of views and practices. Their move towards the mainstream of biblical and theological scholarship has alienated many Fundmentalists who hold unswervingly to their own concept of inerrancy. In the meantime, older leaders like Carl F. H. Henry, Bernard Ramm, Daniel Fuller, and Clark Pinnock, while holding views which place them perhaps a bit left of center in the evangelical spectrum, have maintained their positions of intellectual leadership among the new Evangelicals. Despite their diversities, new Evangelicals appear to remain united in their affirmation of the Lordship of Christ, of the necessity of an experience of regeneration, and of the supreme authority of the Scriptures.

Although the new Evangelical is far apart from the contemporary liberal, theologically speaking, their respective quests at one point may be described as being quite similar. Both of them are seeking the answer to a profoundly important question, namely: How can one be a Christian and a modern man at the same time?

Are Baptists Evangelicals?

Bernard Ramm, a leading new evangelical theologian who is also a Baptist, has the following to say about what constitutes a "fundamental" doctrine: "A fundamental doctrine is one of such importance to the Christian faith that if denied the faith itself would collapse. . . . The fundamentals are therefore that cluster of doctrines that are nonnegotiable; they have no viable alternatives."[51]

If we should assume that Baptists are not Evangelicals, we should still be pleased to admit that the Evangelicals and the Baptists share vast areas of the same doctrinal heritage and very many of the same beliefs. Most probably both Evangelicals and Baptists, for example, would subscribe to the doctrinal content of the Apostles' Creed, although members of both groups would likely "scratch their heads" over the declaration that Christ "descended into hell" [or "hades"].

On the other hand, if an Evangelical is a person who has been saved by the grace of God through Jesus Christ, and who has taken upon himself

---

[50]Cited in ibid., p. 106.

[51]Ramm, *The Evangelical Heritage*, pp. 91-92.

the joy and obligation to witness and live for Christ, we should by this definition assert that Baptists are Evangelicals. However, as we have observed in the foregoing discussion, Fundamentalists and new Evangelicals would impose further restrictions upon what constitutes an Evangelical—restrictions which would rule out, possibly, a large number of Baptists. Our problem then boils down to this: are we going to accept the broad, historical use of the term to define what an Evangelical is, or are we going to accept the more restrictive definition(s) which the Fundamentalists and the new Evangelicals would like to impose upon us? Should Evangelicals who make up a large contingent of the Christian family allow themselves to be disfranchised from the evangelical fellowship by a much smaller group who would like to use the "evangelical" designation for their own sectarian purposes? Perhaps our principal authors will take up these questions in the discussions which follow.

In order to determine whether Baptists are Evangelicals, perhaps we should follow an insightful lead suggested by Dr. Ramm. We might set forth a core cluster of evangelical beliefs, look further at a core cluster of Baptists beliefs, compare these "clusters" with each other to determine whether they are compatible, and conclude whether one cluster contains non-negotiable terms which are violated or compromised by that of the other.

We do not have ample space to do this here, but we can point out a few lines of thought which may merit further discussion. For example, if we should accept the five points of Fundamentalism and new Evangelicalism as criteria for defining the boundaries of Evangelicalism, would Baptists be able to meet the test? Vast numbers of Baptists would do so, no doubt. In the minds of the Evangelicals (using the term in its restrictive sense), the five points are nonnegotiable doctrines. But many Baptists would argue with one or more of these points.

That the Scriptures are for Christians an authority of supreme value would be for most Baptists an essential conviction, but if a Baptist rejects the doctrine of inerrancy, is he denied an essential qualification for being a "true" Baptist? Or a "true" Evangelical? The incarnation of God in Jesus Christ would to the great majority of Baptists be a nonnegotiable conviction, but does a person have to believe in the virgin birth of Christ in order to be a Christian? A Baptist? An Evangelical? Baptists have believed that salvation comes to us by the grace of God through the atoning life and death of Jesus Christ. But is one compelled to believe in the theory of the penal substitutionary death of Christ in order to be an

Evangelical? Or a Baptist? Baptists traditionally have held firmly to the belief that Christ rose triumphant over death, sin, and hell in a bodily resurrection from the dead. But if a Baptist believes that Christ, without the resuscitation of his dead body, now lives at the right hand of God, in the lives of his disciples, and works for the redemption of the world, can he be a *true* Baptist? Or in any sense an Evangelical? A vast number of Baptists have believed in the physical return of Christ to this earth to claim victory and rule over his enemies, and to consummate his everlasting kingdom. But if a Baptist believes that Christ's triumph will not be evidenced in a premillennial return to earth, can he be a *true* Baptist? A *true* Evangelical?

No doubt a Fundamentalist or a new Evangelical would answer each one of these questions stated above with resounding "No." To deny the five points as they are stated in their classical form would be "cutting out the very core of Christianity." But would all true Baptists agree with respect to every one of the five points? In other words, does a person have to be a Fundamentalist or a new Evangelical to be a true Baptist?

Subsidiary questions (not so "subsidiary," perhaps, to a Fundamentalist) follow. Must a Baptist renounce evolution, higher criticism of the Scriptures, and the National Council of Churches in order to be a true Baptist? Can a "Liberal," or even a "Modernist" be a born-again Christian? And if he is one, does his deviation at certain points from evangelical orthodoxy remove him from the pale of Evangelicalism? Or from the fellowship of "true" Baptists?

Since the Baptist movement began (at least in its modern phase) in seventeenth century England around concerns about the nature and function of the church, most of its distinctives have been in the area of ecclesiology. Baptist life began when a small group of Christian separatists took their stand on the principle of a regenerate church membership with its corollary, the baptism of believers only. They stood unequivocally for religious freedom, with its corollary, the separation of church and state. They believed that they derived these convictions from the Scriptures, which they sought to follow consistently as an authority subordinate only to the authority of God in Christ.

Very much bound up with Baptist ecclesiology is what has been affirmed to be the central Baptist principle, namely, "the direct, unmediated, undelegated lordship of Jesus Christ." An implication of this Baptist stand involves what Dr. E. Y. Mullins called "the competency of the individual soul before God." The lordship of Christ and the competency of the person signify that no priest, church, or earthly government has a right to interpose itself between God and the human soul. This twin affirmation involves the authority of the Scriptures, for no ecclesiastical institution has the right to interject a creed or a prescribed practice which infringes upon the right of private interpretation. It involves the belief in the "New Testament as our only rule of faith and practice." Without any denigration of the Old Testament, this principle asserts that the Old Testament must be interpreted in the light of the New, and that the witness of the New Testament to Christ is the criterion by which the Old Testament revelation is to be evaluated and judged.

The Baptist convictions stated above would be considered in the Baptist fellowship to be statements of nonnegotiable principles. One can be an Evangelical in virtually any ecclesiastical setting, accept a state church, a hierarchial church government, infant baptism, and still be, apparently, an "Evangelical." But not a Baptist. Baptists profess the acceptance of "no creed except the Bible." When some Baptists attempt to impose a man-made creed upon the Baptist fellowship, does this effort stem from a Baptist, or from, let us say, a fundamentalist, mentality? Some Baptists have been Calvinists, others Arminians, Fundamentalists, Liberals, tongue-speakers, faith-healers, evolutionists, non-evolutionists, premillennialists, postmillennialists, amillennialists, ecumenists, nonecumenists, and so forth, but none of these ideological factors made them Baptists. A real Baptist is a believer who holds tenaciously, courageously, and charitably, to Baptist convictions. Whether or not a Baptist is also an "Evangelical" is the question which will be addressed by Professors Garrett and Hinson in the pages that follow.

Part One

"Evangelicals" and Baptists —Is There a Difference?

by James Leo Garrett, Jr.

Chapter One

Who Are the
"Evangelicals"?

Pollsters and news media in the United States proclaimed the presidential election year of 1976 as "the year of the Evangelical."[1] Estimates as to the number of "Evangelical Christians" in the United States have ranged from thirty-three million to forty-five and one-half million.[2] One historian reported that Jimmy Carter was only the fifth "born-again"

[1]See David Kucharsky, "Year of the Evangelical," *Christianity Today* 21 (22 October 1976): 12-13; "1976: 'The Year of the Evangelical,' " *The Christian Century* 93 (29 December 1976): 1165-66. Carl F. H. Henry, however, writing early in 1977, warned that the Evangelical upsurge must be balanced with a realistic recognition of the pervasive secularization of and secularism in American society: "Evangelical Summertime?" *Christianity Today* 21 (1 April 1977): 38, 40. Similarly, reflecting on the year 1977, Henry asserted that "the thrusting evangelical movement, which might have shifted into overdrive, has slipped instead into second gear." The year proved to be one "of disconcerting losses" as well as "a time of noteworthy constructive gains": "Evangelical Profits and Losses," *The Christian Century* 95 (25 January 1978): 69-70. George Gallup's Princeton Religious Research Center predicted that 1978 would be another "year of the evangelical"; see Albert J. Menendez, "Who Are the Evangelicals?" *Christianity Today* 22 (27 January 1978): 42.

[2]Richard Quebedeaux, *The Young Evangelicals: Revolution in Orthodoxy* (New York: Harper & Row, 1974), p. 47, has referred to "about 33 million churchgoing Evangelicals in America," but admittedly his total does not include the Jesus People, Catholic Charismatics, or Evangelicals in the American Lutheran Church. "Back to That Oldtime Religion," *Time* 110 (26 December 1977): 53, has estimated that there are 45.5 million Evangelicals "on the U.S. church rolls."

president of the United States.[3] Books on or by the Evangelicals became best sellers, television programs designed to propagate the message of Evangelicals increased markedly in numbers and in viewers, and the general consciousness of "Evangelicals" reached a new peak.

The task of defining or identifying the "Evangelicals" is fraught with complications. For example, soon after his election as pope in 1978, John Paul II was said by a television commentator to have spoken "in an evangelical manner." Furthermore, during the open-air mass at Grant Park in Chicago on 5 October 1979, concelebrated by John Paul II, the well-known evangelical hymn, "Amazing Grace," was sung.[4]

Is it not appropriate, therefore, that some serious inquiry should be made as to the origin and usages of the term "Evangelical"[5] and concerning the beliefs and practices of those termed "Evangelicals"?

The term itself derives from the Greek word for "gospel" or "good news," εὐαγγέλιον. Within the New Testament writings the word was used to refer to the good news of Jesus Christ,[6] as in Mark 1:1 and Romans 1:16. It also came to be used in reference to a category of ancient literature concerning the life, ministry, death, and resurrection of Jesus of Nazareth, of which there came to be two types: canonical gospels, of which there were four, and apocryphal gospels, of which there were a considerable number.

Hence etymology shows that Evangelicals are in some sense "gospel people." Presumably they have a concern for the good news and attach

---

[3]Paul F. Boller, Jr., "Religion and the U. S. Presidency," *Journal of Church and State* 21 (Winter 1979): 5-7.

[4]"John Paul II: Papal Mass, Chicago, October 5, 1979" (Chicago: Roman Catholic Archdiocese of Chicago, 1979), p. 14.

[5]Lerond Curry, "Will the Real Evangelical Please Stand Up?" *The Christian Century* 93 (26 May 1976): 512-16, has deplored the "one-upmanship" of those "Evangelicals" who apply the term within severe limits to their own group to the exclusion of others and has advocated the laying aside of this and other labels. On the other hand, Joseph Bayly, "Yes, There Are Semi-Evangelicals," *Christianity Today* 21 (29 July 1977): 23, has defended, against Martin E. Marty, the propriety of the use of John Warwick Montgomery's term "semi-evangelical."

[6]Ernst Kinder, *Evangelical: What Does It Mean?*, trans. Edward and Marie Schoeder (St. Louis: Concordia Publishing House, 1968), p. 12, has differentiated *two* meanings of the term "Gospel" in the New Testament: (1) "the *message* spoken by the apostles and repeated to this day by the church," and (2) the saving *"act of God* [in Christ] itself." It is doubtful, however, whether the saving act of God in Christ was ever "good news" apart from interpretation.

high importance to its proclamation. But the actual usages of the term "Evangelicals" must be sought out and discovered within the history of Western Christianity during and since the sixteenth-century Reformation.

The present study will not undertake, as Bernard L. Ramm has already done, "to trace the history of evangelicalism through the great theological crises of the church."[7] The present investigation of the term "Evangelical," being essentially semantic, will rather concentrate on four geographical areas: Continental Europe, the British Isles, Latin America, and the United States. In the outset of such a geographical-semantic inquiry note should be taken of Bruce L. Shelley's definition of Evangelicalism, which, except for Latin America, embraces all the geographical areas to be presently investigated:

> The word "evangelical" is used in our time to designate a group of Protestant churches in Germany, Low Church sympathies in the Church of England, Christians in the Wesleyan tradition, and American fundamentalists. It is most accurately employed, however, in referring to all Christians within Protestant Christianity who emphasize salvation by faith in the atoning death of Jesus Christ through personal conversion, the authority of Scripture, and the importance of preaching in contrast to ritual as a means of saving grace.[8]

Continental Europe

The term "Evangelical" (German, *evangelische*; French, *évan-*

---

[7]*The Evangelical Heritage* (Waco, TX: Word Books, 1973), p. 16. Ramm's tracing of the "Evangelical heritage" suffers from his highly dubious effort to exclude the sixteenth-century Anabaptists from that heritage, ibid., pp. 47-48, fn. 5. Furthermore, Ralph Winter, "Who Are the Evangelicals?" *Christianity Today* 20 (9 April 1976): 35-38, has criticized Ramm for wholesale neglect of the (mid-eighteenth-century) Evangelical Awakening, the Protestant missionary movement, and the ministry of Billy Graham.

[8]*Evangelicalism in America* (Grand Rapids: William B. Eerdmans Publishing Company, 1967), p. 14. Martin E. Marty, "The Revival of Evangelicalism and Southern Religion," in David Edwin Harrell, Jr., ed., *Varieties of Southern Evangelicalism* (Macon, GA: Mercer University Press, 1981), pp. 9-10, has defined "evangelical" as "a Jesus-centered form of Protestantism that emerged during the last quarter millennium largely on Anglo-American soil. It is generated through the call for a turning from the old self and world, in a conversion through an intense experience of Jesus Christ by the power of the Holy Spirit. This conversion it reinforces with a fresh resort to biblical authority supported by high claims for the literal accuracy of the Bible. Evangelicalism then issues in a plea for ordered moral behavior and efforts to witness to and share the faith in the form of evangelism."

gélique) has been used within Protestantism in Continental Europe since the time of the Reformation. Desiderius Erasmus referred in one of his letters to a group as being "evangelicals" and added, "for so they rejoice to be called."[9] "An observer in Italy reported that in the years 1526 and 1527 the evangelical faith was preached so widely and publicly that 'one could see the number of Lutherans who had taken the name Evangelicals increase daily'."[10] In the First Helvetic Confession (1536), framed by representatives of the Protestant cantons, chapter twelve is entitled "The Purpose of Evangelical Doctrine."[11] Sebastian Castellio, in his *Counsel to France in Her Distress* (1562), consistently referred to the Protestants in France as "the Evangelicals."[12] Such sixteenth-century usage of the term "Evangelical" suggests that it was synonymous with the term "Protestant," which originated with the *Protestatio* by the pro-Luther princes and representatives of cities at the Second Diet of Speier in 1529. "Evangelical" was also interchangeable, at least prior to the end of the sixteenth century, with the term "reformed," the first official use of which seems to have been by Theodore Beza at the Colloquy of Poissy in France in 1561.[13] It was not until the end of that century, following controversy over the Lord's Supper, that the term "Lutheran" was used officially and confes-

---

[9]Cited by Heinrich Heppe, *Ursprung und Geschichte der Bezeichnungen "reformirte" und "lutherische" Kirche* (Gotha: Verlag von Friedrich Andreas Perthes, 1859), p. 2, as quoted by M. Eugene Osterhaven, *The Spirit of the Reformed Tradition* (Grand Rapids: William B. Eerdmans Publishing Company, 1971), pp. 171, 177: "...*evangelicos, sic enim appellari gaudent.*"

[10]Osterhaven, *The Spirit of the Reformed Tradition*, pp. 171, 177, quoting from Heppe, *Ursprung und Geschichte*, p. 3: "...*l'on voyait augmenter tous les jours le nombre des Lutheriens, qui avoient pris le nom d'Evangeliques.*"

[11]Arthur C. Cochrane, *Reformed Confessions of the 16th Century* (Philadelphia: Westminster Press, 1966), p. 104.

[12]Sebastian Castellio, *Concerning Heretics . . . together with Excerpts from Other Works of Sebastian Castellio*, trans. and ed. Roland H. Bainton, "Records of Civilization: Sources and Studies," no. 22 (New York: Columbia University Press, 1935), pp. 358-64.

[13]Osterhaven, *The Spirit of the Reformed Tradition*, p. 172. Beza, *Histoire Ecclésiastique des Églises Réformées au Royaume de France* (Lille: Imprimerie de Leleux, Grand Place, 1841), 1: 374, as quoted by Osterhaven, *The Spirit of the Reformed Tradition*, pp. 172, 177, referred in his account of the colloquy to the dogma of transubstantiation "which is disapproved of by the common accord of all the reformed churches both in Germany and elsewhere" (. . . *laquelle est réprouvée par le commun accord de toutes les églises réformées, taut en Allemagne, qu'ailleurs*).

sionally,[14] for even the *Formula of Concord* (1577) did not use the term "Lutheran" but did speak of its churches as "Evangelical Christian churches"[15] and as "our reformed churches."[16] Likewise, it was not until his very late writings that John Calvin used the term "Reformed," and "it was not until the end of the century that 'Reformed' was used as a designation of the non-Lutheran Churches of Germany."[17]

After the end of the sixteenth century, when "Lutheran" and "Reformed" had become antithetical confessional or denominational labels, the term "Evangelical" continued to have a more general usage. Although Pietism, according to Donald G. Bloesch,[18] was one of the principal sources of modern Evangelicalism, Pietists seemingly did not make an exclusive claim to the term "Evangelical." In 1817 in Prussia under the initiative of King Friedrich Wilhelm III the newly formed united church embracing both Lutherans and Calvinists was called the Church of the Evangelical Union. Certain of the Protestant missionary societies organized during the nineteenth century contained the term "Evangelical" in their titles; for example, Basel Evangelical Missionary Society (1815) and the Leipzig Evangelical Lutheran Mission (1836).[19] Today in the two Germanies virtually all the Lutheran territorial churches *(Landeskirchen)* contain in their official titles the hyphenated word *"Evangelisch-lutherische."* The union churches (that is, Lutheran and Reformed) of Berlin-Brandenburg, Saxony, the Rhineland, Silesia, Westphalia, Hesse-Nassau, Kurhessen-Waldeck, and Anhalt all contain the term *"Evangelische"* in their titles. The Reformed Church of Baden calls itself *"Evangelisch-protestantische,"* and the Reformed Church of Bremen calls itself *"Evangelische."*[20] Lest one should conclude, however,

---

[14]Osterhaven, *The Spirit of the Reformed Tradition*, p. 172.

[15]*Formula of Concord*, part 2, "Solid Declaration," preface, in *The Book of Concord: The Confessions of the Evangelical Lutheran Church*, trans. and ed. Theodore G. Tappert (Philadelphia: Muhlenberg Press, 1959), pp. 501-502.

[16]Ibid., part w, "Solid Declaration," "Summary Formulation, Basis, Rule, and Norm...," parag. 3, in *The Book of Concord*, ed. Tappert, p. 504.

[17]Osterhaven, *The Spirit of the Reformed Tradition*, pp. 172, 176.

[18]*The Evangelical Renaissance* (Grand Rapids: William B. Eerdmans Publishing Company, 1973), ch. 5.

[19]Williston Walker, *A History of the Christian Church*, rev. Cyril C. Richardson, Wilhelm Pauck, and Robert T. Handy (New York: Charles Scribner's Sons, 1959), p. 506.

[20]Carl E. Lund-Quist et al., *Lutheran Churches of the World* (Minneapolis: Augsburg Publishing House, 1957), pp. 320-21.

that only to Lutheran and Reformed churches in Continental Europe is the term "Evangelical" applied, it should be noted that the two Baptist unions in the two Germanies have the names *Bund Evangelisch-Freikirchlicher Gemeinden in Deutschland* and *Bund Evangelisch-Freikirchlicher Gemeinden in der DDR.*[21]

Karl Barth, whose theology is usually identified in the Anglo-American sphere as "Neo-Orthodox" rather than as "Evangelical," nevertheless entitled his volume of lectures delivered on his only trip to the United States in 1962: *Evangelical Theology: An Introduction.*[22] Such Continental Protestant authors as G. C. Berkouwer, Hendrikus Berkhof, Helmut Thielicke, Jacques Ellul, Walter Künneth, and Francis Schaeffer may in general terms and perhaps to varying degrees be described as Evangelicals.[23]

The British Isles

However much theological similiarity there may have been between English Puritans of the sixteenth and seventeenth centuries and later Evangelicals, the Puritans by and large did not take the name "Evangelicals." Following and as a consequence of the Evangelical Revival, in which George Whitefield and the Wesleys gave leadership, there developed within the Church of England a party known as the "Evangelicals" or the "Low Church" party. George Reginald Balleine[24] has even traced the Evangelical party to 1729, the year of the formation of the Holy Club at Oxford. The Low Church party was in contrast to the Anglo-Catholic or

---

[21]*New People for a New World—Through Christ: Official Report of the Thirteenth Congress, Baptist World Alliance, Stockholm, Sweden, July 8-13, 1975,* ed. Cyril E. Bryant and Debbie Stewart (Nashville: Broadman Press, 1976), p. 309.

[22]Trans. by Grover Foley (New York: Holt, Rinehart and Winston, 1963).

[23]Bloesch, *The Evangelical Renaissance,* pp. 31-32.

[24]*A History of the Evangelical Party in the Church of England* (London: Longmans, Green, and Co., 1908), p. 1: "Evangelical Churchmen trace their pedigree to the Puritans, the Reformers, and the Lollards, to all within the National Church who have learned to love a simple worship and a spiritual religion; but as a party their existence dates from the Great Revival of the eighteenth century. The story opens at Oxford in 1729. . . ." J. S. Reynolds, *The Evangelicals at Oxford, 1735-1871: A Record of an Unchronicled Movement* (Oxford: Basil Blackwell, 1953), p. 1, has used the word "Evangelical" "to describe a theological position, rather than an ecclesiastical allegiance. It designates 'that school of Protestants which maintains that the essence of the "gospel" consists in the doctrine of salvation by faith in the atoning death of Christ, and denies that either good works or the sacraments have any saving efficacy.' "

High Church party, and in the nineteenth century it would also be differentiated from the Broad Church party. Early Evangelicals included William Grimshaw, Henry Venn, Joseph and Isaac Milner, John William Fletcher, Samuel Walker of Truro, John Berridge, John Newton, William Cowper, and Robert Raikes,[25] but the leading preacher-theologian, who also preserved Anglican polity and helped to keep the Evangelicals within the Church of England,[26] was Charles Simeon of Cambridge.[27] One of the leading evangelical centers of strength was Clapham, a parish near London of which John Venn, the son of Henry Venn, was rector from 1792 to 1813. Clapham men and other Evangelicals founded the Church Missionary Society in 1799.[28] One of the Clapham circle, William Wilberforce, led in the movement to abolish the slave trade (1807) and to abolish slavery (1833) in the British Empire.[29] These Evangelicals, Balleine declared,

> did not invent any new theology. They simply taught the old doctrines of the Reformation—the doctrine of the Trinity (as opposed to the current semi-Socinianism), the guilt of man, his acceptance only through the merits of Christ, renewal and sanctification by the Holy Spirit, and the obligation of universal holiness. They accepted the Thirty-Nine Articles as an almost perfect summary of the Faith.[30]

[25]Balleine, *A History of the Evangelical Party in the Church of England*, pp. 55-56, 72-78, 82-89, 94-96, 98-113, 139-41.

[26]Charles Smyth, *Simeon and Church Order: A Study of the Origins of the Evangelical Revival in Cambridge in the Eighteenth Century* (Cambridge: Cambridge University Press, 1940), esp. ch. 6.

[27]The role of Cambridge as the matrix of Anglican Evangelicals, as it had been of Puritans, has been frequently emphasized. Cf. Balleine, *A History of the Evangelical Party in the Church of England*, pp. 126-33, and Marcus L. Loane, *Cambridge and the Evangelical Succession* (London: Lutterworth Press, 1952). But the presence and activity of Evangelicals at Oxford, even after the expulsion of six Evangelical students in 1768 and even outside St. Edmund's Hall, must also be recognized; cf. Balleine, *A History of the Evangelical Party in the Church of England*, pp. 124-26, 133; Reynolds, *The Evangelicals at Oxford, 1735-1871*; and Marcus L. Loane, *Oxford and the Evangelical Succession* (London: Lutterworth Press, 1950).

[28]Balleine, *A History of the Evangelical Party in the Church of England*, pp. 146-65, and Eugene Stock, *The History of the Church Missionary Society: Its Environment, Its Men and Its Work*, 4 vols. (London: Church Missionary Society, 1899, 1916), 1:31-80.

[29]See John Charles Pollock, *Wilberforce* (New York: St. Martin's Press, 1978), and Oliver Warner, *William Wilberforce and His Times* (London: B. T. Batsford, Ltd., 1962).

[30]*A History of the Evangelical Party in the Church of England*, p. 135.

Some were Calvinists, others were Arminians, and the majority stood somewhere between the two postures. Their innovations seemed to have been the introduction of hymn singing in Anglican worship, of Sunday schools, of the Sunday evening services, and of missionary, tract, and Bible societies.[31] Evangelicals continued to retain an identity and to exert influence within the Anglican communion during the nineteenth and twentieth centuries not only in England but also in the Commonwealth nations and the United States. Among today's leaders of the Evangelical party are Bishop Stephen C. Neill, Donald Coggan, until recently Archbishop of Canterbury, James I. Packer, John R. W. Stott, and Leon Morris of Sydney.

The term "Evangelical" was not normally used by the various Nonconformist or Free church bodies in England to identify themselves. For those who were veering toward unitarian beliefs the term would have been inappropriate. By those whose basic doctrines, apart from church order and polity, would be akin to those of Anglican Evangelicals, the title would not have been disowned. In the late eighteenth century the Church of Scotland had an Evangelical party, one of whose leaders was John Witherspoon, which party controverted the prevailing Moderate party.[32]

The term "Evangelical" was also significantly employed in the name of an international and interconfessional organization of individual Protestant Christians which was founded in London in August-September 1846: the Evangelical Alliance (EA). Formed by individuals from the British Isles, the United States, Canada, and Continental Europe, the Alliance had as its basis the following " 'great evangelical principles,' " which were said not to be formally " 'a Creed or Confession' ":

- The Divine Inspiration, Authority, and Sufficiency of the Holy Scriptures.
- The Right and Duty of Private Judgement in the Interpretation of the Holy Scriptures.
- The Unity of the Godhead, and the Trinity of Persons therein.
- The utter Depravity of Human Nature, in consequence of the Fall.

---

[31]Ibid., pp. 135-36, 137-43, 147, 105, 159-86.

[32]Walker, *A History of the Christian Church*, p. 464.

- The Incarnation of the Son of God, His work of Atonement for sinners of mankind, and His Mediatorial Intercession and Reign.
- The Justification of the sinner by Faith alone.
- The work of the Holy Spirit in the Conversion and Sanctification of the sinner.
- The Immortality of the Soul, the Resurrection of the Body, the Judgement of the World by our Lord Jesus Christ, with the Eternal Blessedness of the Righteous, and the Eternal Punishment of the Wicked.
- The Divine institution of the Christian Ministry, and the obligation and perpetuity of the ordinances of Baptism and the Lord's Supper.

Anglican Evangelicals, English Nonconformists, Free Church of Scotland leaders, Lutherans and Reformed from the Continent, especially those influenced by Pietism, and American and Canadian Protestants from various denominations constituted the EA. Anti-papal and anti-Tractarian in stance, it sponsored an annual week of united prayer, stimulated missionary activity, and promoted a sense of unity among "Evangelicals," but resisted efforts to make it a confederation of churches. Its American branch, delayed by the divisive issue of slavery, was constituted in 1867.[33]

Latin America

With the coming of Protestant Christianity to Latin America during the nineteenth and twentieth centuries, either by immigration, as in the case of German Lutherans, or by missionary work, either from North America or Europe, as in the case of virtually all other Protestant bodies, and with its numerical growth, those belonging to the Protestant com-

---

[33]Ruth Rouse, "Voluntary Movements and the Changing Ecumenical Climate," in Ruth Rouse and Stephen Charles Neill, eds., *A History of the Ecumenical Movement, 1517-1948*, 2nd ed. (Philadelphia: Westminster Press, 1967), pp. 318-24, the nine principles being quoted on p. 320, fn. 1; Henry Renaud Turner Brandreth, "Approaches of the Churches towards Each Other in the Nineteenth Century," in ibid., pp. 638-39; and Don Herbert Yoder, "Christian Unity in Nineteenth-Century America," in ibid., pp. 245, 255-59. According to Yoder (p. 256), the EA in the United States was largely "a dead letter after 1900," but "continued to exist on paper until 1944, when the corporation was dissolved and the funds were transferred to the Federal Council."

munity in Latin America have preferred to speak of themselves as "Evangelicals" rather than as "Protestants." The word is identical in Spanish and Portuguese: *Evangélicos*. The authors of English-language works on Latin American Protestantism tend to use the terms "Protestant" and "Evangelical" interchangeably.[34]

John A. Mackay has summarized the rationale for use of the term "Evangelicals" by Latin American adherents as follows:

> It is profoundly significant that Protestant Christians in the Southern continent prefer to call themselves "Evangelicals," rather than "Protestants." It is not that they are unaware of the theological implications and historic witness of Protestantism, or that they are ashamed of being known as Protestants. Their preference, however, for being known as "Evangelicos" is twofold. In the first place, the associations which many years ago became attached to the term "Protestant" in religious and cultural circles in the Hispanic world, tended to be of a purely negative and derogatory character. In the second place, it was easier for Latin American Protestants to render positive and meaningful witness in their environment if the name they bore did not appear to suggest mere protest or dissent, but affirmed positively the truth for which they stood, a truth which constitutes the very core of the Christian religion. By adopting, therefore, the generic term "evangelicos" to describe

---

[34]See Erasmo Braga and Kenneth George Grubb, *The Republic of Brazil: A Survey of the Religious Situation* (London, New York: World Dominion Press, 1932), esp. chs. 3-6; John A. Mackay, *The Other Spanish Christ: A Study in the Spiritual History of Spain and South America* (New York: Macmillan Company, 1932), pp. 231-75; ibid., *That Other America* (New York: Friendship Press, 1935), pp. 141-202; W. Stanley Rycroft, *On This Foundation: The Evangelical Witness in Latin America* (New York: Friendship Press, 1942), pp. 68-96; ibid., *Religion and Faith in Latin America* (Philadelphia: Westminster Press, 1958), pp. 139-41, 147-77; and William R. Read, Victor M. Monterroso, and Harmon A. Johnson, *Latin American Church Growth* (Grand Rapids: William B. Eerdmans Publishing Company, 1969), esp. pp. 35-47, although in the remainder of the book the term "Evangelical" predominates. On the other hand, Kenneth George Grubb, *Religion in Central America* (London, New York: World Dominion Press, 1937), pp. 28-48, used interchangeably "Evangelical" and "non-Roman," and W. Stanley Rycroft and Myrtle M. Clemmer, *A Factual Study of Latin America* (New York: Commission on Ecumenical Mission and Relations, United Presbyterian Church in the U.S.A., 1963), pp. 183, 193-96, 205-206, 217-33, distinctly preferred the term "Protestant." The widespread contemporary usage of *Evangélicos* in Latin America has been confirmed by interviews with Jerry S. Key, professor, Baptist Seminary of South Brazil, 9 October 1979, and with Roy L. Lyon, former rector, Baptist Seminary of Venezuela, 17 October 1979.

themselves, they were in fact quietly proclaiming that devotion to the Gospel, which centers in Christ and is the main theme of the Bible, is what makes people truly Christian across all denominational boundaries. They were in effect setting personal obedience to Christ and the Gospel over and above nominal unreflective membership in an institution called the Church.[35]

Latin American Evangelicalism today includes theologians of liberation such as Rubem Alves, Brazilian Presbyterian, and José Míguez-Bonino, Argentine Methodist, pastors such as Nilson Fanini, Brazilian Baptist, radio preachers such as David Gomes, Brazilian Baptist, and evangelists such as Argentine-born Luis Palau.[36]

The United States

Much of American Protestantism from the colonial period to the end of the nineteenth century can be generally described as "Evangelical," in the sense of being gospel-oriented and Bible-oriented, but the term was not a generally accepted or frequently used label.

Part of the Name for Denominational Bodies. In the United States the term "Evangelical" has often formed part of the official name of various Protestant denominational bodies. This has been particularly true of Lutheran bodies, German Reformed bodies, German-language Methodist bodies, and Swedish independent bodies.

Following the German and Scandinavian practice in Europe, various Lutheran synods and one synodical conference in the United States have placed the term "Evangelical" in their names. A partial list includes the following, most of which have by virtue of church unions ceased to bear these titles:

- Evangelical Lutheran Church of North America (1846), also

---

[35]*The Latin American Churches and the Ecumenical Movement* (New York: Committee on Cooperation in Latin America, Division of Foreign Missions, National Council of the Churches of Christ in the U.S.A., 1963), p. 23. Mackay also affirmed that Latin American Evangelicals had become "heirs of a great lost tradition in Hispanic Christianity . . . profoundly evangelical in character" which embraced "Theresa of Avila, John of the Cross and Luis de Leon, the brothers Juan and Alfonso Valdes, Casiodoro de Reina and Cipriano de Valera."

[36]Palau is affiliated with Overseas Crusades, Palo Alto, California.

called Eielsen Synod, which became Hauge's Norwegian Evangelical Lutheran Synod in America (1876)

- Norwegian Evangelical Lutheran Church of America (1853), or Norwegian Synod
- Scandinavian Evangelical Lutheran Augustana Synod of North America (1860), which became Swedish Evangelical Lutheran Augustana Synod (c. 1870), which in turn became Evangelical Lutheran Augustana Synod in North America (c. 1895), which in turn became Augustana Evangelical Lutheran Church (1948)
- Evangelical Lutheran Synodical Conference of North America (1872)
- Danish Evangelical Lutheran Church in America (1872), which became American Evangelical Lutheran Church (1953)
- Icelandic Evangelical Lutheran Synod of America (1885)
- Finnish Evangelical Lutheran Church in America (1890), or Suomi Synod
- United Danish Evangelical Lutheran Church (1896), which became United Evangelical Lutheran Church (1946)
- Finnish Evangelical Lutheran National Church of America (1898), which became National Evangelical Lutheran Church (1946)
- Slovak Evangelical Lutheran Church of America (1902), which became Synod of Evangelical Lutheran Churches (1959)
- Evangelical Lutheran Joint Synod of Wisconsin and Other States (1919), which became Wisconsin Evangelical Lutheran Synod (1959)
- Evangelical Lutheran Church (1946), formerly Norwegian Lutheran Church of America.[37]

In 1840 a small group of German Reformed pastors in the vicinity of St. Louis formed *Der Deutsche Evangelische Kirchenverein*[38] *des*

---

[37]Abdel Ross Wentz, *A Basic History of Lutheranism in America* (Philadelphia: Muhlenberg Press, 1955), passim; E. Clifford Nelson, *Lutheranism in North America, 1914-1970* (Minneapolis: Augsburg Publishing House, 1972), p. 77, chart on inside cover.

[38]"The term *Verein* was variously translated in contemporary documents as 'society,' 'synod,' 'association,' 'conference,' or 'union.' " David Dunn et al., *A History of the Evangelical and Reformed Church* (Philadelphia: Christian Education Press, 1961), p. 171.

Westens. By 1866 the term *"Kirchenverein"* was Anglicized as "Synod," by 1872 the Synod of the West merged with two other German Reformed synods, and the resultant German[39] Evangelical Synod of North America expanded in the western states. In 1934 this body united with another German Reformed body, the Reformed Church in the United States, whose first synod had been formed by Michael Schlatter (1716-1790) in 1747, whose synodical history dated from 1793, and whose membership was primarily in the eastern states. The roots of the Reformed Church in the United States were in the "union" Church of the Palatinate, whereas the origins of the Evangelical Synod of North America could be traced to the Church of the Prussian Union (1817). Hence neither was hostile to the Lutheran heritage. The merged church bore the name: the Evangelical and Reformed Church. Its separate existence continued until 1957, when it united with the majority of the Congregational Christian Churches to form the United Church of Christ.[40]

Among Lutherans and German Reformed in the United States the term "Evangelical" tended to connote adherence to various Lutheran and/or Reformed confessions of faith. Moreover, the catechism and the sacraments tended to be emphasized more than conversion, and doctrine to be stressed more than experience.

Inasmuch as some German immigrants were influenced by Wesleyan Methodism, two German-language church bodies came into existence in Pennsylvania at the beginning of the nineteenth century. One, the Church of the United Brethren in Christ, organized in 1800, was the fruit of the labors of Philip Wilhelm Otterbein (1726-1813), Pietistic German Reformed immigrant preacher, and Martin Boehm (1725-1812), former Mennonite. The other, the Evangelical Association, originated in the same year under the ministry of Jacob Albright (1759-1808). A division within the Evangelical Association resulted in the organization in 1894 of the United Evangelical Church, but that body and the Evangelical Association reunited in 1922 to form the Evangelical Church.[41] Some of the United Evangelical Church did not reunite and continue to exist as the

---

[39]The word "German" was dropped in 1927, ibid., p. 275.

[40]Ibid., pp. 169-72, 190, 202-206, 233-47, 293, 283-90, 37-39, 51-52, 340-42, 331-36.

[41]Augustus Waldo Drury, *History of the Church of the United Brethren in Christ* (Dayton, Ohio: Otterbein Press, 1924), pp. 27-250, 265-70; Raymond W. Albright, *A History of the Evangelical Church* (Harrisburg, Pa.: Evangelical Press, 1942), pp. 45-56, 58-62, 88, 330-33, 377-89.

Evangelical Congregational Church.[42] In 1946 the Evangelical Church and the Church of the United Brethren in Christ merged to form the Evangelical United Brethren Church, and in 1968 the latter united with the much larger Methodist Church to form the United Methodist Church. Those Evangelical-United Brethren who did not participate in this merger formed in 1968 the Evangelical Church of North America.[43]

Certain Scandinavian immigrants to the United States, reacting against the state churches of their native lands, formed "free" churches of an "evangelical" type with congregational polity and utilized the term "Evangelical" in the names of their movements. The Norwegian-Danish Free Church Association of North America traces its history to 1884 in Boston, and in the same year the Swedish Evangelical Free Church of America had its beginning in Boone, Iowa. The former was renamed the Evangelical Free Church Association, and the latter became the Evangelical Free Church of America. The two merged in 1950 to form the Evangelical Free Church of America. Pretribulational premillennialism and biblical inerrancy are among its doctrines.[44] The Evangelical Free Church of America is a member of the National Association of Evangelicals.[45]

Swedish immigrants who had been influenced by the Mission Friends (*Missionsväonner*) in Sweden, an indigenous mid-nineteenth-century lay-oriented, house-church, and missionary movement with roots in German Pietism and English Wesleyanism but still within the Church of Sweden, constituted in 1873 in Iowa the Evangelical Lutheran Mission Synod of America. The practice of receiving unbelievers as well as believers into Lutheran churches was given as the reason for non-affiliation with a general Lutheran synod. In 1874 in Galesburg, Illinois, other Mission Friends organized the Evangelical Lutheran Ansgarius Synod but decided to join the Lutheran General Synod. The Ansgarius Synod severed its ties

---

[42]Frank S. Mead, *Handbook of Denominations in the United States*, 6th ed. (Nashville: Abingdon Press, 1975), p. 137.

[43]Ibid., pp. 136-37.

[44]Arnold Theodore Olson, *This We Believe: The Background and Exposition of the Doctrinal Statement of the Evangelical Free Church of America* (Minneapolis: Free Church Publications, 1961), pp. 8, 92, 137, 317-28, 136, 187-90.

[45]James DeForest Murch, *Cooperation without Compromise: A History of the National Association of Evangelicals* (Grand Rapids: William B. Eerdmans Publishing Company, 1956), p. 202.

with the Lutheran General Synod in 1882 and dissolved itself in 1885. Despite strong currents toward congregational independency, various Mission Friends organized in Chicago in 1885 the Swedish Evangelical Mission Covenant of America, composed of churches and societies. In 1920 a proposed union with the Swedish Evangelical Free Church of America failed.[46] The denominational name was changed in 1957 to the Evangelical Covenant Church of America.[47]

Two Baptist bodies currently have the word "Evangelical" in their official names. One of these is the National Baptist Evangelical Life and Soul Saving Assembly of the U.S.A., which was formed in 1920 in Kansas City, Missouri, as part of the National Baptist Convention, U.S.A. (unincorporated), but became independent in 1937. The other is the General Conference of the Evangelical Baptist Church, Inc., which was organized among Free Will Baptists in 1935 and is similar to Free Will Baptists.[48]

Two Mennonite bodies bear the name "Evangelical": the Evangelical Mennonite Church, which originated in 1858 and was until 1948 known as the Defenseless Mennonite Church; and the Evangelical Mennonite Brethren Conference, which dates from 1889 and insists "on a definite Christian experience as a prerequisite for baptism."[49] Both of these bodies are members of the National Association of Evangelicals.[50] The Evangelical Methodist Church, which separated from the Methodist Church in 1946 over issues of polity and "modernism," is a congregationally governed group.[51]

The Name for the Transformed of Fundamentalism. By far the most important usage of the term "Evangelical" for the contemporary Christian scene is that which in the United States grew out of Fundamentalism

---

[46]C. V. Bowman, *The Mission Covenant of America* (Chicago: Covenant Book Concern, 1925), chs. 1-6, 8, 10, 16; David Nyall and Karl A. Olsson, *The Evangelical Covenant Church* (Chicago: Covenant Press, 1954), ch. 4.

[47]F. E. Mayer, *The Religious Bodies of America*, 4th ed. rev. by Arthur Carl Piepkorn (St. Louis: Concordia Publishing House, 1961), p. 341.

[48]Mead, *Handbook of Denominations in the United States*, 6th ed., pp. 55, 54.

[49]Annie Dyck, ed., *Mennoniten in aller Welt/Mennonites around the World* (Basel: Agape-Verlag, 1967), p. 63.

[50]Murch, *Cooperation without Compromise*, p. 202.

[51]*The History of American Methodism*, ed. Emory Stevens Bucke et al., 3 vols. (Nashville: Abingdon Press, 1964), 3:593-94; Murch, *Cooperation without Compromise*, p. 202.

following its controversy with Modernism and which has developed during the period of about forty years, that is, since about 1940. It is not possible here to review in detail the course of the Fundamentalist-Modernist Controversy, which may indeed have been the Fundamentalist-Conservative-Liberal-Modernist Controversy, or its effects upon the major Protestant denominations.[52] It is not necessary to settle finally the question of the influence of the prophetic and Bible conferences of the late nineteenth century upon Fundamentalism. It is sufficient to acknowledge that the term "fundamentals" derives from the series of books entitled *The Fundamentals: A Testimony to the Truth*[53] and published in 1910-1915 under the successive editorship of Amzi Clarence Dixon, Louis Meyer, and Reuben A. Torrey and with the financial backing of two brothers, Lyman and Milton Stewart of Los Angeles. The term "fundamentalist" was coined by Curtis Lee Laws, editor of the (Baptist) *Watchman-Examiner*, in 1920 when he used it to refer to those "who mean to do battle royal for the fundamentals."[54]

One should note that the list of the so-called five "fundamentals" has not always appeared in identical form. Cole (1931)[55] attributed to the Niagara Bible Conference of 1895 five fundamentals, although the fifth had two parts (inerrancy of the Bible; deity of Christ; virgin birth of Christ; substitutionary atonement of Christ; and bodily resurrection and second coming of Christ to earth), and seemingly assumed that these were the five points of later Fundmentalism. Furniss (1954)[56] listed five points allegedly based on the volumes entitled *The Fundamentals*; in doing so he deleted the deity of Christ and split into two points the bodily resurrection of Christ and the second coming of Christ. Gasper (1963)[57] listed the five points as had Cole and held these to have been expressed

---

[52]The first two histories of Fundamentalism, both written by strong critics of the movement, traced the effects upon the major denominations during the 1920s: Stewart G. Cole, *The History of Fundamentalism* (New York: Richard R. Smith, Inc., 1931); Norman F. Furniss, *The Fundamentalist Controversy, 1918-1931* (New Haven: Yale University Press, 1954). Furniss tended to make evolution the central issue.

[53]12 vols. in 4 (Chicago: Testimony Publishing Company, 1910-1915?).

[54]"Convention Side Lights," *Watchman-Examiner* 8 (1 July 1920): 834.

[55]Cole, *The History of Fundamentalism*, p. 34.

[56]Furniss, *The Fundamentalist Controversy, 1918-1931*, p. 13.

[57]Louis Gasper, *The Fundamentalist Movement* (The Hague: Mouton & Co., 1963), pp. 11, 12.

identically at Niagara Falls in 1895 and by Fundamentalists in 1910, but Gasper's listing of the five points as derived from the volumes entitled *The Fundamentals* did not include the deity of Christ except in a supplementary list of four doctrines. Sandeen (1970)[58] corrected Cole by pointing out that fourteen doctrines, not five, had been affirmed by the Niagara Bible Conference and that first in 1878, not in 1895. Sandeen pointed to the five doctrines (inerrancy of Scripture; virgin birth of Christ; atonement of Christ; resurrection of Christ; and miracle-working power of Christ) adopted by the General Assembly of the Presbyterian Church, U.S.A. in 1910 and reaffirmed in 1916 and 1923, and concluded that the five Presbyterian doctrines were not millenarian, whereas the Niagara articles had been clearly premillennial. Such a labyrinthine tracing of the five points can lead to the conclusion that, whereas there may never have been a fully agreed upon list of five fundamentals, all the items that have appeared in such lists had strong support among Fundamentalists.

Sandeen (1968, 1970)[59] has provided a religio-theological interpretation of Fundamentalism which was lacking in the earlier histories of Fundamentalism and has treated it as a "movement" and not just as a "controversy" during the 1920s. Theological interpretation is especially important for the understanding of the post-1940 usage of the term "Evangelical." Sandeen's thesis is that Fundamentalism "was comprised of an alliance between two newly formulated nineteenth-century theologies, dispensationalism and the Princeton Theology which, though not wholly compatible, managed to maintain a united front against Modernism until about 1918."[60] Dispensationalism and the Princeton theology, of course, differed on the doctrines of eschatology, inasmuch as the Princeton theologians (Charles Hodge, Benjamin Breckinridge Warfield) were postmillennialists. But the Princeton doctrine of Scripture as verbally inspired, inerrant, and rationally defensible had been appro-

---

[58]Ernest R. Sandeen, *The Roots of Fundamentalism: British and American Millenarianism, 1800-1930* (Chicago: University of Chicago Press, 1970), pp. xiv-xv.

[59]Ibid., esp. pp. ix-xiv, and *The Origins of Fundamentalism: Toward a Historical Interpretation,* "Facet Books, Historical Series," no. 10 (Philadelphia: Fortress Press, 1968).

[60]*The Origins of Fundamentalism,* p. 3. Shelley, *Evangelicalism in America,* pp. 63-67, had anticipated Sandeen's thesis by pointing to two nineteenth-century sources of Fundamentalism: "the Old School Presbyterians headed by Princeton Theological Seminary and the premillennial thought expressed in the Bible conference movement." Shelley differentiated "historic" premillennialism and Dispensationalism.

priated by Dispensationalists, whose roots were traceable to John Nelson Darby and the Plymouth Brethren. Furthermore, Bloesch (1973) sought to correct or expand Sandeen's thesis by asserting that Fundamentalism "represents a union of scholastic orthodoxy (both Reformed and Lutheran) and latter-day Pietism, which includes both premillennial and perfectionist strands."[61] Thus Sandeen saw British millenarianism of the nineteenth century as a major source of Fundamentalism, whereas Bloesch gave stress to Continental Pietism as a source of Fundamentalism; yet both Sandeen and Bloesch acknowledged post-Reformation Protestant orthodoxy or its late American expression at Princeton as a major source.

The image of Fundamentalism in the United States during the 1930s and later was not a favorable one. H. L. Mencken and the American press described Fundamentalists most unfavorably. The *Scopes* trial made it easier to do, and the negative withdrawal and bitter denunciations of others that characterized many Fundamentalists added to the unfavorable image. Fundamentalism had no social ethic, and it sometimes showed little of its professed personal ethic. But it did, however, during the 1930s begin to constitute outside the structures of the older Protestant denominations a network of Bible institutes, liberal arts colleges, summer assemblies, radio programs, foreign mission agencies, and publication outlets.[62] But how, indeed, did Fundamentalism, especially of the 1920s, become Evangelicalism? One of the key events in such a transition was the formation in St. Louis in April 1942 of the National Association of Evangelicals (NAE) with Harold John Ockenga as its first president. Composed of denominations, independent religious organizations, local churches, groups of churches, and individuals, the NAE sought to provide channels for united action by Evangelicals in the national use of radio, church-state separation, relations with government, preservation of freedom for home and foreign missions, evangelism, Christian education, and evangelical cooperation within local communities and to act as a counter-

[61]*The Evangelical Renaissance*, p. 143. Shelley, *Evangelicalism in America*, pp. 25-63, listed as "roots" of modern "Evangelicalism": Puritanism, Pietism, Methodism, Anglican Evangelicals, Evangelical Nonconformity (in Britain), the Great Awakening, revivalism, perfectionism, voluntary societies, the Holiness movement, Pentecostalism, and Fundamentalism.

[62]Joel A. Carpenter, "Fundamentalist Institutions and the Rise of Evangelical Protestantism," *Church History* 49 (March 1980): 62-75.

force to the Federal Council of the Churches of Christ in the U.S.A. (FCC). Its sevenfold doctrinal affirmation included the "fundamentals" of Fundamentalism but also specifically stressed "regeneration by the Holy Spirit," godly living by the indwelling of the Holy Spirit, "the spiritual unity of believers" in Christ, and dual eternal destiny.[63] Preceded by the New England Fellowship (1929),[64] the NAE became the rallying point for the smaller denominations that had continued to be "evangelical," those "evangelicals" in the larger denominations that were resisting "Liberalism" or "Modernism," and the numerous independent "evangelical" churches and para-church organizations that had been formed during the twentieth century. The NAE spawned such allied organizations as the Evangelical Foreign Missions Association (1945), the National Sunday School Association (1945), the Accrediting Association of Bible Institutes and Bible Colleges (1947), the National Association of Christian Day Schools (1947), the Evangelical Press Association (1948), and the Evangelical Theological Society (1949), and on an international scale the World Evangelical Alliance (1951).[65] By 1956 the NAE had forty-one member denominations and a total membership of more than two million persons.[66] It did not deny membership to local churches that belonged to denominations that in turn belonged to the FCC or its successor, the National Council of the Churches of Christ in the U.S.A.[67]

Prior to the organization of the NAE in 1942, two other organizations destined to influence Evangelicalism had come into being. In 1940 the Inter-Varsity Christian Fellowship (IVCF), which could trace its beginning to the University of Cambridge in the 1870s, took organizational form in the United States and began to constitute chapters on university campuses. Hence an increasing number of university graduates began to be influenced toward Evangelicalism. IVCF's five doctrinal

---

[63]Murch, *Cooperation without Compromise*, pp. 52-71, 202-204. Southern Baptists who were participants in the formation or early history of the NAE include Dr. R. G. Lee, Dr. Robert J. Bateman, Dr. Russell Bradley Jones, Dr. Victor I. Masters, Judge John W. McCall, and Dr. O. W. Taylor, ibid., pp. 54 (fn. 6), 56, 57, 58, 60-61, and 67 (fn. 4), and Southern Baptist Convention *Annual* (1942), pp. 542, 537, 541, 490, 8, and 545.

[64]Murch, *Cooperation without Compromise*, pp. 51-52.

[65]Ibid., esp. pp. 102, 124, 90, 91, 173-74, 93, and 184-89.

[66]Ibid., pp. 202-203.

[67]Gasper, *The Fundamentalist Movement*, p. vi; cf. Shelley, *Evangelicalism in America*, pp. 69-109.

articles included the "fundamentals" of Fundamentalism; the atonement and the resurrection of Christ were united as one article; regeneration by the Holy Spirit was added; but the article on the Bible did not utilize the terms "inerrancy" or "infallibility."[68]

In September 1941 the Bible Presbyterian Church and the Bible Protestant Church, formerly the Methodist Protestant Church, led in the formation of the American Council of Christian Churches (ACCC) with Carl McIntire, Bible Presbyterian pastor, as its first president.[69] Designed to resist the "apostasy" of the Modernists,[70] the ACCC accepted the five articles of Fundamentalism[71] and established a policy of exclusivism or separation which barred "individual churches and denominations from its membership as long as any of them were associated with modernism or remained affiliated with the Federal Council."[72] The leaders who were in 1941 bringing into existence the NAE conferred with ACCC leaders but decided that the two bodies had different methods and ideals and should not coalesce.[73] Indeed, the NAE and the ACCC did represent different postures toward non-Evangelicals and did pursue different objectives. In 1948 the ACCC led in forming in Amsterdam the International Council of Christian Churches as a countermovement to the World Council of Churches, but by 1956 McIntire's critics within the Bible Presbyterian Church were able to withdraw that denomination from the ACCC. In 1957 the ACCC reported fourteen "constituent" member denominations. McIntire and others were active in the anti-Communist crusade, in criticism of the Revised Standard Version of the Bible, and in

---

[68]Gasper, *The Fundamentalist Movement*, pp. 90-92; Murch, *Cooperation without Compromise*, pp. 94-96; Richard Quebedeaux, *The Worldly Evangelicals* (New York: Harper & Row, 1978), pp. 101-103. The Young Life movement, founded in 1941 by Jim Rayburn of Dallas, has sought to evangelize high school and junior high school youth; see Quebedeaux, *The Worldly Evangelicals*, pp. 104-105.

[69]Gasper, *The Fundamentalist Movement*, pp. 21-23.

[70]Carl McIntire, *Twentieth Century Reformation* (Collingswood, N.J.: Christian Beacon Press, 1944), esp. chs. 4-6, 18-20.

[71]McIntire, in ibid., pp. 11-15, also claimed that the ACCC was in agreement with the nine articles of faith adopted by the Evangelical Alliance in London in 1846 and that the ACCC was "in a sense a continuation of the testimony of the Alliance" (p. 14).

[72]Gasper, *The Fundamentalist Movement*, p. 24.

[73]Murch, *Cooperation without Compromise*, pp. 53, 57-58. For McIntire's account of these negotiations, see *Twentieth Century Reformation*, pp. 191-98.

repudiating the entire Ecumenical movement.[74] McIntire generally preferred the term "Protestant" to the term "Evangelical." By 1970 he had lost his control of the ACCC.

The formation of the NAE did not mean that the term "Fundamentalist" would cease to be used and the term "Evangelical" would be its invariable replacement. Although the term "Fundamentalist" was more aptly and self-consciously applied to the ACCC and although the term "Evangelical" came to be favored by the NAE leadership, the American public and the American press were hardly aware of such a distinction during the 1940s, the 1950s, and the early 1960s.

From the end of World War II (1945) to the election of John F. Kennedy as president (1960) the Evangelical movement was engaged in constructing its structures and moving out of the matrix of Fundamentalism. The structures were formed in respect to youth movements, mass evangelism, educational institutions, and publications. In 1945 Torrey Johnson led in the organization of Youth for Christ, International; its first field representative was Billy Graham (1918—   ), and its Saturday night rallies were held in numerous cities in the United States and abroad.[75] In 1951 Bill Bright founded Campus Crusade for Christ, a movement that was to expand greatly during the 1960s and 1970s.[76]

Although nationwide radio broadcasts such as Charles E. Fuller's "Old Fashioned Revival Hour"[77] and Walter A. Maier's preaching on "The Lutheran Hour"[78] preceded the 1950s, it was Billy Graham's evangelistic crusades in numerous cities, beginning in Los Angeles in 1949, and his "Hour of Decision" (1955), both undergirded by the Billy Graham Evangelistic Association (1950), that elevated mass evangelism and the Evangelical movement to a new level of visibility, acceptance, and influence. In

---

[74]Gasper, *The Fundamentalist Movement*, pp. 44-51, 33-37, 39, 59-69, 71-74, 69-71. For McIntire's criticism of the World Council of Churches, see especially his *Modern Tower of Babel* (Collingswood, N.J.: Christian Beacon Press, 1949). For a critical interpretation of McIntire and the ACCC, see Ralph Lord Roy, *Apostles of Discord: A Study of Organized Bigotry and Disruption on the Fringes of Protestantism* (Boston: Beacon Press, 1953), pp. 165-68, 185-202, 204-27, 238-42.

[75]Gasper, *The Fundamentalist Movement*, pp. 85-89, 130.

[76]Quebedeaux, *The Young Evangelicals: Revolution in Orthodoxy*, pp. 30-31; Quebedeaux, *The Worldly Evangelicals*, pp. 55-59.

[77]Gasper, *The Fundamentalist Movement*, pp. 77-78.

[78]Murch, *Cooperation without Compromise*, pp. 49, 72.

Graham's 1957 crusade in New York City the criticism by ACCC leaders McIntire, John R. Rice, and Bob Jones, Sr., of Graham's nonseparatism or inclusivism became prime evidence that Fundamentalism and Evangelicalism were not only distinguishable but also divergent.[79]

Numerous Bible institutes and Bible colleges were constituted, especially during the 1930s and 1940s, and these belong to the story of Evangelicalism's emergence from Fundamentalism.[80] Wheaton College, Wheaton, Illinois, continued to grow in influence and to move into Evangelicalism, whereas Bob Jones University, which moved from Cleveland, Tennessee, to Greenville, South Carolina, in 1947, became markedly identified with separatist Fundamentalism.[81] Fuller Theological Seminary, founded in Pasadena, California, in 1947, was destined to identify with the emerging Evangelicalism.[82] In 1949 the Evangelical Theological Society, with its single condition of membership, namely, belief in the inerrancy of the autographs of the Bible, was organized.[83]

In 1956 Graham and others established a fortnightly Evangelical magazine, *Christianity Today*, with Carl F. H. Henry as its first editor. It served as the Evangelical "counterpart" to *The Christian Century* and *Christianity and Crisis*.[84] A group of theologians, including Henry, Edward John Carnell, Bernard Ramm, and others, began to write and publish prolifically under the label of "Neo-Evangelical" theologians. Certain bookstores, especially Eerdmans, Baker, and Zondervan in Grand Rapids, Michigan, which had specialized in "selling used and rare orthodox books which the traditional Eastern publishers neglected and allowed to go out of print," became publishers of an increasing and more widely circulating Neo-Evangelical literature.[85]

---

[79]Gasper, *The Fundamentalist Movement*, pp. 130-47, 78-79; Quebedeaux, *The Worldly Evangelicals*, p. 54.

[80]Gasper, *The Fundamentalist Movement*, pp. 93-103.

[81]Ibid., pp. 104-109; Quebedeaux, *The Young Evangelicals*, pp. 22, 29-30.

[82]Quebedeaux, *The Young Evangelicals*, pp. 69-72.

[83]Quebedeaux, *The Worldly Evangelicals*, pp. 33-34.

[84]Quebedeaux, *The Young Evangelicals*, pp. 13, 28, 36.

[85]See Shelley, *Evangelicalism in America*, pp. 111-20. Ronald H. Nash, *The New Evangelicalism* (Grand Rapids: Zondervan Publishing House, 1963), interpreted Neo-Evangelicalism's rise out of Fundamentalism (esp. ch. 2), differentiated the two movements, and defended the case for Neo-Evangelicalism. Writing to refute Robert Lightner, *Neo-Evangelicalism* (Findlay, Ohio: Dunham Publishing Col., 1962), esp. in chs. 10-11,

"Evangelicals" were not only to be found in the denominations that were members of the NAE and among the supporters of the Billy Graham Evangelistic Association, Campus Crusade for Christ, Fuller Theological Seminary, and the like but also in the congregations of other denominations, namely, the Southern Baptist Convention, the Lutheran Church-Missouri Synod, the Christian Reformed Church, and to a lesser extent the Presbyterian Church in the United States.

The "Evangelicals" who had come out of the matrix of Fundamentalism were not in the vanguard of the Civil Rights movement or of media attention during the 1960s. Trinity Evangelical Divinity School, an institution of the Evangelical Free Church of America, however, was restructured in 1963 and began to expand, and Gordon-Conwell Theological Seminary was created by the merger of Gordon Divinity School and the Conwell School of Theology.

A Name Embracing Pentecostalists, Neo-Pentecostalists, and the Jesus Movement. The turbulent 1960s brought two unexpected accessions to American Evangelicalism. Bursting onto the American scene was the Neo-Pentecostal or Charismatic movement with its emphasis on baptism of the Holy Spirit as evidenced by speaking in tongues, direct divine healing, and other charisms. It had no direct links to the older or classical Pentecostal churches that had originated early in the twentieth century. It perhaps did have the worldwide Pentecostal leader, David DuPlessis, the Full Gospel Business Men's Fellowship International, established in 1951 by Armenian-American dairyman Demos Shakarian, and the ministry of Oral Roberts as its active precursors.[86] Neo-Pentecostalism quickly spread into mainline Protestant churches and subsequently into the Roman Catholic Church. Traceable to St. Mark's Episcopal Church, Van Nuys, California, the reception of the baptism of the Holy Spirit by its rector, Dennis Bennett, and by some seventy other members, and Bennett's resignation as rector in April 1960,[87] the move-

---

Nash (pp. 13-14) attributed the term "new evangelicalism" to Harold John Ockenga, "The New Evangelicalism," *The Park Street Spire*, February 1958. On the publishing houses in Grand Rapids, see Gasper, *The Fundamentalist Movement*, p. 121.

[86]Richard Quebedeaux, *The New Charismatics: The Origins, Development, and Significance of Neo-Pentecostalism* (Garden City, N.Y.: Doubleday & Company, Inc., 1976), pp. 53-54; Erling Jorstad, comp., *The Holy Spirit in Today's Church: A Handbook of the New Pentecostalism* (New York: Abingdon Press, 1973), pp. 16-17.

[87]Quebedeaux, *The New Charismatics*, pp. 54-57.

ment in its Protestant phase came to be expressed in such forms as the Blessed Trinity Society (1961-1966), Oral Roberts University (1965), Melodyland Christian Center and its charismatic clinics, Kathryn Kuhlman's healing campaigns, Logos International publishers, the Society for Pentecostal Studies (1971),[88] Pat Robertson's Christian Broadcasting Network, and the Beverly Hills Baptist Church of Dallas, Texas. Its Roman Catholic phase began in 1967 on the campuses of Duquesne University, the University of Notre Dame, and Michigan State University, spread to other campuses and cities, and was fostered by annual national Catholic Pentecostal conferences.[89] It was obvious from the early years of Neo-Pentecostalism that, despite its common ground with classical Pentecostalism on Spirit-baptism and glossolalia, the two movements were marked by genuine and significant differences. Richard Quebedeaux has identified seven of these differences. Neo-Pentecostalism is characterized by " 'progressive evangelicalism' " rather than "rigid fundamentalism," by the "quiet spirit" rather than a "spirit of confusion," by "ecumenism" instead of "sectarianism," by "intellectual motivation" and not by "anti-intellectualism," by a "social conscience" rather than by "social unconcern," by "culture affirmation" instead of "culture rejection," and by a "middle-class" rather than a "working-class" identity.[90]

But one is entitled to ask whether and to what extent either or both of these movements, classical Pentecostalism and Neo-Pentecostalism, should be reckoned among the "Evangelicals." Classical Pentecostalists, represented by the beliefs of the major Pentecostal bodies such as the Assemblies of God, the Church of God (Cleveland, Tennessee), the United Pentecostal Church, the Church of God in Christ, and the International Church of the Foursquare Gospel, by virtue of their views of the inspiration and authority of the Bible, the deity of Christ, his virgin birth, substitutionary atonement, bodily resurrection, and second coming,

---

[88]Ibid., pp. 57-76, 102-104; 87-92, 58, 69, 103, 105-108, 110, 122-23, 155-56; 77, 84-87, 141, 183; 69, 77, 81-82; 69, 155, 172. See Steve Durasoff, *Bright Wind of the Spirit: Pentecostalism Today* (Englewood Cliffs, N.J.: Prentice-Hall, Inc., 1972), chs. 7, 8, 10.

[89]Quebedeaux, *The New Charismatics*, pp. 63-68, 70, 120-21, 165, 170, 177. See Edward D. O'Connor, C. S. C., *The Pentecostal Movement in the Catholic Church* (Notre Dame, Ind.: Ave Maria Press, 1971); Kevin Ranaghan and Dorothy Ranaghan, *Catholic Pentecostals* (Paramus, N.J.: Paulist Press, 1969), chs. 1-2; Rene Laurentin, *Catholic Pentecostalism*, trans. Matthew J. O'Connell (Garden City, N.Y.: Doubleday & Company, Inc., 1977), pp. 11-17; and Durasoff, *Bright Wind of the Spirit*, ch. 6.

[90]*The New Charismatics*, ch. 6.

should be reckoned as "Evangelicals" even though they do not share the Calvinistic orientation of the Neo-Evangelicals who came out of Fundamentalism and instead make Pentecost and the gifts of the Holy Spirit central.[91] A similar affirmative answer is to be given concerning Neo-Pentecostalists, most of whom have remained within their former denominations, most of which are members of the National Council of Churches. These persons tend to have a high view of the authority of the Bible; to affirm clearly the deity of Christ and of the Holy Spirit, and hence the Trinity; to be conscious of salvation by grace; and to emphasize the life in and the gifts of the Spirit. Neo-Pentecostalists tend also to embody the ecumenism of the charisms.

The other unexpected accession to Evangelicalism during the 1960s, less numerous than Neo-Pentecostalism, consisted of those who came from the Jesus Movement. Unlike most Neo-Pentecostalists whose backgrounds were mainstream, the Jesus people came from the counterculture of the 1960s and retained deep concern for the transformation of American society.[92] In 1969 there was founded in Berkeley, California, by persons working with Campus Crusade for Christ an evangelistic and "socially concerned street and campus ministry as an alternative to the . . . Third World Liberation Front," namely, the Christian World Liberation Front (CWLF). After a schism in 1975 CWLF was renamed the Berkeley Christian Coalition (BCC). This community publishes *Radix* (formerly

---

[91]For "Statement of Fundamental Truths" of the Assemblies of God, see William W. Menzies, *Anointed to Serve: The Story of the Assemblies of God* (Springfield, Mo.: Gospel Publishing House, 1971), pp. 385-90; for "Church of God Teachings" and "Declaration of Faith" of the Church of God (Cleveland, Tenn.), see Charles W. Conn, *Like a Mighty Army Moves the Church of God, 1886-1955* (Cleveland, Tenn.: Church of God Publishing House, 1955), pp. 311-13; for an interpretation of the doctrines of the Church of God in Christ, the Pentecostal Holiness Church, the Pentecostal Church of God of America, Inc., and the International Church of the Foursquare Gospel, see John Thomas Nichol, *Pentecostalism* (New York: Harper & Row, 1966), pp. 102-108, 114-16, 120-22. On the contrary, two Pentecostal bodies are non-Trinitarian by virtue of their teaching a unitarianism of Jesus and practicing baptism in the name of Jesus only: the Pentecostal Assemblies of the World (black) and the United Pentecostal Church (white); see Nichol, *Pentecostalism*, pp. 116-19.

[92]For general treatments of the Jesus Movement, see Edward E. Plowman, *The Jesus Movement in America*, 2d ptg. (Elgin, Ill.: David C. Cook Publishing Co., 1971); Ronald M. Enroth, Edward E. Ericson, Jr., and C. Breckinridge Peters, *The Jesus People: Old-Time Religion in the Age of Aquarius* (Grand Rapids: William B. Eerdmans Publishing Company, 1972); Erling Jorstad, *The New-Time Religion: The Jesus Revival in America* (Minneapolis: Augsburg Publishing House, 1972); and Robert S. Ellwood, Jr., *One Way: The Jesus Movement and Its Meaning* (Englewood Cliffs, N.J.: Prentice-Hall, Inc., 1973).

Right On), engages in various diaconal ministries, and sustains the Spiritual Counterfeits Project as a means of studying and counteracting religious cults.[93] In Deerfield, Illinois, in 1971, Jim Wallis, a student with a Plymouth Brethren background and involvement with the New Left who had dropped out of Trinity Evangelical Divinity School, together with others founded the People's Christian Coalition (PCC). Moved first to Chicago and then in 1975 to Washington, D. C., this community publishes *Sojourners* (formerly *Post-American*), which

> focuses especially upon capitalist exploitation in the United States and abroad, and upon violence, racism, sexism, militarism, materialism, and the foibles of both conservative and liberal Christendom and their equal alignment with the dominant American culture.

Wallis's *Agenda for Biblical People* has been termed by Quebedeaux "the radical evangelicals' foremost manifesto."[94] Quebedeaux finds that both BCC and PCC "are gradually moving toward an espousal of some form of Christian socialism, tinged with Marxism,"[95] These radical new expressions of Evangelicalism share some basic theology with traditional Evangelicals, but their very different social-ethical orientation is both obvious and significant.

Social radicalism during the 1960s, however, had another quite different effect; namely, the formation of Evangelical caucuses of protesting groups within certain mainline, ecumenically oriented, theologically liberal denominations: the Fellowship of Witness (1965) in the Episcopal Church; the Presbyterian Lay Committee (1965) and Presbyterians United for Biblical Concerns (1965) in the United Presbyterian Church in the U.S.A., and Good News (1967) in the United Methodist Church.[96]

Evangelicals in the 1970s: Nature and Classification. During the 1970s Evangelicalism came to center stage in the United States, or, as Quebedeaux has stated, "emerged from its anticultural ghetto into the mainstream of American life."[97] What did Jimmy Carter, Mark Hatfield,

---

[93]Quebedeaux, *The Young Evangelicals*, pp. 94-97; Quebedeaux, *The Worldly Evangelicals*, pp. 151-52.

[94]Quebedeaux, *The Worldly Evangelicals*, pp. 149-50.

[95]Ibid., p. 152. Quebedeaux's judgment concerning BCC seems as of 1982 to be unwarranted.

[96]Ibid., pp. 44-51.

[97]Ibid., p. xi.

Harold Hughes, John Anderson, Jeb Magruder, Charles Colson, Eldridge Cleaver, Pat Boone, Johnny Cash, Anita Bryant, Tom Landry, Graham Kerr, Wallace Johnson, Nelson Hunt, Bruce Metzger, David Hubbard, and Leighton Ford all have in common? They were "Evangelical Christians."

It was the decade of noteworthy Evangelical youth gatherings: the IVCF's triennial international missionary conventions at Urbana, Illinois (1970, 1973, 1976), and Explo '72, sponsored by Campus Crusade, in Dallas. It was a decade of focus on evangelism: Key '73, an ad hoc interdenominational effort, and the 1974 International Congress on World Evangelization in Lausanne.[98] It was the decade of rapid expansion of nationwide Evangelical television: Rex Humbard, Oral Roberts, Pat Robertson's Christian Broadcasting Network and the "700 Club," Jerry Falwell's "Old-Fashioned Gospel Hour," and Jim Bakker's "PTL Club."[99] In the Evangelical theological seminaries, both nondenominational and those of the Southern Baptist Convention, enrollments rapidly increased, and new records were set.[100] Book publishers featuring Evangelical authors had increasing sales; these included not only the Grand Rapids three but also Word, InterVarsity, Creation House, Fleming H. Revell, Moody, Logos International, and Bethany Fellowship, as well as Harper and Row, Lippincott, and Doubleday.[101] It was the era when black Evangelicals gained considerable visibility: the National Black Evangelical Association (1963), Tom Skinner Associates, and John Perkins's Voice of Calvary in Mississippi.[102]

Following the burgeoning and changing Evangelicalism of the 1970s is it possible to reclassify Evangelicals in the United States so as to clarify the theological, ethical, and attitudinal differences among them? Quebedeaux attempted such a reclassification in *The Young Evangelicals* (1974). In doing so he sharpened the distinctions between Fundamentalism and Evangelicalism and faulted "mainstream Ecumenical Liberal-

---

[98]Bloesch, *The Evangelical Renaissance*, p. 13; Quebedeaux, *The Worldly Evangelicals*, pp. 59-61, 83, 102-103.

[99]Quebedeaux, *The Worldly Evangelicals*, pp. 67-69.

[100]Quebedeaux, *The Young Evangelicals*, p. 50; Quebedeaux, *The Worldly Evangelicals*, pp. 85, 90-92.

[101]Bloesch, *The Evangelical Renaissance*, p. 14; Quebedeaux, *The Young Evangelicals*, pp. 49-50, 145; Quebedeaux, *The Worldly Evangelicals*, p. 69.

[102]Quebedeaux, *The Worldly Evangelicals*, pp. 156-59.

ism" for failing to make such distinctions. Accordingly, Quebedeaux identified two types of Fundamentalism (Separatist and Open) and two types of Evangelicalism (Establishment and New). Separatist Fundamentalism, insistent upon total separation from Evangelicals as well as Liberals, biblical inerrancy, and premillennial, and usually Dispensationalist (hence, pretribulational) eschatology, as well as the "five points" of earlier Fundamentalism, embraces, according to Quebedeaux, Bob Jones University, Carl McIntire, the ACCC and ICCC, Billy James Hargis's Christian Echoes National Ministry, William Steuart McBirnie's "Voice of Americanism," Fred Schwarz's Christian Anti-Communism Crusade, and Edgar Bundy's Church League of America.[103] Open Fundamentalism, also Dispensationalist and insistent on biblical inerrancy, takes a less severe separation, disclaims anti-intellectualism, and "repudiates the explicit alliance of Fundamentalism with ultraconservative politics." Here one finds Dallas Theological Seminary and *Bibliotheca Sacra*, Moody Bible Institute, Talbot Theological Seminary, and Hal Lindsey.[104] Furthermore, Establishment Evangelicalism shares with Fundamentalism belief in the inspiration and the authority of the Bible but is not limited to a literal hermeneutic and continues to reckon with the issue of inerrancy. It professes "to have a social conscience and a biblically based social ethic," practices dialogue rather than rigid separatism, and finds defections from or rejections of Dispensationalism in its ranks. It includes, according to Quebedeaux, the NAE and its member denominations, the Billy Graham Evangelistic Association, *Christianity Today*, most Southern Baptists and Missouri Synod Lutherans, certain smaller nonaligned denominations, some congregations and individuals within NCC-WCC-related denominations, Wheaton College (Illinois), Westmont College, Fuller Theological Seminary, Trinity Evangelical Divinity School, Gordon-Conwell Theological Seminary, Asbury Theological Seminary, Campus Crusade for Christ, Youth for Christ, and so forth.[105] Finally, New Evangelicalism, with which Quebedeaux himself identifies,

---

[103]Quebedeaux, *The Young Evangelicals*, pp. 18-25.

[104]Ibid., pp. 25-28. Probably Francis Schaeffer should be added; cf. *The Worldly Evangelicals*, pp. 107-109.

[105]Quebedeaux, *The Young Evangelicals*, pp. 28-37. Cf. Quebedeaux, *The Worldly Evangelicals*, pp. 36-44, 54-59. Whether Quebedeaux in 1974 considered Neo-Pentecostals to be part of Establishment Evangelicalism is not clear.

is less precisely defined and illustrated. It teaches that the Bible is inerrant in matters of doctrine and practice, emphasizes sanctification as well as regeneration, rejects Dispensationalism, seeks to apply the gospel toward social change, has dialogue with Liberals and with non-Chistians, and seeks compatibility with science.[106] Quebedeaux named as representative of New Evangelicalism "Clarence Bass, Vernon Grounds, George Ladd, David Moberg, J. Rodman Williams," and the late Edward John Carnell, and obliquely referred to Carl F. H. Henry.[107] Probably BCC and PCC should be added, although Quebedeaux seems to place such communities "beyond" Evangelical social action.[108]

Whether Quebedeaux's fourfold typology is valid and, if so, will continue to be valid must be determined by further observation and study. It serves as a useful working hypothesis for understanding who the "Evangelicals" are in the United States today. As a consequence of his clear differentiation of Evangelicals and Fundamentalists and in order to demarcate Evangelicals from all non-Fundamentalist non-Evangelicals, Quebedeaux has articulated a threefold test as to who are "Evangelicals." They affirm

> (1) the complete reliability and final authority of Scripture in matters of faith and practice; (2) the necessity of a *personal* faith in Jesus Christ as Savior from sin and consequent commitment to Him as Lord; and (3) the urgency of seeking actively the conversion of sinners to Christ.[109]

---

[106]Quebedeaux, *The Young Evangelicals*, pp. 37-39. New Evangelicalism is not to be confused with the earlier Neo-Evangelicals, who now belong to Establishment Evangelicalism (p. 37). Quebedeaux acknowledged his dependence on Bloesch, *The Evangelical Renaissance*, pp. 33-37.

[107]Quebedeaux, *The Young Evangelicals*, p. 40.

[108]Quebedeaux, *The Worldly Evangelicals*, esp. p. 143.

[109]Quebedeaux, *The Young Evangelicals*, pp. 3-4. Quebedeaux's more recent acceptance of a role as "a consulting coordinator of various kinds of ecumenical conferences sponsored by the Unification Church" raises among Evangelical Christians serious questions about the validity of Quebedeaux's assessment of the teachings of the Unification Church but need not invalidate his earlier research and writing about Evangelicals. The reporters for *The Wittenburg Door*, after interviewing Quebedeaux, "were not sure whether Mr. Quebedeaux is an evangelical, a Moonie, an evangelical Moonie, an academic evangelical Moonie, or an evangelical who moons Moonies." "Door Interview: Richard Quebedeaux," *The Wittenburg Door* (February-March 1981): 9, 12-13, 16-18.

The threefold test is less inclusive than the five fundamentals of earlier Fundamentalism, especially concerning Christ's virgin birth, substitutionary atonement, bodily resurrection, and second coming, and it is more experience-oriented than those five fundamentals. Can expanding Evangelicalism in the early 1980s find these three affirmations accurate and adequate to identify rational Evangelicals and experiential Evangelicals, Calvinist Evangelicals and Arminian Evangelicals, denominational Evangelicals and nondenominational Evangelicals, politically liberal Evangelicals and politically conservative Evangelicals, premillennial and amillennial Evangelicals?

Whatever the number or identity of the minimal tests for identifying today's Evangelicals in the United States, a concluding observation seems necessary. The burgeoning Evangelicalism seems not to have produced, as J. Edwin Orr has pointed out,[110] a clearly discernible spiritual awakening resulting in changes in both private and public morality. It seems to be facing, as Quebedeaux implies throughout *The Worldly Evangelicals*,[111] the dangers of "success" with and acceptance by the American populace.

The quest for answers to the question, "Who are the 'Evangelicals'?" now comes to an end. In Continental Europe, especially the Germanies, the term has continued as part of the official name of various Lutheran, Union, and Reformed territorial churches and carries confessional and sacramental connotations. In the British Isles, especially England, the term identifies one of the major parties within the Anglican tradition, which party has a clearly identifiable doctrine of salvation and missionary outreach. In Latin America the term is used instead of the word "Protestant" to identify virtually all Protestant Christians. In the United States, whereas it has been used in the official names of various Lutheran, Reformed, German-oriented Wesleyan, Swedish independent, Baptist, Mennonite, and Methodist denominational bodies, the term's principal contemporary usage derives from Fundamentalism. It applies not only to the less strict heirs of Fundamentalism but also to those who from charismatic, social-revolutionary, or older denominational origins have

---

[110]"There is truly a moving of the Spirit today, but it does not compare with previous great awakenings in its impact on private and corporate morality. Even the evangelism of some movements of today is lacking in the preaching of repentance, which is one reason why there is so little change in public morality." J. Edwin Orr to James Leo Garrett, Jr., 24 July 1980, files of recipient.

[111]Especially ch. 2.

begun to or have continued to insist upon the supremacy of Scripture, the all-sufficiency of the divine-human Jesus Christ, the necessity of the transforming experience of being born anew or justified by grace through faith, and the inner compulsion to share one's faith in Christ with those who do not yet believe.[112]

---

[112]Ellwood, *One Way: The Jesus Movement and Its Meaning*, p. 24, has written: "Wherever there is [*sic*] Protestant simplicity, melodious hymns, warm and emotional preaching, and felt personal conversions to Christ, where there are revival meetings and perhaps gifts of the Spirit such as speaking in tongues, where the Bible is believed quite literally and the church tries above all to relive the New Testament, there is evangelicalism."

Chapter Two

What Evangelicals
Believe and Practice

Following the quest for the varied usages of the term "Evangelical" it is proper to ask whether those called "Evangelicals" have had and do now have any common beliefs and common practices that differentiate them from other Christians or at least clearly characterize them.

Doctrine

Recent writers as diverse as Bruce Shelley[1] and Robert S. Ellwood, Jr.[2] have emphasized that Evangelicalism is not an organization or a theological system so much as it is a "mood." Clear and recognizable conclusions to the quest for basic doctrines, therefore, must indeed be justified. Have there been and are there today basic doctrines or beliefs that are common to the various Christians to be denominated as "Evangelicals"?

Some of the basic beliefs of those previously identified as "Evangelicals" may be summarized in the chart printed on the dust jacket.

An examination of the chart makes evident that there have been three areas of doctrinal emphasis or agreement among Evangelicals: (1) the nature and necessity of justification or regeneration or salvation; (2) the

---

[1] *Evangelicalism in America*, p. 7.

[2] *One Way: The Jesus Movement and Its Meaning*, p. 25.

nature and supreme authority of the Bible; and (3) the deity of Jesus
Christ together with certain events of His "holy history," namely, virginal conception, atoning death, bodily resurrection, and second coming.
Justification or salvation by grace through faith, coupled with regeneration experienced as conversion, and the inspiration, reliability, and
supreme authority of the Bible are the most frequently recurring doctrinal affirmations of Evangelicals on the chart. Slightly less frequently
recurring is the cluster of affirmations concerning Jesus Christ. This
cluster was strongly affirmed during and after the Modernist-
Fundamentalist Controversy but less emphasized prior to that time.[3]
Other doctrines such as entire sanctification, baptism of the Holy Spirit as
evidenced by charisms, the secondary authority of confessions of faith,
dual eternal destiny (heaven and hell), the obligation of witnessing and
missions, and sacraments as means of grace appear on the chart but may
not have been clearly and specifically affirmed by a majority of Evangelicals. The doctrine of the millennium, including the major schools (historic premillennialism, amillennialism, postmillennialism, and
dispensational premillennialism), has not been consistently included on
the chart because of the difficulty in securing accurate information for all
groups of Evangelicals or because of the lack in some cases of explicit,
published affirmation.[4] The obligation of witnessing and missions, commonly practiced by most Evangelicals, may not appear more frequently
on the chart because it may have been regarded as something practiced

---

[3]Kenneth S. Kantzer, "Unity and Diversity in Evangelical Faith," in David F. Wells
and John D. Woodbridge, eds., *The Evangelicals: What They Believe, Who They Are,
Where They Are Going*, rev. ed. (Nashville: Abingdon Press, 1975; Grand Rapids: Baker
Book House, 1977), pp. 58-87, has interpreted contemporary Evangelicalism in terms of
the formal and material principles of the sixteenth-century Reformation, i.e., "the
enduring authority of Scripture in matters of faith and conduct" and "the good news of
how man can be rightly related to God," but he also has acknowledged (pp. 73-74) that
"certain teachings regarding the person and work of Christ" [Kantzer delineates twelve of
these] which were "highly mooted by nonevangelicals of the last century" "served to unify
fundamentalism in its battle against liberal theology and continue to unite the evangelical
movement of the last quarter of the twentieth century." ©1975 by Abingdon Press, and
used by permission.

[4]Kantzer, in ibid., p. 79, has stated concerning the late 1970s: "Premillennialism . . . is
the characteristic stance of the majority of American evangelicals. At the same time, it has
ceased its rapid gains of the early middle part of the century and has probably come to a
sort of stalemate with amillennialism, both being accepted as legitimate within the
framework of consistent evangelicalism, while the postmillennial view for all practical
purposes has dropped out of sight."

rather than something believed.[5]

Evangelicals within the Lutheran, Reformed, and Anglican traditions tend to emphasize and articulate the Reformation doctrine of justification by grace through faith and that not on the basis of works. They posit a basic identification with the doctrine as formulated by Luther, Zwingli, Calvin, and Cranmer. They accept Luther's affirmation of *sola gratia* and *sola fides*. Bernard Ramm has summarized the deviations of Luther's doctrine of justification from that of late medieval Roman Catholicism: (1) "righteousness was not only the retributive justice of God but something believers possessed"; (2) "righteousness was received by imputation, by God's verdict, and not by "infusion"; (3) the word "alone" excluded both "the Mosaic law" and "ecclesiastical works (or good works or works of love or so-called worthy acts of penance)"; (4) "the combination of sanctifying grace or infused grace of justification, regeneration, and sanctification" was "broken up by Luther into three separate though conjoined acts of God"; (5) all believers were priests in the sense that "each believer was to be a priest to every other believer," and hence "the entire church" was "the people of God and a kingdom of priests."[6] Sometimes the term "salvation" tends to be used instead of the term "justification."

Present-day Evangelicals, however, who have been influenced by the Anabaptist, the Pietistic, and/or the Wesleyan traditions tend to express how sinful human beings may be rightly related to God by the concept of regeneration, or being born again by the Holy Spirit. Without downplaying the impossibility of righteousness by works or by keeping the law, such usage stresses the indispensability of the new birth and the transformation which the new life brings to the reborn.

In addition to the differing emphases on justification and regeneration, present-day Evangelicals continue to be characterized by the historic theological differences between Calvinists and Arminians, especially on the issue of perseverance or apostasy. Those who have been deeply influenced by the Calvinistic tradition, for example, Presbyterians and Reformed, non-Arminian Baptists, and Anglican Evangelicals, continue to affirm the perseverance of all true believers (that is, the elect) to final salvation. On the other hand, those who have been deeply influenced by

---

[5]See Morris A. Inch, *The Evangelical Challenge* (Philadelphia: Westminster Press, 1978), pp. 63, 76-97.

[6]*The Evangelical Heritage*, pp. 35-36.

Luther or by the Arminian heritage, for example, Lutherans, Wesleyans, Holiness people, Pentecostals, and Free Will Baptists, continue to teach the possibility that true believers may cease to believe and lapse from salvation.

The second area of common doctrinal affirmation among Evangelicals, namely, the inspiration and supreme authority of the Bible, is today marked by intense theological conflict over the issue of the inerrancy of the Bible. It is noteworthy that the supreme authority of the Bible as a truth to be confessed is not currently at issue among Evangelicals. Although Lutheran and Reformed churches especially emphasize the secondary authority of confessions of faith and although Pentecostals and Neo-Pentecostals put great stress on the experience of the baptism of the Holy Spirit, Evangelicals do not differ essentially among themselves as to the supreme or final authority of Scripture. Likewise, the present-day conflict does not center on various theories of the mode of biblical inspiration, although these may be drawn into controversy. Rather the focal point of contemporary controversy is the question of the inerrancy of the Bible, that is, on two levels: (1) whether the Bible is without error not only in matters of doctrine and ethics but also in historical, geographical, and scientific matters; and (2) whether the Bible is genuinely without error in all matters of doctrine and ethics.

Jack Bartlett Rogers has traced the inerrancy doctrine on the first level to François Turretin (1623-1687), Genevan theologian and author of *Institutio theologiae elencticae* (1679-1685), has noted that "Turretin utilized the Aristotelian-Thomistic method of putting reason before faith to develop this theology," and has pointed out that Turretin's *Institutio* "was the principal textbook in systematic theology at Princeton Seminary for sixty years until Charles Hodge's *Systematic Theology* replaced it in 1872."[7] Harold Lindsell has asserted that "for two thousand years the Christian church has agreed that the Bible is completely trustworthy; it is

---

[7]"The Church Doctrine of Biblical Authority," in Jack Bartlett Rogers, ed. *Biblical Authority* (Waco, Tex.: Word Books, 1977), pp. 30-31, 37. Rogers (pp. 31-35, 41-44) has interpreted the Westminster Confession of Faith, the Scottish theologian James Orr, and Dutch Reformed theologians Herman Bavinck, Abraham Kuyper, and G. C. Berkouwer as not supportive of the doctrine of inerrancy. This interpretation of key representatives of the Reformed tradition as non-inerrantists has been elaborated and set in a larger historical framework in Jack Bartlett Rogers and Donald Keith McKim, *The Authority and Interpretation of the Bible: An Historical Approach* (San Francisco: Harper & Row, 1979).

infallible or inerrant." Lindsell has undertaken no fresh examination of the works of the Church Fathers, medieval churchmen, or the Protestant Reformers as to the question of inerrancy but has instead relied upon George Duncan Barry's *The Inspiration and Authority of Holy Scripture: A Study in the Literature of the First Five Centuries* (1919) for the patristic age and upon secondary writers who have interpreted Luther and Calvin. Lindsell has bypassed the medieval writers and has used the terms "inspiration" and "inerrancy" virtually as synonyms.[8] It remains to be seen, however, whether the doctrine of inerrancy can be accurately and specifically traced to leading Christian thinkers prior to Turretin and to his Lutheran contemporary, J. A. Quenstedt (1617-1688). The controversy concerning inerrancy has been recently ignited in a special sense by *God's Inerrant Word*, edited by John Warwick Montgomery,[9] by Harold

---

[8]*The Battle for the Bible* (Grand Rapids: Zondervan Publishing House, 1976), pp. 19, 41-71. George Duncan Barry's book, published in 1919 by the Society for Promoting Christian Knowledge in London and treating the Church Fathers through Augustine of Hippo Regius, is primarily concerned with the nature of the inspiration of the Bible (especially the interrelation of the divine and the human), the reliability and authority of the Bible, the canon of each of the testaments, the relation of the two testaments, and biblical hermeneutics as taught by the various writers of the patristic age. The volume only quite secondarily treats the theme of inerrancy or errancy. According to Theophilus of Antioch (p. 52), the biblical writers never contradicted each other and were "preserved from error" in describing "events which preceded their own time." For Irenaeus (pp. 53, 55, 57) the "words" of the biblical writers were not to be corrected, and the apostles could not make false statements, but there are "syntactical errors" in Paul's writings. Origen (p. 86) found "discrepancies" among the four Gospels but saw their resolution through allegorical interpretation. For John Chrysostom (p. 121) there was "divergence" among the narratives of the four Gospels but "no contradiction." According to Augustine (p. 142) there were "no contradictions" among the four Gospels. Jerome (p. 137) found "grammatical errors" in the Bible, but these posed no problem for him. For Augustine (pp. 140, 146) both the Hebrew Old Testament and the Septuagint were "equally inspired, despite their great differences and manifest inconsistencies" and " 'no single error due to the author is found in any one' " (Epistle 82) of the biblical books. Philo, Josephus, Clement of Rome, Ignatius of Antioch, Papias, Polycarp, the *Epistle to Diognetus*, Barnabas, Justin Martyr, Athenagoras, Tatian, Tertullian, Cyprian, Clement of Alexandria, Athanasius, Cyril of Jerusalem, Gregory of Nyssa, Gregory of Nazianzus, Basil, Diodore of Tarsus, Theodore of Mopsuestia, and Theodoret of Cyrus provide, according to Barry, no evidence on the issue of inerrancy. Yet fourteen of these twenty-two authors are cited by Lindsell, *The Battle for the Bible*, pp. 46-52, as supporters of his own doctrine of inerrancy. If the famous test of apostolic tradition set forth by Vincent of Lerins in his *Commonitory* (2:6) in the fifth century A.D., namely, "that which has been believed everywhere, always, and by all," is to be applied to the doctrine of biblical inerrancy, more patristic evidence will be necessary if the doctrine is to pass the Vincentian test.

[9]*An International Symposium on the Trustworthiness of Scripture* (Minneapolis: Bethany Fellowship, 1974).

Lindsell's books *The Battle for the Bible* and *The Bible in the Balance*,[10] and by Francis Schaeffer's *No Final Conflict: The Bible without Error in All That It Affirms*,[11] all of which defend inerrancy; and by Dewey M. Beegle's *The Inspiration of Scripture*[12] and *Biblical Authority*, edited by Jack Bartlett Rogers, both of which deny biblical inerrancy on the first level.[13] For Lindsell the defense of biblical inerrancy must necessarily be coupled with the rejection of the historical-critical method of interpreting the Bible.[14] Schaeffer has identified the issue of inerrancy as "the watershed of the evangelical world,"[15] and Lindsell, although acknowledging that a host of those Evangelicals who no longer hold to inerrancy are still "relatively evangelical," has refused to "concede . . . that in a technical sense anyone can claim the evangelical badge once he has abandoned inerrancy."[16] Indeed, for Lindsell, "any definition of what evangelicals believe must include biblical inerrancy."[17]

The differentiation of a second level for consideration of the issue of biblical inerrancy, namely, inerrancy in matters of doctrine and ethics, is not unlike Stephen T. Davis's distinction between "inerrancy," which he rejects on the basis of so-called errors of fact, and "infallibility," which he applies to matters of doctrine and ethics and which he defends.[18] The second level, however, has seemingly been challenged by Paul King Jewett in his *Man as Male and Female*,[19] wherein he rejected the teaching

---

[10](Grand Rapids: Zondervan Publishing House, 1979).

[11](Downers Grove, Ill.: InterVarsity Press, 1975).

[12](Philadelphia: Westminster Press, 1963); revised, enlarged, and reissued under the title, *Scripture, Tradition, and Infallibility* (Grand Rapids: William B. Eerdmans Publishing Company, 1973).

[13]Robert K. Johnston, *Evangelicals at an Impasse: Biblical Authority in Practice* (Atlanta: John Knox Press, 1979), pp. 22-28, has classified Beegle's view under "partial infallibility." Concerning the debate on inerrancy, see also Carl F. H. Henry, *Evangelicals in Search of Identity* (Waco, Tex.: Word Books, 1976), ch. 5.

[14]*The Bible in the Balance*, ch. 7.

[15]*No Final Conflict*, p. 13.

[16]*The Battle for the Bible*, p. 210.

[17]*The Bible in the Balance*, p. 306.

[18]*The Debate about the Bible: Inerrancy versus Infallibility* (Philadelphia: Westminster Press, 1977).

[19](Grand Rapids: William B. Eerdmans Publishing Company, 1975). On Jewett's book see Henry, *Evangelicals in Search of Identity*, pp. 55-56; Lindsell, *The Battle for the Bible*, pp. 117-21; Lindsell, *The Bible in the Balance*, pp. 184, 193-95, 308, 333-34; Johnston,

of the Apostle Paul concerning the submission of wives to husbands and concluded that there are inconsistencies in the Pauline teaching about women.

The controversy concerning biblical inerrancy threatens to divide Evangelicals in the United States at precisely that time in their history when they have begun to be conscious of their increasing numbers, their genuine diversity, and their potential influence upon American life and society.

The third area of common doctrinal affirmations among Evangelicals, that is, those related to the person and work of Jesus Christ or to His "holy history," has been summarized by Kenneth S. Kantzer under twelve topics:

> (1) the eternal preexistence of the Son as the second person of the one God; (2) the incarnation of God the Son in man as the divine-human person—two natures in one person; (3) the virgin birth, the means by which God the Son entered into the human race and, without ceasing to be fully God, became also fully man; (4) the sinless life of Christ while sharing the life and experiences of alien men apart from sin; (5) the supernatural miracles of Christ as acts of his compassion and signs of his divine nature; (6) Christ's authoritative teaching as Lord of the church; (7) the substitutionary atonement in which God did all that was needed to redeem man from sin and its consequences; (8) the bodily resurrection of Christ as the consummation of his redemptive work and the sign and seal of its validity; (9) the ascension and heavenly mission of the living Lord; (10) the bodily second coming of Christ at the end of the age; (11) the final righteous judgment of all mankind and the eternal kingdom of God; (12) the eternal punishment of the impenitent and disbelieving wicked of this world.[20]

Concerning the doctrines commonly affirmed by Evangelicals, therefore, it may be concluded that there have been and continue to be three such doctrinal areas: justification by grace through faith, or regeneration by the Holy Spirit; the inspiration and supreme authority of the Bible;

Evangelicals at an Impasse, pp. 34-35, 56-62, 148.

[20]"Unity and Diversity in Evangelical Faith," pp. 73-74.

and the holy history of Jesus as the Son of God, incarnate, crucified, risen, and coming again.

Ethics

What has been the ethical teaching and practice of those whom we may denominate as "Evangelicals"? To what extent have they agreed on ethical matters? Have there been any significant changes in the ethical concerns of Evangelicals? It will be useful to treat separately personal ethics and social ethics.

Evangelicals, especially in the United States, have tended to magnify abstinence from various personal "sins" which they have associated with "worldliness" and have regarded as incompatible with a Christian life style. Utilizing Quebedeaux's classification, one may posit that Separatist Fundamentalists, Open Fundamentalists, and Establishment Evangelicals have tended to frown upon or reject the following: drinking alcoholic beverages; smoking tobacco; social dancing; all forms of gambling (sometimes also card-playing); attendance at the theater and/or movies; use of narcotics; immodest dress; rock music; and the wearing of long hair by men.

Not all Evangelicals, however, have rejected all these practices. Evangelicals in Continental Europe and those in the United States whose ecclesiastical roots are in Continental Europe, that is, Lutherans and Reformed, practice moderation rather than abstinence in the drinking of alcoholic beverages and tend to accept forms of gambling. Southern Baptists, especially those in tobacco-producing areas, tend to accept the smoking of tobacco; moreover, considerations of health have served to bring a restatement of the prohibition. The widespread use of television has tended to nullify the rejection of offensive plays and movies. The advent of Christian rock music has somewhat softened the criticism of rock music. But the Young Evangelicals, according to Quebedeaux, tend to regard such frowned upon practices as part of the legacy of Puritanism and nineteenth-century revivalism and to reject strict abstinence from these as normative for Young Evangelicals.[21]

In the arena of social ethics two statements have frequently been made concerning Fundamentalism: that it tended to be allied with the political far right wing, and that it lacked a specific social ethic that would point to much-needed changes in contemporary society. Erling Jorstad

---

[21]*The Young Evangelicals*, pp. 129-34; *The Worldly Evangelicals*, pp. 117-19.

documented that alliance of "far right" Fundamentalists such as Carl McIntire, Billy James Hargis, Edgar C. Bundy, and Verne P. Kaub and conservative Republicans, especially in support of the presidential candidacy of Senator Barry Goldwater in 1964.[22] Richard V. Pierard found the "unequal yoke" with political and economic conservatism to involve more of the Evangelical constituency than the right wing.[23] Meanwhile, Evangelical historians were making it evident that nineteenth-century American Protestantism even in its revivalistic expressions had been productive of social change. Timothy L. Smith found this to have been true after the awakening of 1858, especially in respect to grappling with poverty and abolishing slavery.[24] Donald W. Dayton traced the postmillennial social activism of Jonathan Blanchard, Charles G. Finney and Oberlin College, Theodore Dwight Weld, Arthur and Lewis Tappan, and the Wesleyan Methodists, especially concerning the abolition of slavery.[25] It was becoming apparent that Fundamentalism as the confluence of the old Princeton Theology and the new premillennialism had indeed been deficient in its social ethic and its impact on social problems. As early as 1947 Carl F. H. Henry had sounded the critical note in his *The Uneasy Conscience of Modern Fundamentalism*,[26] in which he deplored Fundamentalism's lack of a social ethic. Later Henry developed positively the theme in his *Aspects of Christian Social Ethics*.[27] Sherwood Elliot Wirt

---

[22]*The Politics of Doomsday: Fundamentalists of the Far Right* (Nashville: Abingdon Press, 1964). See also John Harold Redekop, *The American Far Right: A Case Study of Billy James Hargis and Christian Crusade* (Grand Rapids: William B. Eerdmans Publishing Company, 1968). For an interpretation of the sociopolitical posture of far right Fundamentalists such as Hargis, McIntire, and Fred Schwarz written by a Unitarian, see Brooks R. Walker, *The Christian Fright Peddlers* (Garden City, N.Y.: Doubleday & Company, Inc., 1964), esp. chs. 3, 4, 9.

[23]*The Unequal Yoke: Evangelical Christianity and Political Conservatism* (Philadelphia: J. B. Lippincott Company, 1970).

[24]*Revivalism and Social Reform in Mid-Nineteenth-Century America* (Nashville: Abingdon Press, 1957).

[25]*Discovering an Evangelical Heritage* (New York: Harper & Row, 1976). Dayton (pp. 128-32) has provided an interesting contrast between the societal reformism of Charles G. Finney, based on the doctrine of redemption and considerable "identification with the poor, the slave, and the masses," and the social conservatism of Charles Hodge, based on the doctrine of sin and "closely tied to the aristocracy and higher social classes."

[26](Grand Rapids: William B. Eerdmans Publishing Company).

[27](Grand Rapids: William B. Eerdmans Publishing Company, 1964). Henry treated social transformation, daily work, legislation, and social ideals.

probed "the social conscience" of Evangelicals,[28] Vernon C. Grounds criticized Evangelicals for their "conservatism," "quietism," "pietism," "perfectionism," "legalism," "nationalism," and "pessimism,"[29] and David O. Moberg called for the reversal of the "Great Reversal" that had occurred between 1910 and the 1930s, that is, the demise of Evangelical "social concern."[30] Fundamentalism tended to assume either that reborn persons would automatically and almost effortlessly produce a better society or that society was so corrupt as to be in view of the imminent second advent of Jesus beyond any redemption.

In the 1970s the Young Evangelicals, together with others from Establishment Evangelicalism, have undertaken the reversal of the Great Reversal by developing a new Evangelical social ethic and action[31] that goes beyond, but includes, diaconal ministries. Grounded in an awareness of the social characteristics of sin,[32] it was articulated in the Thanksgiving Declaration framed by a group of Evangelical leaders in 1973 in Chicago. The text of "A Declaration of Evangelical Social Concern" reads as follows:

> As evangelical Christians committed to the Lord Jesus Christ and the full authority of the Word of God, we affirm that God lays total claim upon the lives of his people. We cannot, therefore, separate our lives in Christ from the situation in which God has placed us in the United States and the world.
>
> We confess that we have not acknowledged the complete claims of God on our lives.
>
> We acknowledge that God requires love. But we have not demonstrated the love of God to those suffering social abuses.
>
> We acknowledge that God requires justice. But we have not proclaimed or demonstrated his justice to an unjust American society. Although the Lord calls us to defend the social and

---

[28]*The Social Conscience of the Evangelical* (New York: Harper & Row, 1968).

[29]*Evangelicalism and Social Responsibility*, "Focal Pamphlet," no. 16 (Scottdale, Pa.: Herald Press, 1969), pp. 4-6.

[30]*The Great Reversal: Evangelism versus Social Concern* (Philadelphia: J. B. Lippincott Company, 1972). Moberg (p. 153) emphasized both activism and pietism.

[31]Quebedeaux, *The Young Evangelicals*, pp. 99-129.

[32]Moberg, *The Great Reversal*, ch. 7.

economic rights of the poor and the oppressed, we have mostly remained silent. We deplore the historic involvement of the church in America with racism and the conspicuous responsibility of the evangelical community for perpetuating the personal attitudes and institutional structures that have divided the body of Christ along color lines. Further, we have failed to condemn the exploitation of racism at home and abroad by our economic system.

We affirm that God abounds in mercy and that he forgives all who repent and turn from their sins. So we call our fellow evangelical Christians to demonstrate repentance in a Christian discipleship that confronts the social and political injustice of our nation.

We must attack the materialism of our culture and the maldistribution of the nation's wealth and services. We recognize that as a nation we play a crucial role in the imbalance and injustice of international trade and development. Before God and a billion hungry neighbors, we must rethink our values regarding our present standard of living and promote more just acquisition and distribution of the world's resources.

We acknowledge our Christian responsibilities of citizenship. Therefore, we must challenge the misplaced trust of the nation in economic and military might—a proud trust that promotes a national pathology of war and violence which victimizes our neighbors at home and abroad. We must resist the temptation to make the nation and its institutions objects of near-religious loyalty.

We acknowledge that we have encouraged men to prideful domination and women to irresponsible passivity. So we call both men and women to mutual submission and active discipleship.

We proclaim no new gospel, but the gospel of our Lord Jesus Christ, who, through the power of the Holy Spirit, frees people from sin so that they might praise God through works of righteousness.

By this declaration, we endorse no political ideology or party, but call our nation's leaders and people to that righteousness which exalts a nation.

We make this declaration in the biblical hope that Christ is coming to consummate the Kingdom and we accept his claim on our total discipleship till he comes.[33]

The Young Evangelicals and many Establishment Evangelicals, including Evangelicals in the historic peace churches, though not Fundamentalists, have manifested an increasing concern for and activity regarding racial justice,[34] world peace,[35] overcoming poverty,[36] and the dangers of nationalism and civil religion[37] and of the cultural captivity of

[33]Ronald J. Sider, ed., *The Chicago Declaration* (Carol Stream, Ill.: Creation House, 1974), cover, pp. 1-2.

[34]Thomas Bufford Maston, *Segregation and Desegregation: A Christian Approach* (New York: Macmillan Company, 1959); Maston, *The Bible and Race* (Nashville: Broadman Press, 1959); and Columbus Salley and Ronald Behm, *Your God Is Too White* (Downers Grove, Ill.: InterVarsity Press, 1970). Quite significant is the growing literature by black Evangelicals: e. g., William E. Pannell, *My Friend, the Enemy* (Waco, Tex.: Word Books, 1968); Tom Skinner, *How Black Is the Gospel?* (Philadelphia: J. B. Lippincott Company, 1970); Skinner, *Words of Revolution: A Call to Involvement in the Real Revolution* (Grand Rapids: Zondervan Publishing House, 1970); John Perkins, *Let Justice Roll Down* (Glendale, Calif.: Regal Books, 1976); and Perkins, *A Quiet Revolution: The Christian Response to Human Need; A Strategy for Today* (Waco, Tex.: Word Books, 1976).

[35]Culbert G. Rutenber, *The Dagger and the Cross: An Examination of Christian Pacifism* (Nyack, N.Y.: Fellowship Publications, 1958; first publ. in 1950); Frank H. Epp, *A Strategy for Peace: Reflections of a Christian Pacifist* (Grand Rapids: William B. Eerdmans Publishing Company, 1973); John Howard Yoder, *Nevertheless: A Meditation on the Varieties and Shortcomings of Religious Pacifism* (Scottdale, Pa.: Herald Press, 1971); Yoder, *The Original Revolution: Essays on Christian Pacifism* (Scottdale, Pa.: Herald Press, 1971); Pierard, *The Unequal Yoke*, ch. 5; Robert G. Clouse, "The Christian, War, and Militarism" in Robert G. Clouse, Robert D. Linder, and Richard V. Pierard, eds., *The Cross and the Flag* (Carol Stream, Ill.: Creation House, 1972), ch. 12; Vernard Eller, *King Jesus' Manual of Arms for the Armless: War and Peace from Genesis to Revelation* (Nashville: Abingdon Press, 1973).

[36]Pierard, *The Unequal Yoke*, ch. 6; James Johnson, "Evangelical Christianity and Poverty," in Clouse, Linder, and Pierard, eds., *The Cross and the Flag*, ch. 9; Vernard Eller, *The Simple Life: The Christian Stance toward Possessions* (Grand Rapids: William B. Eerdmans Publishing Company, 1973); W. Stanley Mooneyham, *What Do You Say to a Hungry World?* (Waco, Tex.: Word Books, 1975); Ronald J. Sider, *Rich Christians in an Age of Hunger: A Biblical Study* (Downers Grove, Ill,: InterVarsity Press, 1977).

[37]Pierard, *The Unequal Yoke*, ch. 4; Mark O. Hatfield, *Between a Rock and a Hard Place* (Waco, Tex.: Word Books, 1976), esp. ch. 7; Thomas Howard, "The Evangelical Christian and the American Civic Religion," in Clouse, Linder, and Pierard, eds., *The Cross and the Flag*, ch. 3; James E. Wood, Jr., *Nationhood and the Kingdom* (Nashville: Broadman Press, 1977); Robert D. Linder and Richard V. Pierard, *Twilight of the Saints: Biblical Christianity and Civil Religion in America* (Downers Grove, Ill.: InterVarsity Press, 1978).

the churches.[38] Evangelicals increasingly reckon an active role in politics to be highly desirable.[39] Some have set forth a theology of politics in the Calvinistic tradition,[40] others have done so in the Anabaptist tradition,[41] and yet others have provided critical analyses of current political options and trends.[42]

A school of relational theology has arisen among Evangelicals that, "influenced by the secular human potential movement,"[43] has stressed acceptance and love of other persons.[44] Some Evangelicals, both men and women, have continued to defend the subordination of women to men on the basis of Pauline exhortations as expressive of submission to God.[45]

---

[38]Calvin Redekop, *The Free Church and Seductive Culture* (Scottdale, Pa.: Herald Press, 1970); John Lee Eighmy, *Churches in Cultural Captivity: A History of the Social Attitudes of Southern Baptists* (Knoxville: University of Tennessee Press, 1972); Jim Wallis, *Agenda for Biblical People* (New York: Harper & Row, 1976).

[39]Robert G. Clouse, Robert D. Linder, and Richard V. Pierard, eds., *Protest and Politics: Christianity and Contemporary Affairs* (Greenwood, S. C.: Attic Press, Inc., 1968); John B. Anderson, *Between Two Worlds: A Congressman's Choice* (Grand Rapids: Zondervan Publishing House, 1970); Richard J. Mouw, *Political Evangelism* (Grand Rapids: William B. Eerdmans Publishing Company, 1973); Robert D. Linder and Richard V. Pierard, *Politics: A Case for Christian Action* (Downers Grove, Ill.: InterVarsity Press, 1973); and Paul B. Henry, *Politics for Evangelicals* (Valley Forge, Pa.: Judson Press, 1974).

[40]Richard J. Mouw, *Politics and the Biblical Drama* (Grand Rapids: William B. Eerdmans Publishing Company, 1976); Robert Duncan Culver, *Toward a Biblical View of Civil Government* (Chicago: Moody Press, 1974).

[41]John Howard Yoder, *The Politics of Jesus: Vicit Agnus Noster* (Grand Rapids: William B. Eerdmans Publishing Company, 1972).

[42]Stephen V. Monsma, *The Unraveling of America* (Downers Grove, Ill.: InterVarsity Press, 1974); John B. Anderson, *Vision and Betrayal in America* (Waco, Tex.: Word Books, 1975).

[43]Quebedeaux, *The Worldly Evangelicals*, p. 96.

[44]Bruce Larson, *Ask Me to Dance* (Waco, Tex.: Word Books, 1972); Larson, *The Relational Revolution* (Waco, Tex.: Word Books, 1976).

[45]Charles Caldwell Ryrie, *The Role of Women in the Church* (Chicago: Moody Press, 1970); Larry Chistenson, *The Christian Family* (Minneapolis: Bethany Fellowship, 1970); Marabel Morgan, *The Total Woman* (Old Tappan, N.J.: Fleming H. Revell Company, 1973); Morgan, *Total Joy* (Old Tappan, N.J.: Fleming H. Revell Company, 1976); Elizabeth Elliott, *Let Me Be a Woman: Notes on Womanhood for Valerie* (Wheaton, Ill.: Tyndale House Publishers, Inc., 1976), esp. ch. 39. For a defense of "the exclusion of women from the ruling-teaching function of the church," see George W. Knight, III, *The New Testament Teaching on the Role Relationship of Men and Women* (Grand Rapids: Baker Book House, 1977), esp. ch. 3 and p. 57.

Other Evangelical women, prodded by the study of Russell C. Prohl[46] and by the rise of the feminist movement in American society, have advocated feminine liberation within a Christian context[47] and have formed the Evangelical Women's Caucus.[48] Their hermeneutic makes Galatians 3:28 to be central and seeks to revise the traditional male-dominated hermeneutic.[49] Paul King Jewett[50] and Virginia Ramey Mallenkott[51] have taken the liberation argument one basic step further by insisting that Paul's admonitions to female submission were indeed contradictory to certain basic biblical truths and hence that Paul, being influenced by a patriarchal society and rabbinic traditions, was clearly wrong. Lewis B. Smedes[52] and Tim and Beverly La Haye[53] have given specific attention to sexuality.

On the controversial contemporary issue of homosexuality, Smedes, although arriving at orthodox conclusions on most issues involving sex outside heterosexual marriage, has called for compassion and understanding.[54] But the issue of homosexuality has clearly divided the Evangelical community. Some agree with Anita Bryant's position,

> that, biblically speaking (citing Leviticus and the Pauline injunctions), homosexual practice is contrary to the will of God, that it threatens the nuclear family by providing bad role models to impressionable children, and that it is actually

---

[46]*Woman in the Church: A Restudy of Woman's Place in Building the Kingdom* (Grand Rapids: William B. Eerdmans Publishing Company, 1957). Prohl (ch. 2), following Emil Brunner, differentiated between the order of creation, in which woman was subordinate, and the order of redemption, in which woman's inequality has been removed.

[47]Nancy Hardesty, "Women and Evangelical Christianity," in Clouse, Linder, and Pierard, eds., *The Cross and the Flag*, ch. 4: Letha Scanzoni and Nancy Hardesty, *All We're Meant to Be: A Biblical Approach to Woman's Liberation* (Waco, Tex.: Word Books, 1974); and to a lesser extent, Patricia Gundry, *Woman Be Free!* (Grand Rapids: Zondervan Publishing House, 1977).

[48]Quebedeaux, *The Worldly Evangelicals*, p. 122.

[49]Ibid., p. 123.

[50]*Man as Male and Female* (Grand Rapids: William B. Eerdmans Publishing Company, 1975).

[51]*Women, Men and the Bible* (Nashville: Abingdon Press, 1977).

[52]*Sex for Christians: The Limits and Liberties of Sexual Living* (Grand Rapids: William B. Eerdmans Publishing Company, 1976).

[53]*The Act of Marriage* (Grand Rapids: Zondervan Publishing House, 1976).

[54]*Sex for Christians*, p. 138.

dangerous, because homosexuals (gay men, presumably) are especially prone to seduce young boys. . . .[55]

Don Williams forcefully contends that revelation, not observation (the social sciences), and Genesis 1-3, not the biblical texts about homosexuality, should be the beginning-point for consideration of the contemporary issue and concludes that homosexual acts violate the order and purpose of creation of male and female and hence reflect the fall, not the creation. Williams emphasizes that homosexuals can be changed by Christ and the gospel and calls the church from its "homophobia" to a ministry to homosexuals, but he opposes the ordination to the ministry of "avowed and practicing homosexuals."[56] Others, such as Smedes, would sanction "the possibility of *continued* homosexual practice among Christians when successful therapy or celibacy are not realistic options."[57] Ralph Blair, founder of Evangelicals Concerned in Miami in 1976, seeks a realistic ministry to homosexuals, both gay men and lesbians, and differentiates the "unnatural acts" mentioned by Paul from the *"natural"* inclinations of "true homosexuals." Troy Perry leads the Universal Fellowship of Metropolitan Community Churches, a group of gay congregations with Evangelical beliefs.[58]

Evangelicals in the recent past in their quest for holiness have often called for abstention from specific personal practices as sins, although consensus regarding such is not presently discoverable. Evangelicals, deploring Fundamentalism's lack of a social ethic, have become increasingly concerned about and active regarding racism, militarism, poverty, hunger, materialism, sexism, nationalism, cultural captivity, and other great social issues. Evangelicals are less united in confronting such specific issues as homosexuality, abortion, women's liberation, and women's ordination.

Evangelism and Missions

The impulse and obligation to share the gospel of Christ with others has been basic for those who can be properly called Evangelicals. Hence Richard Quebedeaux's third mark of contemporary Evangelicals, namely,

---

[55]Quebedeaux, *The Worldly Evangelicals*, p. 128.

[56]*The Bond That Breaks: Will Homosexuality Split the Church?* (Los Angeles: BIM, Inc., 1978), pp. 105-32.

[57]Quebedeaux, *The Worldly Evangelicals*, p. 128; see Smedes, *Sex for Christians*, p. 73.

[58]Quebedeaux, *The Worldly Evangelicals*, pp. 130-31, 129-30.

"the urgency of seeking actively the conversion of sinners to Christ"[59] is not without foundation and may serve to dispel the concept, sometimes articulated earlier in the present century, that one could be "evangelical" without being "evangelistic."

Anglican Evangelicals founded and supported the Church Missionary Society. Certain Protestant foreign missions societies in Switzerland and Germany which were formed during the nineteenth century bore the name "Evangelical." Both foreign and home mission work were characteristic of virtually all Protestant denominations in the United States after the first quarter of the nineteenth century. American Protestants played an increasing role in world missions during what Kenneth Scott Latourette called "the great century."[60]

Fundamentalist churches, at least after the intense controversy with Modernism during the 1920s, gave attention both to local evangelistic work and to the sending and support of foreign missionaries. New mission societies or boards, some of which were denominational and others of which were nondenominational, were formed. Cooperative structures for these various mission societies seemed to be needed; hence the Evangelical Foreign Mission Association (EFMA) was organized in 1945 under the aegis of the NAE;[61] the Interdenominational Foreign Mission Association (IFMA) had come into existence in 1917 to serve the nondenominational societies or faith missions that would not be related to the NAE.[62] The Foreign Mission Board of the Southern Baptist Convention (FMB-SBC) withdrew in 1950 from the Foreign Missions Conference of North America when it became apparent that the latter would become a department of the new National Council of the Churches of Christ in the U.S.A. (NCC).[63]

Especially during the 1960s the increase in the number of overseas missionary personnel supported by societies related to the EFMA or to

---

[59]*The Young Evangelicals*, p. 4.

[60]*A History of the Expansion of Christianity*, 7 vols. (New York: Harper & Brothers, 1937-45), vols. 4-6.

[61]Murch, *Cooperation without Compromise*, p. 102.

[62]Harold Lindsell, ed., *The Church's Worldwide Mission: An Analysis of the Current State of Evangelical Missions, and a Strategy for Future Activity* (Waco, Tex.: Word Books, 1966), pp. 271-73.

[63]William Wright Barnes, *The Southern Baptist Convention, 1845-1953* (Nashville: Broadman Press, 1954), p. 277.

the IFMA or by the FMB-SBC became apparent and stood in contrast to the decrease in the number of overseas missionary personnel supported by denominations that were members of the NCC and the World Council of Churches (WCC). The following chart displays these increases and decreases between 1958 and 1971.

Foreign Missionary Personnel[64]

	1958	1971
Six selected denominations that are members of the NCC and the WCC		
American Baptist Convention	407	290
Episcopal Church	395	138
Presbyterian Church, U.S.	504	391
United Church of Christ	496	356
United Methodist Church (incl. Evangelical-United Brethren)	1453	1175
United Presbyterian Church, U.S.A.	1293	810
TOTAL	4548	3160
Agencies related to the EFMA (and hence the NAE)	4688	7479
Agencies related to the IFMA	5902	6164
Wycliffe Bible Translators (affiliated with IFMA in 1958, but not in 1971)	(705)	1762
FMB-SBC	1186	2494

In 1973 in the United States of the ten agencies sending and supporting overseas Protestant missionaries that reported[65] the largest number of missionaries eight or nine were distinctly Evangelical:

---

[64]"The Missionary Retreat," *Christianity Today* 16 (19 November 1971): 188-89.

[65]"Overseas Missions: Stalled?" *Christianity Today* 18 (7 December 1973): 320-21, based on William L. Needham, "North American Protestant Ministries Overseas 1973: An Analysis of the Survey," in Edward R. Dayton, ed., *Mission Handbook: North American Protestant Ministries Overseas*, 10th ed. (Monrovia, Calif.: Mission Advanced Research and Communication Center, 1973), p. 89. By 1976 the Wycliffe Bible Translators had 2,693 missionaries, and the FMB-SBC had 2,667 missionaries. "More for Missions," *Christianity Today* 21 (4 March 1977): 660, based on Edward R. Dayton, ed., *Mission Handbook: North American Protestant Ministries Overseas*, 11th ed. (Monrovia, Calif.: Mission Advanced Research and Communication Center, 1976), pp. 367, 319.

1. SBC-FMB	2,507
2. Wycliffe Bible Translators	2,200
3. Churches of Christ	1,623
4. Seventh-Day Adventists	1,546
5. Youth with a Mission	1,009
6. Assemblies of God	967
7. United Methodist Church	951
8. Evangelical Alliance Mission	922
9. Sudan Interior Mission	818
10. Christian and Missionary Alliance	803

Ralph D. Winter has described the missionary expansion of Christianity during the period from 1945 to 1969, despite "the cutting of roots" (that is, ties with sending agencies), "the closing of doors," "the deepening pessimism," and "the turmoil in mission theory," as "the twenty-five unbelievable years."[66]

During the quarter of a century after the close of World War II Evangelical campus ministries in the United States were effective both in winning high school, college, and university students to Jesus Christ and in challenging numbers of them to Christian ministerial and missionary service. These ministries included InterVarsity Christian Fellowship (IVCF), whose triennial student missionary conventions at Urbana, Illinois,[67] were a potent missionary influence; Campus Crusade for Christ, which expanded in ministry beyond campuses; Youth for Christ; Young Life; and denominational student movements such as the SBC's Baptist Student Union. In 1965 Fuller Theological Seminary established its School of World Mission,[68] which has provided graduate study in missiology and stimulated research and writing, especially by Donald A. McGavran,[69] the father of the Church Growth movement, J. Edwin Orr,[70] the

---

[66]*The Twenty-Five Unbelievable Years, 1945-1969* (South Pasadena, Calif.: William Carey Library, 1970), esp. pp. 9-10, 47-64, 74-84.

[67]See John R. W. Stott et al., *Christ the Liberator* (Downers Grove, Ill.: InterVarsity Press, 1971), the volume of addresses given at the 1970 convention. C. Peter Wagner (pp. 93-101) identified *"presence evangelism"* as *"good,"* *"proclamation evangelism"* as *"better,"* and *"persuasion evangelism"* as *"best."* The first arouses "a *social* conscience," the second arouses *"spiritual conviction,"* but the third has "as its goal nothing less than making disciples."

[68]Quebedeaux, *The Worldly Evangelicals*, p. 85.

[69]*The Bridges of God: A Study in the Strategy of Missions* (New York: Friendship Press, 1955); *How Churches Grow: The New Frontiers of Mission* (London: World

leading authority on spiritual awakenings, C. Peter Wagner,[71] and Winter.[72] During the latter 1960s James D. Kennedy, senior minister of Coral Ridge Presbyterian Church, Fort Lauderdale, Florida, launched Evangelism Explosion, an evangelistic training program for lay Christians.[73] World Vision International, founded in 1950 by Bob Pierce to provide for Korean War orphans and engaging in various diaconal ministries overseas, has an important missionary statistics-gathering arm, Missions Advanced Research and Communications Center.[74] Harold Lindsell,[75] John R. W. Stott,[76] and D. Elton Trueblood[77] have restated the Evangelical case for world missions, J. Herbert Kane[78] has provided basic textbooks in Christian missions, and Michael Green[79] has treated the role of

Dominion Press, 1959); ed., *Church Growth and Christian Mission* (New York: Harper & Row, 1965); *Understanding Church Growth* (Grand Rapids: Williams B. Eerdmans Publishing Company, 1970); and ed., *Crucial Issues in Missions Tomorrow* (Chicago: Moody Press, 1972).

[70]*The Second Evangelical Awakening in Britain* (London: Marshall, Morgan & Scott, 1949); *The Light of the Nations: Evangelical Renewal and Advance in the Nineteenth Century* (Grand Rapids: William B. Eerdmans Publishing Company, 1965); *The Eager Feet: Evangelical Awakenings, 1790-1830* (Chicago: Moody Press, 1975); *The Fervent Prayer: The Worldwide Impact of the Great Awakening of 1858* (Chicago: Moody Press, 1974); *The Flaming Tongue: The Impact of Twentieth Century Revivals* (Chicago: Moody Press, 1973); *Evangelical Awakenings in Southern Asia* (Minneapolis: Bethany Fellowship, 1975); *Evangelical Awakenings in Eastern Asia* (Minneapolis: Bethany Fellowship, 1975); *Evangelical Awakenings in Africa* (Minneapolis: Bethany Fellowship, 1975); *Evangelical Awakenings in the South Seas* (Minneapolis: Bethany Fellowship, 1976); and *Evangelical Awakenings in Latin America* (Minneapolis: Bethany Fellowship, 1978).

[71]*Frontiers in Missionary Strategy* (Chicago: Moody Press, 1971) and *Our Kind of People: The Ethical Dimensions of Church Growth in America* (Atlanta: John Knox Press, 1979).

[72]See fn. 66.

[73]Quebedeaux, *The Worldly Evangelicals*, pp. 61-62.

[74]Ibid., pp. 110-11.

[75]*A Christian Philosophy of Mission* (Wheaton, Ill.: Van Kampen Press, 1949).

[76]*Our Guilty Silence* (Grand Rapids: William B. Eerdmans Publishing Company, 1969), and *Christian Mission in the Modern World* (Downers Grove, Ill.: InterVarsity Press, 1975).

[77]*The Validity of the Christian Mission* (New York: Harper & Row, 1972).

[78]*A Global View of Christian Missions: From Pentecost to the Present* (Grand Rapids: Baker Book House, 1971) and *Christian Missions in Biblical Perspective* (Grand Rapids: Baker Book House, 1976).

[79]*Evangelism in the Early Church* (Grand Rapids: William B. Eerdmans Publishing Company, 1970).

evangelism in early Christian history. Under the sponsorship of the EFMA and the IFMA a Congress on the Church's Worldwide Mission was held at Wheaton College in April 1966.[80] Third-world-formed and supported Evangelical missions, operative in various nations, including the United States, demonstrate the vitality of Evangelicalism outside the European and American spheres and may point the direction of tomorrow's Christian world mission.[81]

For the past thirty years the Billy Graham Evangelistic Association has deeply influenced the evangelistic activity of Evangelicals and other Christians both in the United States and in other nations through the Graham crusades, the "Hour of Decision," and *Decision* magazine. Under its initiative an International Congress on World Evangelization was held in July 1974 in Lausanne, Switzerland.[82] A covenant expressive of Evangelical beliefs was drawn up and signed,[83] and Latin American speakers "criticized American imperialism" and "the 'culture Christianity' inherent in the American way of life."[84] The Young Evangelicals during the mid-1970s, however, became critical of Billy Graham because of his close association with U.S. political leaders, especially President Richard M. Nixon, and because they alleged that he was preaching believing without discipleship, and they were more attracted to his brother-in-law, Leighton Ford.[85]

Evangelicals have been among the leading participants in developing new stress upon contextualization in the writing of theology. Contextualization, a step beyond indigenization in missions, is the direct formulation of Christian theology on the basis of the Bible in non-western cultures without dependence upon the western Christian theologies of the past and present. Careful to warn of the dangers of syncretism in

---

[80]Lindsell, ed., *The Church's Worldwide Mission.*

[81]C. Peter Wagner, "Missions from the Third World," *Christianity Today* 17 (22 June 1973): 987-90.

[82]James Dixon Douglas, ed., *Let the Earth Hear His Voice: International Congress on World Evangelization, Lausanne, Switzerland* (Minneapolis: World Wide Publications, 1975).

[83]John R. W. Stott, *The Lausanne Covenant: An Exposition and Commentary* (Minneapolis: World Wide Publications, 1975).

[84]Quebedeaux, *The Worldly Evangelicals*, p. 60.

[85]Quebedeaux, *The Young Evangelicals*, pp. 81-90, and *The Worldly Evangelicals*, pp. 54-55; Richard V. Pierard, "Billy Graham and the U.S. Presidency," *Journal of Church and State* 22 (Winter 1980): 107-27.

improper contextualization, Evangelical missiologists have nevertheless advocated the rightful use of contextualization.[86]

Evangelical Christians in the United States, if unspoiled by their popularity and cultural accommodation during the 1970s and unrent by antagonisms and schisms over secondary issues,[87] have with their common doctrinal affirmations, expanding ethical concerns, and unparalleled technology in communications a significant evangelistic and missionary opportunity at the beginning of the 1980s.

---

[86]David J. Hesselgrave, *Communicating Christ Cross-Culturally* (Grand Rapids: Zondervan Publishing House, 1978), esp. chs. 12-19; David J. Hesselgrave, ed., *Theology and Mission: Papers and Responses Prepared for the Consultation on Theology and Mission, Trinity Evangelical Divinity School, School of World Mission and Evangelism, March 22-25, 1976* (Grand Rapids: Baker Book House, 1978), esp. Norman R. Ericson, "Implications from the New Testament for Contextualization," pp. 71-85, and James O. Buswell, III, "'Contextualization: Theory, Tradition and Method," pp. 87-111; David J. Hesselgrave, ed., *New Horizons in World Missions; Evangelicals and the Christian Mission in the 1980s: Papers and Responses Prepared for the Consultation on Theology and Mission, Trinity Evangelical Divinity School, School of World Mission and Evange-lism, March 19-22, 1979* (Grand Rapids: Baker Book House, 1979), esp. Gleason L. Archer, Jr., "Contextualization: Some Implications from Life and Witness in the Old Testament," pp. 199-216, and Paul G. Hiebert, "Sets and Structures: A Study of Church Patterns," pp. 217-27; Bruce J. Nicholls, *Contextualization: A Theology of Gospel and Culture*, "Outreach and Identity: Evangelical Theological Monographs," no. 3 (Downers Grove, Ill.: InterVarsity Press, 1979); Charles H. Kraft, *Christianity in Culture: A Study in Dynamic Biblical Theologizing in Cross-Cultural Perspective* (Maryknoll, N.Y.: Orbis Books, 1979), esp. ch. 15; John Stott and Robert T. Coote, eds., *Gospel & Culture: The Papers of a Consultation on the Gospel and Culture, Convened by the Lausanne Commit-tee's Theology and Education Group* (Pasadena, Calif.: William Carey Library, 1979), esp. Bruce J. Nicholls, "Towards a Theology of Gospel and Culture," pp. 69-82, C. Rene Padilla, "Hermeneutics and Culture: A Theological Perspective," pp. 83-108, and Charles H. Kraft, "The Church in Culture: A Dynamic Equivalence Model," pp. 285-312; and Ebbie C. Smith, "Contextualization: The Current Discussion in Missionary Theology" (unpub-lished paper delivered to World Missions-Church Growth Conference, Southwestern Baptist Theological Seminary, October 9, 1980).

[87]This is the underlying theme of Quebedeaux's *The Worldly Evangelicals*; see especially ch. 2.

Chapter Three

Are Southern Baptists "Evangelicals"?

A considerable number of conservative Protestant religious bodies in the United States readily identify themselves as "Evangelical Christians" or "Evangelicals." Southern Baptists, however, have not generally been inclined to use the term as a self-descriptive denominational label or category of classification. By the term "Southern Baptists" we mean the members of the churches affiliated with the Southern Baptist Convention. The non-employment of the term "Evangelical" by Southern Baptists in reference to themselves may have been due to several factors such as the following: (1) the desire not to be identified with the Fundamentalism the Fundamentalist-Modernist Controversy; (2) the self-image of denominational independence which allows for neither conciliar Protestant nor conservative Protestant interdenominational affiliations; and (3) the preference for the terms "conservative," "evangelistic," and "missionary" rather than for "Evangelical."

During the 1970s the emergence to visibility in the United States of a larger community of Evangelical Christians that transcends any structures or organizations has compelled the more thoughtful among Southern Baptists to ask and to seek to answer the question, "Are Southern Baptists 'Evangelicals'?"

Who Are Southern Baptists?
A Look at History

Southern Baptists, especially since the centennial anniversary of their convention in 1945,[1] have become increasingly conscious of their own denominational history, including the various movements, influences, and controversies that have shaped their own denominational existence in the present.[2] Southern Baptists at the beginning of the 1980s are the product of a confluence of historical movements which together serve to identify, at least to an extent, who, despite their diversity, Southern Baptists actually are.

Calvinist Rather than Arminian, But Very Moderately Calvinist. The earliest Baptists in the South were immigrants from Great Britain who had belonged either to the Particular (or Calvinistic) Baptists or the General (or Arminian) Baptists and who constituted congregations of either of those types in the Southern colonies.[3] These groups of Baptists were separated from each other by those doctrines of predestination, atonement, grace, faith, and perseverance that had distinguished the Bezan Calvinists from the Arminians in continental Europe.[4] The Particular Baptists, who had come to be known in the American colonies as Regular Baptists, came to be more prevalent by the latter eighteenth century, being aided in their numerical expansion by the Great Awakening. The South especially was to be deeply influenced by another result of the Great Awakening, that is, the Separate Baptists, who under the leadership of Shubal Stearns (1706-1771) spread over the Southern frontier with their evangelistic, conversion-centered, and simplified Cal-

---

[1]Southern Baptist awareness of the beginnings of Baptist history in England may be said to have been kindled by the Whitsitt Controversy during 1896-1899. See Walter B. Shurden, *Not a Silent People: Controversies That Have Shaped Southern Baptists* (Nashville: Broadman Press, 1972), pp. 21-33, and James Thomas Meigs, "The Whitsitt Controversy," *The Quarterly Review* 31 (January-February-March 1971): 41-61.

[2]See William Wright Barnes, *The Southern Baptist Convention, 1845-1953* (Nashville: Broadman Press, 1954); Robert Andrew Baker, *The Southern Baptist Convention and Its People, 1607-1972* (Nashville: Broadman Press, 1974); Shurden, *Not a Silent People*; and Albert McClellan, "The Shaping of the Southern Baptist Mind," *Baptist History and Heritage* 13 (July 1978): 2-11.

[3]Baker, *The Southern Baptist Convention and Its People*, pp. 15-27.

[4]See David N. Steele and Curtis C. Thomas, *The Five Points of Calvinism: Defined, Defended, Documented*, "International Library of Philosophy and Theology" (Philadelphia: Presbyterian and Reformed Publishing Co., 1963), esp. pp. 16-19.

vinism.[5] The union of Regulars and Separates, especially in Virginia and North Carolina, integrated the Calvinistic Baptists and led to participation by such Baptists in the South as well as the North in the developing missionary consciousness which found organizational expression in the General Missionary Convention of the Baptist Denomination in the United States of America for Foreign Missions—better known as "the Triennial Convention," organized in 1814 in Philadelphia. Arminian Baptists continued their separate existence but enjoyed less numerical growth. The Freewill Baptists of the Northern states merged with the Northern Baptist Convention in 1911,[6] but the Free Will Baptists in the Southern and Western states still have their own denominational structure.[7] Baptists in the South, even in the colonial era, never fully embraced all the doctrines of Augustinianism or Bezan Calvinism; especially was this true of irresistible grace.[8] That doctrine of the atonement which limited its intention to the elect did not prevail among Southern Baptists after the nineteenth century,[9] and predestination came to be interpreted

---

[5]See William L. Lumpkin, *Baptist Foundations in the South: Tracing through the Separates the Influence of the Great Awakening, 1754-1787* (Nashville: Broadman Press, 1961).

[6]See Norman Allen Baxter, *History of the Freewill Baptists: A Study in New England Separatism* (Rochester, N.Y.: American Baptist Historical Society, 1957), ch. 6.

[7]See Damon C. Dodd, *The Free Will Baptist Story* (Nashville: Executive Department of the National Association of Free Will Baptists, 1956).

[8]The Philadelphia Confession (art. 3.1), declared that God's eternal decree is such that no "violence [is] offered to the will of the Creature, nor yet is the liberty, or contingency of second causes taken away, but rather established." The New Hampshire Confession (1833) affirmed that (art. 9) election is "perfectly consistent with the free agency of man" and that (art. 6) "nothing prevents the salvation of the greatest sinner on earth except his own voluntary refusal to submit to the Lord Jesus Christ." W. L. Lumpkin, *Baptist Confessions of Faith* (Philadelphia: Judson Press, 1959), pp. 254, 364, 363.

[9]According to the Philadelphia Confession (8.8), "To all those for whom Christ hath obtained eternal redemption, he doth certainly, and effectually apply, and communicate the same." This statement means that those who are redeemed through the death of Christ are identical with those who effectually receive Christ's redemption, i.e., the elect. On the other hand, neither the New Hampshire Confession nor the SBC statement of faith (1925) is specific about the scope of the atonement. Lumpkin, *Baptist Confessions of Faith*, pp. 262, 361-67, 393-98. The same lack of specificity may be seen in "The Abstract of Principles of The Southern Baptist Theological Seminary (1858)," *The Southern Baptist Theological Seminary 1978-1980 Catalog*, pp. 13-16, and in the SBC statement of faith (1963), Lumpkin, *Baptist Confessions of Faith*, rev. ed. (Valley Forge, Pa.: Judson Press, 1969), pp. 393-400.

more generally as God's eternal purpose of saving grace.[10] The modifications of Calvinism among Southern Baptists[11] may be seen by contrasting the teachings of their leading nineteenth-century theologians (that is, John Leadley Dagg,[12] James Petigru Boyce[13]) with the teachings of their leading early twentieth-century theologians (that is, Edgar Young Mullins,[14] Walter Thomas Conner[15]). The clearest surviving aspect of the earlier Southern Baptist Calvinism is the doctrine of the perseverance of the saints, known also as the security of the believer or by the less apt, but popular wording, "once saved, always saved."[16] Southern Baptists stand in the heritage of Paul, Augustine of Hippo Regius, Martin Luther, John Calvin, and Andrew Fuller in respect to the necessity of God's grace, understood both as pardon and as power, for the salvation of sinful human beings. But their conception of God's sovereignty is always coupled with and qualified by that of God's gracious purpose to save.[17]

---

[10]According to the Philadelphia Confession (3.3), God's predestination of "some" to eternal life through Christ is "to the praise of his glorious grace," whereas God's leaving of "others . . . to act in their sin to their just condemnation, [is] to the praise of his glorious justice." On the other hand, the New Hampshire Confession (art. 9) defined election as "the gracious purpose of God, according to which he regenerates, sanctifies, and saves sinners." Neither the 1925 nor the 1963 SBC statement of faith contains an article concerning election or predestination. Lumpkin, *Baptist Confessions of Faith*, pp. 254, 364, 393-98; Lumpkin, *Baptist Confessions of Faith*, rev. ed., pp. 393-400.

[11]On the de-Calvinization of Southern Baptist beliefs, see Robert Tillman Kendall, "The Rise and Demise of Calvinism in the Southern Baptist Convention" (M.A. thesis, University of Louisville, 1973).

[12]See his *A Manual of Theology* (Charleston, S.C.: Southern Baptist Publication Society, 1857), esp. pp. 99-110, 152-57, 287-300, 305-38.

[13]See his *Abstract of Systematic Theology* (Philadelphia: American Baptist Publication Society, 1887), esp. chs. 13, 28, 29, 30, 31, and 38.

[14]See his *The Christian Religion in Its Doctrinal Expression* (Philadelphia: Judson Press, 1917), esp. chs. 13-14 and pp. 294-99 and 432-38.

[15]See his *The Gospel of Redemption* (Nashville: Broadman Press, 1945), esp. pp. 22-25, 51, 136, 247-58.

[16]"The New Hampshire Confession" (art. 11), "The Abstract of Principles of The Southern Baptist Theological Seminary" (art. 13), and the 1925 (art. 11) and 1963 (art. 5) SBC statements of faith clearly teach the perseverance of all true believers. Lumpkin, *Baptist Confessions of Faith*, pp. 365, 394-95; Lumpkin, *Baptist Confessions of Faith*, rev. ed., p. 396; *The Southern Baptist Theological Seminary 1978-80 Catalog*, p. 15.

[17]In his delineation of the Great Awakening as the time of transition from the Puritan period to the Evangelical period of the history of American Christianity, Charles L. Chaney, *The Birth of Missions in America* (South Pasadena, Calif.: William Carey Library, 1976), p. 49, has written:

Missionary, Not Antimissionary. The foreign missionary motivation and activity among Baptists originated among English Particular Baptists at the end of the eighteenth century with the labors of their pioneer missionary, William Carey (1761-1834), and his colleagues in India and the Baptist Missionary Society, which was founded in 1792 by certain Particular or Calvinistic Baptists in England. The non-invitation, non-application hyper-Calvinism embraced by John Gill (1697-1771) and certain of his contemporaries had been supplanted by the more evangelical Calvinism of Andrew Fuller (1754-1815), whose theology combined God's sovereign and electing grace with the obligation of Christians to proclaim the gospel to all human beings. It was Fuller's evangelical Calvinism that undergirded both Carey and his colleagues and his supporters at home.[18]

The new foreign missionary impulse attracted the attention of Baptists in the new American nation—that is, in New England, the Middle Atlantic states, and the Southern states. Some Baptists sent contributions to the Baptist Missionary Society; some organized missionary societies of their own.[19]

But the missionary motivation and the activity of Baptists in the American colonies and the new nation were not altogether a response to British happenings. Throughout much of the eighteenth century Baptist farmer-preachers and missionaries sent forth by Baptist churches or by Baptist associations[20] carried the gospel to and planted churches among

---

It is emphasis rather than exact definition which distinguishes the two periods. The major emphasis of the Puritan era was the sovereignty of God while that of the Evangelical period was the reign of Christ. One underlined sovereignty; the other underlined grace. The Puritan age, while it did not negate emotion, demote Jesus Christ, or decry compassion for mankind, accentuated the role and will of the inscrutable God. The new age of American Christianity did not deny God's sovereign rule, but it emphasized the place of the affections in religion, the role of Jesus the Savior, and his free grace to save.

This distinction may indeed apply to and help to explain the differences between the Regular Baptists of the late seventeenth and early eighteenth centuries and the Southern Baptists of the latter nineteenth and the twentieth centuries.

[18]A. C. Underwood, *A History of the English Baptists* (London: Kingsgate Press, 1947), pp. 159-85.

[19]See Albert L. Vail, *The Morning Hour of American Baptist Missions* (Philadelphia: American Baptist Publication Society, 1907), pp. 21-85, 157-94; and Baker, *The Southern Baptist Convention and Its People*, pp. 98-101.

[20]Chiefly the Philadelphia, the Charleston, and the Warren associations.

the Indians and in the new and unchurched settlements.[21]

It was, however, the becoming Baptists of Adoniram (1788-1850) and Ann Judson (1789-1826) and of Luther Rice (1783-1836) after appointment as missionaries of the American Board of Commissioners for Foreign Missions to India and the itinerant missionary statesmanship of Rice that led Baptists from the various states to constitute in Philadelphia in May 1814 the first Baptist structure to be national in scope, the General Missionary Convention of the Baptist Denomination in the United States of America for Foreign Missions. This "convention," after temporary expansion into home missions, education, and publication, became after 1826 strictly a foreign mission society. Whereas participants from the South favored a general multifaceted missionary convention and those from New England were attracted to the single society method—the differences between which contributed to the separation of 1844-1845, all the participants, whether from Southern, Middle, or New England states, were committed as Baptists to the world mission of Christianity.[22]

In addition to the nationwide Baptist societies created from 1814 to 1832 there came to be constituted, especially in the South, state Baptist conventions, designed to conduct various types of missionary and denominational activity. The first of these was formed in South Carolina in 1821. Soon various Baptist colleges were established in the Southern states, especially after the separation of Columbian College in Washington, D.C. Baptists in the South seemed to be on the threshold of great expansion when another controversy divided their ranks, namely, the antimissionary controversy.

Motivated by a tenacious jealousy for local church autonomy and by the fear of centralization, sometimes holding to a hyper-Calvinistic theology, often characterized by ignorance and by a highly polemical spirit, and in places influenced by the anti-society stance of Alexander Campbell (1788-1866) during his years of identification with Baptists (1813-1830),[23] the

---

[21]See Chaney, *The Birth of Missions in America*, pp. 121-26, 141-44, 170-72, and Baker, *The Southern Baptist Convention and Its People*, pp. 97-98.

[22]See Chaney, *The Birth of Missions in America*, pp. 194, 196-99; Jesse C. Fletcher, "The Beginnings," in Baker James Cauthen, et al., *Advance: A History of Southern Baptist Foreign Missions* (Nashville: Broadman Press, 1970), pp. 8-14; and Baker, *The Southern Baptist Convention and Its People*, pp. 104-17. The Baptist General Tract Society was organized in 1824, and the American Baptist Home Mission Society in 1832.

[23]Victor I. Masters, *Baptist Missions in the South* (Atlanta: Home Mission Board of the Southern Baptist Convention, 1915), pp. 114-23. B. H. Carroll, Jr., *The Genesis of*

Antimissionary or "Hardshell" Baptists were opposed to the "Triennial Convention" and its associated societies, to state conventions, to Baptist colleges, to Sunday schools, etc. The struggle was waged for about a quarter of a century and resulted in the permanent separation of the Primitive (or "Hardshell") Baptists and the Missionary Baptists.

Those Baptists who formed the Southern Baptist Convention (SBC) in May 1845 and those who supported it during subsequent decades were clearly and unmistakably Missionary Baptists. The preamble to the constitution of the SBC, adopted in 1845, declares that the convention originated

> for the purpose of carrying into effect the benevolent intentions of our constituents, by organizing a plan for eliciting, combining, and directing the energies of the whole denomination in one sacred effort, for the propagation of the Gospel....[24]

The SBC in 1925 affirmed:

> It is the duty of every Christian man and woman, and the duty of every church of Christ, to seek to extend the gospel to the ends of the earth. The new birth of man's spirit by God's Holy Spirit means the birth of love for others. Missionary effort upon the part of all rests thus upon a spiritual necessity of the regenerate life. It is also expressly and repeatedly commanded in the teachings of Christ. It is the duty of every child of God to seek constantly to win the lost to Christ by personal effort and by all other methods sanctioned by the Gospel of Christ.[25]

American Anti-Missions (Louisville: Baptist Book Concern, 1902), chs. 3-6, gave special attention to the work and thought of Daniel Parker, John Taylor, and Alexander Campbell. Concerning Daniel Parker's teachings, see O. Max Lee, "Daniel Parker's Doctrine of the Two Seeds" (Th.M. thesis, Southern Baptist Theological Seminary, 1962). Lee, having discovered three hitherto thought to be nonextant writings by Parker, *Views on the Two Seeds* (1826), *A Supplement or Explanation of My Views on the Two Seeds* (1826), and *Second Dose on the Two Seeds* (1827), concluded (1) that Parker favored church-centered missions but opposed the societal plan of the "Triennial" Convention (pp. 20-25); (2) that Parker explicated his doctrine of the two seeds as a doctrine of the non-elect, who condemn themselves by their sins rather than be condemned by an eternal decree of God, and hence Parker's two-seed doctrine was designed to modify, not to enhance, hyper-Calvinism (pp. 25-30); and (3) that Parker's anti-missionary society stance and his doctrine of the two seeds "were never intentionally related to each other by Parker himself" (p. 34), but these two had ineptly coalesced by 1827 in the polemic of Parker's opponents (pp. 34-35).

[24]SBC, *Annual*, 1845, p. 3.

[25]Art. 23, in Lumpkin, *Baptist Confessions of Faith*, pp. 397-98.

In 1963 the SBC adopted the same essential statement with slight verbal alterations.[26] Clearly and unmistakably the corporate existence of Southern Baptists as a denomination from 1845 to the present has been primarily due to the missionary imperative and task. The expanding numbers of missionary personnel, both foreign and home, under appointment has been a major development among Southern Baptists during the third quarter of the twentieth century. The Bold Mission Thrust offers an even greater challenge to lay involvement at the onset of the 1980s.

Denominational, But Not Landmarkist. Very soon after the organization of the Southern Baptist Convention within the context of the defense of slaveholders as missionaries there arose within its ranks a movement or party which was to produce controversy for more than half a century and effects upon the Southern Baptist consciousness throughout most of the twentieth century. Called Landmarkism, it took its name from the tract, "An Old Landmark Reset,"[27] written by James Madison Pendleton (1811-1891) and first published in 1854 by James Robinson Graves (1820-1893). Landmarkism arose from queries about the validity of immersions performed by pedobaptist ministers that were published and answered in the *Western Baptist Review* (Louisville) in 1848. It was first given expression by Graves in his questions propounded at Cotton Grove, Tennessee, in 1851. Under the leadership of Graves and Pendleton, Landmarkism became a system of ecclesiological teaching.[28] Unbroken Baptist church succession from the apostolic era to the nineteenth century, traced through various ancient and medieval groups and parties, was affirmed. The Kingdom of God was identified with Baptist churches, and Baptist churches were held to be the "only true" Christian churches. Hence no Baptist pulpit should be open to non-Baptist ministers, no immersion performed by a non-Baptist minister should be reckoned by Baptists as valid, and participation in the Lord's Supper should be limited to members of the celebrating Baptist church. The local Baptist congrega-

---

[26]Art. 11, in Lumpkin, *Baptist Confessions of Faith*, rev. ed., pp. 397-98.

[27]See Prov. 22:28.

[28]For an extended exposition of Landmarkism as a system, see James E. Tull, "A Study of Southern Baptist Landmarkism in the Light of Historical Baptist Ecclesiology" (Ph.D. diss., Columbia University, 1960), chs. 4-6; also see Tull's "The Landmark Movement: An Historical and Theological Appraisal," *Baptist History and Heritage* 10 (January 1975): 3-18.

tion was the key unit in Landmark belief. The Landmark leaders, especially Graves, agitated for their system during the 1850s and, despite their inability to dominate the Southern Baptist Convention, began to enlist a widespread following in the states that did not border the Atlantic Ocean, especially because of Graves's publishing activity.[29]

During the 1880s and 1890s Landmarkism was expressed within the Southern Baptist Convention in four controversies: the Gospel Missionism of Tarleton Perry Crawford (1821-1902), the Whitsitt Controversy, the Hayden-Cranfill Controversy in Texas (1894-1900), and the separation in 1905 led by Ben Marquis Bogard (1868-1951) which resulted in the formation of a Landmark general body, the General Association of Landmark Baptists, the name of which was changed in 1924 to the American Baptist Association.[30]

Although Landmarkers have been institutionally separated from the Southern Baptist Convention for three-fourths of a century, certain effects of Landmarkism have been discernible among Southern Baptists: the importance attached to the independence of the local Baptist congregation apart from cooperation in general bodies; the widespread practice of rejecting so-called "alien immersions" and insistence upon Baptist-administered immersions; the exclusive local church basis of representation in the Southern Baptist Convention;[31] a strong denominational

---

[29]Hugh Wamble, "Landmarkism: Doctrinaire Ecclesiology among Baptists," *Church History* 33 (December 1964): 429-47; Barnes, *The Southern Baptist Convention, 1845-1953*, pp. 98-113; Baker, *The Southern Baptist Convention and Its People, 1607-1972*, pp. 208-19, 248-49; John E. Steely, "The Landmark Movement in the Southern Baptist Convention," in Duke K. McCall, ed., *What Is the Church? A Symposium of Baptist Thought* (Nashville: Broadman Press, 1958), pp. 134-47; W. Morgan Patterson, "Landmarkism," *Encyclopedia of Southern Baptists*, 4 vols. (Nashville: Broadman Press, 1958, 1971, 1982), 2:757; Homer L. Grice, "Graves, James Robinson," ibid., 1:576-78; and Leo T. Crismon and Harold Stephens, "Pendleton, James Madison," ibid., 2:1082-83. On Baptist successionism, see W. Morgan Patterson, *Baptist Successionism: A Critical View* (Valley Forge, Pa.: Judson Press, 1969).

[30]Baker, *The Southern Baptist Convention and Its People, 1607-1972*, pp. 277-84. The American Baptist Association experienced a schism in 1950 with the result that there was formed the North American Baptist Association, the name of which in 1969 became the Baptist Missionary Association of America.

[31]Baker, *The Southern Baptist Convention and Its People, 1607-1972*, pp. 404-6, has noted that the change of the basis of representation in the Southern Baptist Convention made in 1931 provided "a *designated* church representation," not the "*delegated* church representation" advocated by Landmarkers.

self-consciousness; a reluctance to consider Baptists as Protestants; and the insistence upon separation from non-Baptist denominations in any quest for more visible, or ultimately organic, union. But as Southern Baptists have developed during the twentieth century, there have also been evidences of anti-Landmark tendencies: the enlargement and complexification of the denominational organization;[32] the shift from strictly local church participation in the Lord's Supper to a denominational inclusion of those "of like faith and order" or to open communion in which all professing and baptized Christians are invited to partake; the study and teaching of Baptist history which rejects Landmark successionist theory; the allowing of non-Baptist ministers to preach in Baptist pulpits and the willingness of Baptist ministers to preach in non-Baptist pulpits; and the tendency of Southern Baptists to accept the use of the term "church" in reference to non-Baptist congregations or denominations.[33] The seventy-seven years since the Landmark schism (1905) have been the era in which the Southern Baptist Convention on the one hand has affiliated as a convention with and strongly supported the Baptist World Alliance and on the other hand has declined to join the Federal Council of the Churches of Christ in America, the World Council of Churches, the National Association of Evangelicals, or the National Council of the Churches of Christ in the U.S.A. Southern Baptists continue to be denominationalists, but the majority of their number seem unwilling to understand denominationalism in terms of the Landmark system.

Conservative Rather Than Liberal in Theology. The churches of the Southern Baptist Convention were not so seriously affected, so hurtfully divided, or so severely damaged by the Modernist-Liberal-Conservative-Fundamentalist Controversy, which began at the end of the nineteenth century and came to its climax during the 1920s, as were certain other denominational bodies based in the Northern states, namely, the Northern Baptist Convention and the Presbyterian Church in the U.S.A.[34]

---

[32]This evidence has been set forth by Baker, *The Southern Baptist Convention and Its People, 1607-1972*, p. 284.

[33]Graves had insisted that they be called "societies" but not "churches."

[34]Norman F. Furniss, *The Fundamentalist Controversy, 1918-1931* (New Haven: Yale University Press, 1954), p. 119, declared: "Modernism . . . never became a troublesome issue to the Southern Baptists during the 1920's. . . . If conflict over theology was to come at all, it would have to wait until later in the twentieth century." Furniss found one exception, the subject of evolution. According to Shurden, *Not a Silent People: Controver-*

Why was it that Southern Baptists suffered less hurtful effects from this controversy that so deeply affected American Protestantism? The influence of German university scholarship was not so great upon Southern Baptist seminary and college professors as upon some institutions in the North.[35] Industrialization was not coming to the South to the degree it was coming to the North, and hence labor-management tensions were not such a major factor in the South.[36] Southern cities were not yet experiencing the great population expansion that characterized numerous cities in the North, and Southern Protestants were not being significantly displaced by Roman Catholic, Eastern Orthodox, or Jewish immigrants. Neither academia nor the market place nor the local community was making the demands for changes in Bible study, theology, and ethics that were being made in the North. Today scholars continue to debate the degree of the effect of the Social Gospel on the South.[37]

---

sies That Have Shaped Southern Baptists, p. 89: "Modernism never strutted in the South as it had in the North. For Southern Baptists, this meant that the Fundamentalist-Modernist controversy was not as grave an issue as it had been among Northern Baptists. But there was tension. And there would be separation, but it would be small."

[35]Crawford Howell Toy (1836-1919) and William Heth Whitsitt (1841-1911), both of Southern Baptist Theological Seminary, had been influenced by German scholarship, but they were not teaching in that seminary after the opening of the twentieth century. For a study of the changing views of the Bible among Northern Baptists, see Norman H. Maring, "Baptists and Changing Views of the Bible," *Foundations* 1 (July 1958): 52-75 and (October 1958): 30-61.

[36]That industrialization did occur in the South before 1930 has been noted by John Samuel Ezell, *The South since 1865*, 2d ed. (New York: Macmillan, 1975), ch. 8., who cites textiles, cottonseed, cigarettes, iron-coal, sulphur, lumber, hydroelectric power, oil, and railroads.

[37]Baker, *The Southern Baptist Convention and Its People, 1607-1972*, pp. 306-308, has argued that the Social Gospel movement did not squarely face the number one social problem confronting Southern Baptists, namely, race relations, and hence he minimizes the effect of the Social Gospel upon Southern Baptists. Samuel S. Hill, Jr., *Religion and the Solid South* (Nashville: Abingdon Press, 1972), pp. 49, 43, has argued that the effect of the Social Gospel upon the South was minimal, but the reason, he finds, was the "character of Southernness as a cultural system-mythology operating as the model for living." "What was most fundamental to the experience of the people was Southernness, not religious faith, truth, or integrity as such." On the other hand, John Lee Eighmy, *Churches in Cultural Captivity: A History of the Social Attitudes of Southern Baptists* (Knoxville: University of Tennessee Press, 1972), pp. 70-71, has declared: "As compared to the Presbyterians and Methodists of the South, the Baptists had greater difficulty accepting the social-gospel ideology because their religious individualism, theological conservatism, decentralized authority, and denominational isolationism, taken together, formed greater barriers to cooperative social action by churches. The presence of such formidable barriers

Moreover, Southern post-Reconstruction regional isolationism tended to separate Southern Christians and Southern churches from outside influences and to intensify the regional influences upon theology and ethics.[38]

If biblical criticism, the Social Gospel, and liberal Protestant theology were to have limited influence upon Southern Baptists prior to 1930, the same may be said concerning the two streams which, according to Ernest Sandeen, converged to form Fundamentalism, namely, Dispensationalism and the Princeton Theology. Dallas Theological Seminary, today the chief center of dispensational premillennial scholarship and teaching, was not founded until 1924, and none of its "founders" was a Baptist.[39] The only major writing theologian who influenced Southern Baptists prior to 1930 that espoused Dispensationalism was James Robinson Graves,[40] who never cited, it seems, the works of the principal formulator of Dispensationalism, John Nelson Darby (1800-1882), an Anglican who joined and gave leadership to the Plymouth Brethren. James Petigru Boyce (1827-1888), professor of theology in and chairman of the faculty of Southern Baptist Theological Seminary, who himself had studied theology under Charles Hodge of Princeton Theological Seminary,[41] may

---

makes even more remarkable the evidence of social-gospel influence in Southern Baptist life."

[38]Comer Vann Woodward, *The Burden of Southern History*, rev. ed. (Baton Rouge: Louisiana State University Press, 1968), pp. 13-21, has asserted that in contrast to the national or American "myths" of abundance or opulence, success or invincibility, and moral innocence, Southerners have known poverty, military defeat, and the reality of evil. The influence of the South and its culture upon churches may not only be seen in the history of Southern Baptists but also in the history of the Churches of Christ, the Presbyterian Church in the United States, the Methodist Episcopal Church (South)— until 1939, and the various Holiness and Pentecostal church bodies that arose in the South during this period. Ezell, *The South since 1865*, p. 356, confidently asserted: "Yet despite ecclesiastical differences [i.e., of social class or church polity], the basic social philosophy of Southern churches was the same."

[39]Rudolf A. Renfer, "A History of Dallas Theological Seminary" (Ph.D. diss., University of Texas at Austin, 1959), p. 1, chs. 4-6.

[40]See his *The Work of Christ in the Covenant of Redemption; Developed in Seven Dispensations* (Memphis: Baptist Book House, 1883), pp. 159-243, 286-95, 313-37, 379-405, 544-55. Harold Stewart Smith, "A Critical Analysis of the Theology of J. R. Graves" (Th.D. diss., Southern Baptist Theological Seminary, 1966), pp. 113-14, found that Graves did not write about Dispensationalism until 1870 and suggested, on the basis of S. H. Ford's statement in 1900, that he might have derived his Dispensationalism from a Kentucky Presbyterian, Robert J. Breckinridge (1800-1871).

[41]John A. Broadus, *Memoir of James Petigru Boyce, D.D., LL.D.* (New York: A. C. Armstrong and Son; Louisville: Baptist Book Concern, 1893), pp. 72, 73, 304-5, 307, 310,

have provided an important link between the Princeton Theology and the theology taught among Southern Baptists, but Edgar Young Mullins (1860-1928)[42] and Walter Thomas Conner (1877-1952)[43] and most of their teaching colleagues did little to perpetuate that link. The basic theological conservatism of Southern Baptists prior to 1930, therefore, was not consciously and explicitly molded by or dependent on either Dispensationalism or the Princeton Theology.

The Modernist-Liberal-Conservative-Fundamentalist Controversy did, however, to a degree impinge upon and affect Southern Baptists. Of somewhat limited significance was the fact that three Southern Baptist seminary professors contributed articles to *The Fundamentals: A Testimony to the Truth*, a twelve-volume series first issued during 1910-1915,[44] and that a former Southern Baptist pastor was a contributor to

---

asserted that Charles Hodge was "the most influential of all Boyce's instructors at Princeton" [during his two years as a student, 1849-1851] and that "Boyce was more powerfully impressed by Dr. Hodge than by any other Princeton professor" and evaluated Boyce's study under Hodge as "a great privilege to be directed and upborne by such a teacher in studying that exalted system of Pauline truth which is technically called Calvinism. . . ." According to Broadus, Boyce used Charles Hodge's three-volume *Systematic Theology* briefly in 1872 as his own textbook and in his own *Abstract of Systematic Theology* (1887) was, like Hodge, "much influenced as to general method by the great treatise of Turrettin, which he was teaching every year to his smaller class in 'Latin Theology' " and as to content by Calvinism. Compare William A. Mueller, *A History of Southern Baptist Theological Seminary* (Nashville: Broadman Press, 1959), p. 56. Basil Manly, Jr., another of the original faculty of Southern Baptist Theological Seminary, studied at Princeton Theological Seminary from 1845 to 1847, had Charles Hodge as one of his teachers, and was graduated in 1847. Mueller, *A History of Southern Baptist Theological Seminary*, p. 89.

[42]Concerning the rejection by Mullins, president and professor of theology, Southern Baptist Theological Seminary, of limited atonement and irresistible grace and his teaching of election as not being grounded on the faith of true believers, of total depravity, and of the perseverance of the saints, see Bill Clark Thomas, "Edgar Young Mullins: A Baptist Exponent of Theological Restatement" (Th.D. diss., Southern Baptist Theological Seminary, 1963), pp. 258, 266-70, 284-85.

[43]Concerning the silence of Conner, professor of theology, Southwestern Baptist Theological Seminary, on the issues of limited atonement and irresistible grace and his teaching total depravity, election as not being grounded on the faith of true believers, and the perseverance of the saints, see James Leo Garrett, Jr., "The Theology of Walter Thomas Conner" (Th.D. diss., Southwestern Baptist Theological Seminary, 1954), pp. 237-39, 241-67, 273-75.

[44](Chicago: Testimony Publishing Company); also publ. as 4 vols. (Los Angeles: Bible Institute of Los Angeles, 1917). See E. Y. Mullins, "The Testimony of Christian Experience," 3:76-85; J. J. Reeve, "My Personal Experience with the Higher Criticism," 3:98-118; and Charles B. Williams, "Paul's Testimony to the Doctrine of Sin," 8:49-63.

and one of the three consecutive editors of that series.[45] Of greater significance were the evolution crisis in the mid-1920s in the Southern Baptist Convention and the schism led by John Franklyn Norris (1877-1952),[46] pastor of the First Baptist Church, Fort Worth, Texas. Both of these developments were interrelated.

The teaching of some form of the theistic evolution of man had commenced in certain Baptist colleges and universities by the early years of the twentieth century. Such teaching was defended on the basis of academic freedom. One of the leading defenders was William Louis Poteat (1856-1938), president of Wake Forest College, and one of the leading teachers was Grove Samuel Dow,[47] professor of sociology at Baylor University. Norris's attacks upon Dow and the Baylor administration led to the resignation of Dow in 1921, but the Baptist General Convention of Texas refused to reprimand the Baylor administration.[48] The Southern Baptist Convention in its 1922 session received a committee report that posed the irreconcilable nature of the Bible and "the accepted theory of evolution" and heard its president, E. Y. Mullins, advocate "firm faith, and free research" as "our noble Baptist ideal." In

---

Mullins was president of and professor of theology in Southern Baptist Theological Seminary; Reeve was professor of Old Testament and Williams was professor of New Testament in Southwestern Baptist Theological Seminary. The articles by Mullins and by Williams, though valuable in themselves, treated topics that were somewhat adjunctive to the controverted issues. Reeve's short tenure at Southwestern Seminary meant that he had limited influence on Southern Baptists.

[45]Amzi Clarence Dixon, "The Scriptures," 5:72-80. Dixon edited the first five columes of *The Fundamentals*, Louis Meyer edited volumes 6-10, and Reuben A. Torrey edited volumes 11-12, according to "A Statement of the Two Laymen," vol. 12, p. 3. Dixon had been pastor of Southern Baptist churches until 1890 and would later serve as pastor of another Southern Baptist church from 1921 until his death in 1925. From 1906 to 1911 Dixon was pastor of the Moody Church, Chicago, and from 1911 to 1919 was pastor of Metropolitan Tabernacle, London. Helen C. A. Dixon, *A. C. Dixon: A Romance of Preaching* (New York, London: G. P. Putnam's Sons, 1931), and W. H. Brannock, "Dixon, Amzi Clarence," *Encyclopedia of Southern Baptists*, 1:377.

[46]On the life of Norris, see E. Ray Tatum, *Conquest or Failure? Biography of J. Frank Norris* (Dallas: Baptist Historical Foundation, 1966), a psychological study, and Roy Emerson Falls, *A Biography of J. Frank Norris, 1877-1952* (n.p.p.: n.p., 1975), written by one who stands within the Norris movement.

[47]In his *Introduction to the Principles of Sociology* (Waco, Tex.: Baylor University Press, 1920), Dow's emphasis was on the evolution of the family from the horde, of society, and of religion and ethics (pp. 157-67, 207-23, 239-60). He did refer to "primitive man" as being "about halfway between the anthropoid ape and modern man" (p. 211).

[48]Furniss, *The Fundamentalist Controversy, 1918-1931*, pp. 119, 122-23.

the 1923 session President Mullins was more specific about the details of the "firm faith" and sharply differentiated unverified scientific hypotheses from established facts.[49] In 1924 the convention rejected motions to adopt an already formulated doctrinal statement and instead appointed a committee, with Mullins as chairman, "to consider the advisability of issuing another statement of the Baptist faith and message."[50] When that committee reported its proposed statement in 1925, which contained the words, "Man was created by the special act of God, as recorded in Genesis," a member of the committee, Clarence Perry Stealey (1868-1937), editor of the (Oklahoma) *Baptist Messenger*, moved to amend the statement as follows:

> We believe that man came into this world by direct creation of God and not by evolution. This creative act was separate and distinct from any other work of God and was not conditioned upon antecedent changes in previously created forms of life.

The convention declined to accept the Stealey amendment and accepted instead the committee report.[51] In 1926 the convention's president, George White McDaniel (1875-1927), pastor of the First Baptist Church, Richmond, Virginia, concluded his address with these words:

> This Convention accepts Genesis as teaching that man was the special creation of God, and rejects every theory, evolution or other, which teaches that man originated in, or came by way of, a lower animal ancestry.[52]

On motion by Monroe Elmon Dodd (1878-1952), pastor of the First Baptist Church, Shreveport, Louisiana, who sought to terminate the controversy, the convention adopted the McDaniel statement as "the sentiment" of the convention. In the same 1926 session, however, the convention passed a resolution introduced by Selsus Estol Tull (1878-1973), pastor, First Baptist Church, Pine Bluff, Arkansas, that urgently requested all the convention's institutions, boards, and missionaries to

---

[49]Shurden, *Not a Silent People: Controversies That Have Shaped Southern Baptists*, pp. 94-96; W. Morgan Patterson, "The Southern Baptist Theologian as Controversialist: A Contrast," *Baptist History and Heritage* 15 (July 1980): 13.

[50]SBC *Annual*, 1924, p. 95.

[51]SBC, *Annual*, 1925, pp. 72, 76.

[52]SBC, *Annual*, 1926, p. 18.

accept the McDaniel statement. Threatening of the withholding of SBC Cooperative Program funds in Oklahoma and deferrals or refusals to sign by some convention leaders were followed by the demise of controversy about 1927.[53] Evolution ceased to be a major issue before the Southern Baptist Convention.

J. Frank Norris not only powerfully agitated against the teaching of evolution in Baptist institutions of learning but also led a schism from the Southern Baptist Convention. Norris habitually made from his pulpit and through his newspaper, *The Searchlight*, strong attacks upon Southern Baptist leaders, especially those in Texas.[54] The Tarrant County Baptist Association declined to seat messengers from the First Baptist Church, Fort Worth, in 1922 "primarily for his [Norris's] censoriousness and non-cooperation."[55] The Baptist General Convention of Texas, after censoring Norris in 1922, voted in 1924 to disfellowship Norris and his congregation.[56] According to Robert A. Baker, "the overwhelmingly conservative nature of Southern Baptists" made it "difficult" for Norris and his associates "to establish doctrinal grounds for attacking the [Southern Baptist] Convention and its agencies." Hence Norris instead "used fundamentalism as a platform for personal controversy and to further his ambitions."[57] Norris's own conduct contributed to the separation. "Before the civil courts of Texas, Norris was indicted for arson, tried

[53]Ibid., p. 98; Shurden, *Not a Silent People: Controversies That Have Shaped Southern Baptists*, pp. 96-100; Baker, *The Southern Baptist Convention and Its People, 1607-1972*, pp. 398-99; Patterson, "The Southern Baptist Theologian as Controversialist: A Contrast," pp. 13-14; Furniss, *The Fundamentalist Controversy, 1918-1931*, pp. 123-25; Kenneth K. Bailey, *Southern White Protestantism in the Twentieth Century* (New York: Harper & Row, 1964), pp. 64-66, 74.

[54]Especially George Washington Truett, pastor, First Baptist Church, Dallas; Joseph Martin Dawson, pastor, First Baptist Church, Waco, and Lee Rutland Scarborough, president, Southwestern Baptist Theological Seminary.

[55]Shurden, *Not a Silent People: Controversies That Have Shaped Southern Baptists*, p. 92; see William M. Shamburger, "A History of Tarrant County Baptist Association, 1886-1922" (Th.D. diss., Southwestern Baptist Theological Seminary, 1953), pp. 232-43, 288, 291-92, 298-99, 300-10. The Pastors' Conference of Tarrant County Baptist Association had excluded Norris in 1914. Shamburger, "A History of Tarrant County Baptist Association, 1886-1922," p. 240.

[56]Shurden, *Not a Silent People: Controversies That Have Shaped Southern Baptists*, p. 90.

[57]*The Southern Baptist Convention and Its People, 1607-1972*, pp. 397-98.

for perjury, and acquitted on a murder charge."[58] In close cooperation with William Bell Riley (1861-1947), pastor, First Baptist Church, Minneapolis, and Thomas Todhunter Shields (1873-1955), pastor, Jarvis Street Baptist Church, Toronto, Norris participated in the World's Christian Fundamentals Association and organized in 1923 the Baptist Bible Union of North America, which did not survive the 1920s.[59] The churches, chiefly in the Southwest and the Midwest, that came to be allied with Norris were organized in 1933 as the Premillennial Baptist Missionary Fellowship, the name of which was changed in 1938 to the World Fundamental Baptist Missionary Fellowship and later shortened to World Baptist Fellowship. In 1950, two years prior to Norris's death, a deep schism within this movement, which involved a personal clash between Norris and G. Beauchamp Vick (1901-1975), resulted in the formation of the Baptist Bible Fellowship International, with headquarters in Springfield, Missouri. The latter body, as of 1980, consisted of nearly three thousand churches.[60]

Southern Baptists emerged from the 1920s having their boards and institutions heavily in debt and facing the constricting effects of the Great Depression. They had yet to begin their great expansion into states

---

[58]Shurden, *Not a Silent People: Controversies That Have Shaped Southern Baptists*, p. 90.

[59]Ibid., pp. 88-89, 93; Baker, *The Southern Baptist Convention and Its People, 1607-1972*, p. 397.

[60]Royce Measures, "Men and Movements Influenced by J. Frank Norris" (Th.D. diss., Southwestern Baptist Theological Seminary, 1976), esp. chs. 3, 5. Measures (p. 11) sharply differentiated "Norrisism," a term which he attributed to Lee R. Scarborough, from "Fundamentalism" in its more classic usage in the North, on the ground that, although they "coexist in the South and the Southwest, particularly in Texas, and, both share a common theology and ecclesiastical separatism, . . . they differ in origin, in spirit, and in the place of biblical scholarship." David Edwin Harrell, Jr., *White Sects and Black Men in the Recent South* (Nashville: Vanderbilt University Press, 1971), pp. 26-28, perhaps mistakenly understood the World Baptist Fellowship and the Baptist Bible Fellowship International as organizationally distinct but nevertheless as one movement. Concerning the internal affairs of the Baptist Bible Fellowship International, see *Resolution; Amended Constitution; Articles of Faith; Missions Policy* (Springfield, Mo.: Baptist Bible Fellowship International, n.d.). Measures (p. 261, fn. 1) derived the number of churches affiliated with the Baptist Bible Fellowship International, i.e., 2,083, from the 1973 *Fellowship Directory*. But *Baptist Bible Fellowship International Directory, 1980* (Springfield, Mo.: Missions Office, 1979? 1980?) lists 2,997 affiliated churches. For an earlier and more critical interpretation, see Ralph Lord Roy, *Apostles of Discord: A Study of Organized Bigotry and Disruption on the Fringes of Protestantism*, pp. 350-58.

outside the South and Southwest. They had yet to come to grips with the paramount issue of race, and in this respect they mirrored their Southern politics, society, and culture. They had not been deeply influenced by the Social Gospel with its tendency to deemphasize personal regeneration, by liberal Protestant theologies that stressed the immanence of God, the human aspects of Jesus Christ, the goodness of man as God's creature, the perfectibility of society, and eschatological universalism, or by the type of historical-critical interpretation of the Bible that undermined the trustworthiness and authority of the Holy Scriptures. Southern Baptists had specifically closed the door to the non-creationist origin of mankind. Neither had Southern Baptists been significantly attracted to the Dispensationalism of Darby and the *Scofield Reference Bible*,[61] and their bridges to the older Princeton Theology of Hodge and his colleagues were no longer carrying much traffic.

Southern Baptists believed, preached, and taught the gospel of Jesus Christ as found in the inspired Scriptures of the Old and New Testaments. God the Father is transcendent as well as immanent; Jesus the Son is fully divine as well as fully human; and the Holy Spirit is divine yet indwells the believer. Human beings are both unique creatures of God and sinners in rebellion against God. Through the atoning death and triumphant resurrection of Jesus the one way of forgiveness and reconciliation has been provided by a gracious God, who accepts repentant believers, but not on the basis of their human achievements. God, who made anew believers, will continue to make them like Himself within the community of believers and will bring them to the heavenly consummation through the coming again of Jesus and resurrection from the dead. The sharing of this gospel with all humanity in all the nations Southern Baptists regarded as the mandate of Jesus Christ, and to this task they were increasingly committed.

Cooperative as Denominationalists, But Not Ecumenical. Southern Baptists entered the twentieth century as virile, convinced denominationalists. Several factors tend to account for such an attitude. Southern Baptists had a vivid historical recollection of the former persecution and

---

[61]Those Southern Baptists who accepted Dispensationalism probably did not analyze or confront, as J. R. Graves seemingly had not confronted, the contrast, or indeed the contradiction, between the optimistic, future-as-well-as-past Baptist church successionism of Landmarkism and the pessimistic Laodicean interpretation of "the church age" in Dispensationalism.

suffering for their beliefs of certain Baptists in England and in the American colonies, especially Massachusetts and Virginia. Southern Baptists were still involved in the theological justification of believer's baptism by immersion vis-à-vis the defenders of infant baptism, and in that debate most all other denominations were on the pedobaptist side.[62] The influence of Landmarkism was still quite pervasive, and the Whitsitt Controversy had just been settled by the resignation of President Whitsitt. These and other influences made it unlikely that Southern Baptists would be very open to the new currents of Protestant interdenominationalism that would soon be at flood tide.

Somewhat surprising, therefore, to present-day Southern Baptists may be the fact that one of their number, Thomas Treadwell Eaton (1845-1907), pastor of the Walnut Street Baptist Church, Louisville, Kentucky, editor of the *Western Recorder*, and subsequently an adversary to W. H. Whitsitt during the Whitsitt Controversy, in 1889 called for a conference of scholars from the various denominations to engage in a fresh study of the Bible in reference to their own differences in belief. Eaton did not anticipate that such a study would result in complete agreement but rather the removal of unnecessary barriers. The Southern Baptist Convention, meeting in Fort Worth, Texas, in 1890 and acting upon a committee report presented by Eaton, called upon other denominational bodies to appoint such scholars to engage in the biblical study of matters disputed in doctrine and polity and proposed the publication of the findings of such a study.[63] Only the General Christian Missionary Convention (Disciples of Christ) made any specific reply to the Southern Baptist overture, and a series of exchanges between the two bodies during 1890-1895 demonstrated that the two had differing approaches to Christian unity. There ended the Eaton proposal.[64]

---

[62] Alexander Campbell and the Disciples of Christ would seem almost certainly to have been destined to become allies with the Baptists in the debate, but differences as to the meaning of baptism between Disciples of Christ and Baptists prevented any significant long-term sense of togetherness in the advocacy of believer's baptism by immersion.

[63] SBC, *Annual*, 1890, p. 22.

[64] Raymond O. Ryland, "Southern Baptist Convention (U.S.A.)," in James Leo Garrett, Jr., ed., *Baptist Relations with Other Christians* (Valley Forge, Pa.: Judson Press, 1974), pp. 67-70. Ryland noted that Eaton's proposal antedated the better-known proposal by Protestant Episcopal Bishop Charles H. Brent in 1910 for a world conference on faith and order. See also Barnes, *The Southern Baptist Convention, 1845-1953*, pp. 271-75, and Glenn A. Igleheart, "Ecumenical Concerns among Southern Baptists," in William Jerry

In 1911 the Southern Baptist Convention received an invitation from the Protestant Episcopal Church to participate in a world conference on faith and order[65] and voted to accept it. During the next five years the convention through reports of two different committees manifested an openness toward spiritual unity and interdenominational cooperation in moral, social, and civic reforms, though not toward organic church union. But after 1916 and especially in 1919 the convention, under the influence of James Bruton Gambrell (1841-1921),[66] executive secretary of the Baptist General Convention of Texas, and the wartime conditions for ministering to men in military service, became more critical of and resistant to any Southern Baptist involvement with other non-Baptist denominational bodies or with movements eliciting Protestant interdenominational joint activity, such as the Interchurch World Movement of North America, and became more emphatic about Baptist denominationalism.[67]

The Foreign Mission Board of the Southern Baptist Convention participated in the Foreign Missions Conference of North America, an organization of Protestant mission board leadership, from 1893 to 1919, when such participation was terminated because of the convention's aversion to interdenominationalism, and again from 1938 to 1950, when the Foreign Mission Board withdrew in view of the conference's becoming a department of the new National Council of the Churches of Christ in the U.S.A. The Southern Baptist Convention did not become a member of the Federal Council of the Churches of Christ in America at or after its formation in 1908. In 1909 the Southern Baptist Convention granted to its Home Mission Board, following the board's inquiry, liberty to confer with the leadership of the mission agencies of other denominations on matters of common concern but warned against any connection with the

---

Boney and Glenn A. Igleheart, eds., *Baptists and Ecumenism* (Valley Forge, Pa.: Judson Press, 1980), p. 50. On the life of Eaton, see Leo T. Crismon, "Eaton, Thomas Treadwell," *Encyclopedia of Southern Baptists*, 1:385.

[65]Such a conference did not actually convene until 1927 in Lausanne, Switzerland.

[66]Gambrell served as president of the Southern Baptist Convention in 1917, 1918, 1919, and 1920.

[67]Ryland, "Southern Baptist Convention (U.S.A.)," pp. 70-78; Barnes, *The Southern Baptist Convention, 1845-1953*, pp. 277-84; Baker, *The Southern Baptist Convention and Its People, 1607-1972*, pp. 305, 410; William R. Estep, Jr., *Baptists and Christian Unity* (Nashville: Broadman Press, 1966), pp. 150, 152-55; and Igleheart, "Ecumenical Concerns among Southern Baptists," pp. 51-53.

newly formed Home Missions Council that would inhibit Southern Baptist home mission work. The board chose never to join or attend the meetings of the Home Missions Council.[68]

In its 1925 statement of the Baptist Faith and Message, the Southern Baptist Convention declared:

> Christian unity in the New Testament sense is spiritual harmony and voluntary cooperation for common ends by various groups of Christ's people. It is permissible and desirable as between the various Christian denominations, when the end to be attained is self justified, and when such co-operation involves no violation of conscience or compromise of loyalty to Christ and his Word as revealed in the New Testament.[69]

The Southern Baptist Convention has not approved any action that would establish its formal membership in councils of churches or other interdenominational or non-Baptist structures. It has taken no action favorable to interdenominational mergers or visible organic union. In 1932 and again in 1937 the convention declined on the basis of the lack of ecclesial authority to accept an invitation to send delegates to the 1937 World Conference on Faith and Order in Edinburgh, but in 1937 it did ask George W. Truett, then president of the Baptist World Alliance, to attend the 1937 Conference on Church, State, and Community in Oxford as "spokesman" of the Southern Baptist Convention.[70] When Truett because of other commitments indicated that he could not go to Oxford, the SBC Executive Committee named the convention's president, John Richard Sampey (1863-1946), as "the official representative and spokesman of the Southern Baptist Convention" at both the Oxford and

---

[68]Barnes, *The Southern Baptist Convention, 1845-1953,* pp. 275-77; Estep, *Baptists and Christian Unity,* pp. 150-51; and Igleheart, "Ecumenical Concerns among Southern Baptists," pp. 51, 53, 54. E. P. Alldredge, *While Southern Baptists Sleep* (Nashville: author, 1949), pp. 75-76, charged that, although previous executive secretaries of the Foreign Mission Board had attended the meetings of the Foreign Missions Conference of North America, only under the executive secretaryship of M. Theron Rankin did the board contribute to the budget of the conference and have representation on the conference's committees.

[69]Art. 22, in Lumpkin, *Baptist Confessions of Faith,* p. 397. These sentences, slightly revised, appeared in the 1963 statement. See Lumpkin, *Baptist Confessions of Faith,* rev. ed., p. 399.

[70]SBC, *Annual,* 1932, pp. 64, 71; 1937, pp. 39-40, 79-80.

Edinburgh conferences and also designated Mrs. Sampey, J. D. Franks, and Mrs. J. D. Franks as "representatives."[71] These four attended both conferences, and at the Edinburgh conference Sampey in a brief address warned about ecclesiastical and sacramental interference in Christ's salvation of human beings.[72] In 1939-1940 the Southern Baptist Convention declined an invitation to membership in the World Council of Churches, then in process of formation. The declination cited the lack of ecclesial authority, warned of the danger of centralization of power in religion, and endorsed "spiritual fellowship." Nineteen messengers presented what was in effect a minority report favoring membership in the World Council of Churches as a "channel" of "basic spiritual unity."[73] The Southern Baptist Convention took no action to seek membership in the National Association of Evangelicals at or after its formation in 1942.[74] In 1948 the convention declined to send an official "observer" to the first assembly of the World Council of Churches.[75] In 1949 the convention tabled a proposed constitutional amendment by Eugene Perry Alldredge (1875-1953), retired department secretary of the Sunday School Board, which would have prohibited any one "who belongs to or is affiliated with any state or local council of churches . . . connected with or sponsored by the Inter-council Field Department of the Federal Council" from serving on "any board, agency, or institution of this Convention—either as an official, employee, or board member."[76] During 1950-1953 the convention took no action favorable to its membership in the newly formed National Council of the Churches of Christ in the U.S.A. but continued to receive reports strongly opposed to such.[77] These actions were taken while Southern Baptists were involved in geographical expansion into Western and Northern states and in considerable expansion of their

---

[71]SBC, *Annual*, 1938, pp. 35-36.

[72]John Richard Sampey, *Memoirs of John R. Sampey* (Nashville: Broadman Press, 1947), pp. 249-52.

[73]SBC, *Annual*, 1939, p. 99; 1940, pp. 99-100.

[74]Concerning the involvement of individual Southern Baptists in the formation of the National Association of Evangelicals, see above, ch. 1. fn. 63.

[75]SBC, *Annual*, 1948, p. 58.

[76]SBC, *Annual*, 1949, p. 43. See Alldredge's *Unionizing Southern Baptists: A Survey of the Past and Present Efforts to Bring Southern Baptists into "Cooperative Christianity" and the "United Church of America"* (Nashville: Marshall Bruce Co., 1948) and *While Southern Baptists Sleep.*

[77]SBC, *Annual*, 1950, p. 37; 1951, p. 36; 1953, p. 51.

foreign mission work. These actions were explained or defended under four categories of answers: theological differences (that is, the alleged liberalism within the conciliar movement); the lack of ecclesial authority by the Southern Baptist Convention; methodological differences (that is, the diminishing commitment to evangelism and missions within the conciliar movement); and teleological differences (spiritual unity versus organic union).[78]

The decisions of the Southern Baptist Convention not to become a member of national or international councils of churches did not mean that the convention would not affiliate as a convention[79] with other Baptist bodies or that Southern Baptists would engage in no cooperative activity with non-Baptist Christians. Indeed the Southern Baptist Convention from the formation of the Baptist World Alliance in 1905 had been strongly supportive of the new international fellowship.[80] During later decades the convention contributed the major portion of the budget of the Baptist World Alliance, and since 1965, after initial hesitation, the convention has participated in the North American Baptist Fellowship, a regional body of the Baptist World Alliance.[81] In 1941 the convention joined with the Northern Baptist Convention and the National Baptist Convention, U.S.A., Inc., to form the Joint Conference Committee on Public Relations, the name of which was changed in 1950 to the Baptist Joint Committee on Public Affairs and which today is supported by nine Baptist bodies in the United States and Canada.[82]

---

[78]These four answers or "issues" were listed and discussed by Estep, *Baptists and Christian Unity*, ch. 9; Estep, however, interpreted the "theological" issue in terms of the authority of Scripture, a regenerate church membership, and non-sacramentalism.

[79]Membership in the Baptist World Alliance is by conventions, unions, or conferences, not by local churches or messengers therefrom.

[80]The convention encouraged attendance at the first congress in London in 1905, SBC, *Annual*, 1905, pp. 20-21; in 1910 welcomed John Howard Shakespeare, general secretary of the Baptist Union of Great Britain and Ireland, contributed more than $4,000 toward the travel expenses of one hundred delegates from continental Europe who would attend the second congress in Philadelphia in 1911, pledged support of the congress in Philadelphia, and agreed to share in the establishment of a Baptist seminary in continental Europe, the location of which was intended to be in St. Petersburg, Russia, SBC, *Annual*, 1910, pp. 27, 47, 49-50; 1911, p. 50; 1912, pp. 81-82.

[81]SBC, *Annual*, 1965, pp. 85, 86.

[82]Stanley Leroy Hastey, "A History of the Baptist Joint Committee on Public Affairs, 1946-1971," (Th.D. diss., Southern Baptist Theological Seminary, 1973), esp. pp. 17-26, 61, 1.

Southern Baptist churches have often engaged in citywide or communitywide evangelistic campaigns in cooperation with other Protestant churches, and Southern Baptist churches and leaders have frequently joined with their fellow citizens from other denominations in common efforts to secure, amend, or repeal state legislation or community ordinances relating to beverage alcohol, gambling, or the criminal codes. Such instances of ad hoc cooperation, although quite numerous, have yet to be documented fully. Since 1935 the Southern Baptist Convention has received annual reports from the American Bible Society and has regularly encouraged Southern Baptist churches to contribute to the work of the society.[83] But not until the latter 1960s did Southern Baptists give clear evidence of any intention to engage in forms of cooperation that were on the national or denominational level and that would extend beyond Protestant Christians. As president of the Southern Baptist Convention, William Wayne Dehoney (1918-   ) in 1965 advocated, without "abolishing denominationalism," the seeking of "broader channels of communication and cooperation that will not compromise our conscience, our doctrine or our autonomy" and reminded Southern Baptists that their enemies were "the devil and the forces of materialism, secularism and atheism" rather than their fellow Christians or fellow Baptists.[84] During the 1960s and 1970s individual Southern Baptists served as members of commissions of the World Council of Churches and of the National Council of the Churches of Christ in the U.S.A., and certain agencies of the Southern Baptist Convention had working relations with agencies of these councils.[85] In 1965 the Home Mission Board of the Southern Baptist Convention established its Department of Work Related to Nonevangelicals, the name of which was changed in 1970 to Department of Interfaith Witness. Designed to be evangelistic and apologetic, the department has also sponsored local, regional, and national dialogues with representatives of other denominations.[86] In 1967 Southern Baptist Theological Seminary hosted the first Conference on the

---

[83]Barnes, *The Southern Baptist Convention, 1845-1953*, pp. 287-88; Baker, *The Southern Baptist Convention and Its People, 1607-1972*, pp. 445-46. In 1970 gifts from Southern Baptist churches to the society were sufficient to enable them to rank first among all denominations, SBC, *Annual*, 1971, p. 257.

[84]SBC, *Annual*, 1965, p. 95.

[85]Igleheart, "Ecumenical Concerns among Southern Baptists," pp. 58-59.

[86]Ibid., pp. 56, 59-60, 57.

Concept of the Believers' Church, at which Mennonites, Brethren, Quakers, Disciples of Christ, members of the Churches of Christ and others joined with Baptists in exploring the nature and functions of the church of committed believers, which concepts presumably had been basic to the heritage of each group.[87] In 1968 Wake Forest University founded and later in conjunction with Belmont Abbey College maintained an Ecumenical Institute which conducted Southern Baptist-Roman Catholic dialogues.[88] In 1968 a Southern Baptist was named chairman of the newly constituted Commission on Cooperative Christianity of the Baptist World Alliance.[89] After much local Southern Baptist participation in and support of Billy Graham's evangelistic crusades in various cities in the United States, Southern Baptists in limited fashion cooperated in 1973 with other evangelical groups in a concerted evangelistic effort known as Key '73. A Southern Baptist foreign mission executive delivered one of the major addresses at the International Congress on World Evangelization in Lausanne, Switzerland, in 1974.[90]

Southern Baptists, therefore, having repeatedly refused as a denominational body to seek membership in councils of churches on national and world levels and having disassociated themselves from proposals for organic church union, are not ecumenists in a conciliar or structural sense. Nevertheless, they have engaged increasingly in ad hoc cooperation[91] with other Protestants and in dialogues with Roman Catholics, Eastern Orthodox, and Jews.

Advocates of the Primacy of a Historical Method Instead of a Symbolic Method in Interpreting the Bible. During the decade between 1961

---

[87]James Leo Garrett, Jr., ed., *The Concept of the Believers' Church: Addresses from the 1967 Louisville Conference* (Scottdale, Pa.: Herald Press, 1969), and Donald F. Durnbaugh, "Free Churches, Baptists, and Ecumenism," in Boney and Igleheart, eds., *Baptists and Ecumenism*, pp. 7-8.

[88]Igleheart, "Ecumenical Concerns among Southern Baptists," pp. 56, 59, 60. The Department of Interfaith Witness assumed the sponsorship of these dialogues in 1970.

[89]Garrett, ed., *Baptist Relations with Other Christians*, esp. pp. 11-12; "B.W.A. Executive Committee Meets in Monrovia," *Baptist World* 15 (September 1968): 3; and Gerald L. Borchert, "Ecumenical Concerns among Smaller Baptist Denominations," in Boney and Igleheart, eds., *Baptists and Ecumenism*, p. 62.

[90]SBC, *Annual*, 1973, pp. 72, 87-88; R. Keith Parks, "The Great Commission," in *Let the Earth Hear His Voice: International Congress on World Evangelization; Official Reference Volume; Papers and Responses*, ed. J. D. Douglas (Minneapolis: World Wide Publications, 1975), pp. 483-91.

[91]Garrett, "Epilogue," in Garrett, ed., *Baptist Relations with Other Christians*, p. 196.

and 1971 Southern Baptists were engaged in two controversies centering upon biblical interpretation, especially the interpretation of Genesis. One of these focused upon *The Message of Genesis*, written by Ralph Harrison Elliott (1925-   ), professor of Old Testament, Midwestern Baptist Theological Seminary, and published by Broadman Press in July 1961. The other centered upon the Genesis portion, written by Gwynne Henton Davies (1906-   ), principal, Regent's Park College, Oxford, England, of volume one of the *Broadman Bible Commentary*.[92]

Elliott, announcing that it was his purpose "to ferret out and to underscore the foundational theological and religious principles of the stories of Genesis," utilized in the interpretation of Genesis 1-11 a "parabolic and symbolic" method of interpretation. Hence the six "days" of creation were not twenty-four-hour days, the creation of adam was not that of "an individual man" but of "man in a collective sense," the flood was a local Mesopotamian flood, not a universal flood, and the tower of Babel was a "parable" designed to show "the futility and emptiness of human effort divorced from the acknowledgment and service of God" and was therefore a theological explanation of the dispersion of the human race (Gen. 10).[93] Elliott interpreted the test of Abraham's offering to sacrifice Isaac (Gen. 22:1-19) as "not a literal command [from God] to sacrifice a life" or "a voice from Satan" but as Abraham's attributing to a command from God his own introspective yearning to be as dedicated to Yahweh as were his "pagan neighbors" who engaged in child sacrifice.[94]

Elliott's book evoked much sharp criticism and some firm support in the Southern Baptist state papers during 1961-1962. The SBC Sunday School Board in its January 1962 meeting defended the publication policy of Broadman Press under which Elliott's book had been published. In March 1962 a group of critics of the book met in Oklahoma City to discuss the controversy which the book had evoked and probably to formulate plans for influencing the selection of new trustees of Midwestern Baptist

---

[92]Shurden, *Not a Silent People: Controversies That Have Shaped Southern Baptists,* pp. 103-19. Shurden, although recognizing their distinctness (pp. 103-104), subsumed both controversies under the caption, "The 'What about Genesis?' Controversy." According to Tom J. Nettles, four Southern Baptist controversies have dealt with the book of Genesis: the resignaton of Crawford H. Toy from the faculty of Southern Baptist Theological Seminary in 1879, the Evolution Controversy of the 1920s, and the two discussed here.

[93]Elliott, *The Message of Genesis* (Nashville: Broadman Press, 1961), pp. vii, 15, 35, 39-40, 66-67, 72-73.

[94]Ibid., pp. 144-46.

Theological Seminary.[95] The Southern Baptist Convention in its 1962 session approved a recommendation from its Executive Committee that a committee of the various state Baptist convention presidents be constituted to draw up and present to the convention one year later another statement "of Baptist Faith and Message," which would "serve as information to the churches" and "as guidelines to the various agencies of the Southern Baptist Convention." In the same year the convention adopted two motions made by Kenneth Owen White (1902-), pastor, First Baptist Church, Houston, Texas, and rejected a motion by Ben D. Windham of Oregon. White's two motions were as follows:

> That the messengers to this Convention, by standing vote, reaffirm their faith in the *entire* Bible as the authoritative, authentic, infallible Word of God.
>
> That we express our abiding and unchanging objection to the dissemination of theological views in any of our seminaries which would undermine such faith in the historical accuracy and doctrinal integrity of the Bible, and that we courteously request the trustees and administrative officers of our institutions and other agencies to take such steps as shall be necessary to remedy at once those situations where such views now threaten our historic position.

Windham's defeated motion read as follows:

> That this Convention instruct the Sunday School Board to cease publishing and to recall from all distribution channels, the book, *The Message of Genesis*, by Dr. Ralph Elliott.[96]

The Sunday School Board, following the 1962 SBC session in San Francisco, voted not to publish another printing or edition of Elliott's

---

[95]Shurden, *Not a Silent People: Controversies That Have Shaped Southern Baptists*, pp. 105-108. Shurden cited Salvador T. Martinez, "Southern Baptist Views of the Scriptures in Light of the Elliott Controversy" (Th.M. thesis, Southern Baptist Theological Seminary, 1966), pp. 179, 180, for evidence that the majority of the editors of Southern Baptist state papers were anti-Elliott. Also see Davis C. Woolley, "Major Convention Crises over a Century and a Quarter," *Review and Expositor* 67 (Spring 1970): 178-79.

[96]SBC, *Annual*, 1972, pp. 64, 65, 68, 71, 73. Windham's motion was preceded by a virtually identical motion by Ralph F. Powell of Missouri, which was withdrawn by Powell prior to being voted upon by the convention, ibid., pp. 65, 69. The SBC president, Herschel Hobbs (1907-), pastor, First Baptist Church, Oklahoma City, would serve as chairman of the Committee on Baptist Faith and Message, SBC, *Annual*, 1963, pp. 63, 281.

book. Thus, although the convention had refused to ban the book, the Sunday School Board by "administrative decision" declined to reissue it. The trustees of Midwestern Baptist Theological Seminary succeeded in working out with Elliott and the seminary administration an agreement on principles of teaching the Bible, including the use of the historical-critical method, but failed to secure from Elliott a commitment not to seek republication of the book by another publisher and on 25 October 1962 dismissed Elliott from the faculty—not on the issue of heresy but on the basis of insubordination.[97] In its 1963 session in Kansas City, the Southern Baptist Convention adopted, after rejecting proposed amendments, the report of its Committee on Baptist Faith and Message, which was a revision of the 1925 statement but contained no direct references to the hermeneutical issue inherent in the Elliott Controversy. The convention elected a strong anti-Elliott messenger, K. Owen White, as its president and received a detailed report from the trustees of Midwestern Baptist Theological Seminary.[98]

The central issue in the Elliott Controversy, namely, the convention's assignment of priority to a historical method, even in the interpretation of Genesis 1-11, and Elliott's espousal of a symbolic method in interpret-

---

[97]Woolley, "Major Convention Crises over a Century and a Quarter," p. 179; Shurden, *Not a Silent People: Controversies That Have Shaped Southern Baptists,* pp. 109-10; Baker, *The Southern Baptist Convention and Its People, 1607-1972,* p. 416; Leonard E. Hill, "Southern Baptist Convention, The," *Encyclopedia of Southern Baptists,* 3: 1967-68; According to Woolley, "Elliott left Midwestern a victim of the controversy yet 'without the brand of a heretic.' "

[98]SBC, *Annual,* 1963, pp. 63, 269-81, 64, 67-69. On the background of the 1963 statement, see Herschel H. Hobbs, *The Baptist Faith and Message* (Nashville: Convention Press, 1971), pp. 7-17. Shurden, *Not a Silent People: Controversies That Have Shaped Southern Baptists,* pp. 110-11, identified four "results" of the Elliott Controversy: (1) the dismissal of a seminary professor; (2) the adoption by the SBC of another confession of faith; (3) "an intensification and popularization of the suspicion of theological education and publications"; and (4) "a serious injury" to the SBC's newest seminary. Woolley, "Major Convention Crises over a Century and a Quarter," p. 180, found various similarities between the Elliott Controversy and the Whitsitt Controversy:

> The scholarly writings of a seminary professor had been found unacceptable to a large segment of Southern Baptists. The findings of the professor were not denied or retracted by the school, but the scholar was released from the seminary. The use of the historical-critical approach in the study of the Old Testament [church history, in the Whitsitt Controversy] was approved. The diversity of the Convention's make-up was recognized and the basic beliefs of Baptists were restated. The Seminary president was recognized as the administrative officer who needed help in dealing with academic problems.

ing Genesis 1-11, was never properly clarified.[99]

The second controversy over the interpretation of the book of Genesis occurred after the publication of volume one of the *Broadman Bible Commentary* by the SBC Sunday School Board in October 1969. This twelve-volume set of biblical commentaries, a major publication effort, had been "conceived" in 1957 and "approved" by the members of the Sunday School Board in 1961.[100] The first volume consisted of nine general articles on the Bible, an exposition of Genesis by Davies, a British Baptist Old Testament scholar, and an exposition of Exodus by Roy Lee Honeycutt, Jr., professor of Old Testament, Midwestern Baptist Theological Seminary.[101] Criticisms of the Genesis portion of the volume and especially of Davies's interpretation of the Abraham-Isaac narrative (Genesis 22:1-19) began to appear in the editorials of state Baptist papers, especially in Missouri[102] and Oklahoma,[103] but support for the new commentary could also be found among the editors, especially in Kentucky.[104] Davies had refused to interpret the passage as a "parable," insisting that it was "rather the story of something that actually happened." The problem for interpretation lay, according to Davies, in the motivation for offering to sacrifice Isaac.

---

[99]Neither Southern Baptists nor any other body of Baptists has espoused or practiced the exclusive usage of literal interpretation. One could scarcely find a Baptist who would interpret literally Jesus' sayings relative to the Lord's Supper, "This is my body" and "This is my blood of the covenant" (Mark 14:22, 24, RSV) or Jesus' sayings, "I am the bread of life" (John 6:48), "I am the light of the world" (John 8:12), "I am the door of the sheep" (John 10:7), and "I am the true vine" (John 15:1). But in the Elliott Controversy the Southern Baptist Convention refused to allow or sanction the rejection of a historical method in interpreting Genesis 1-11 that was not without literalist features.

[100]James L. Sullivan, "Why the Broadman Commentary Was Published," *Western Recorder* 144 (11 April 1970): 11; Shurden, *Not a Silent People: Controversies That Have Shaped Southern Baptists*, p. 111.

[101]*The Broadman Bible Commentary; Volume 1: General Articles; Genesis-Exodus* (Nashville: Broadman Press, 1969), table of contents.

[102]W. Ross Edwards, "Witnessing to the Truth," *The Word and Way* 107 (8 January 1970): 2.

[103]Jack L. Gritz, "Warning to Our People," *The Baptist Messenger* 59 (15 January 1970): 2.

[104]Chauncey R. Daley, Jr., "In Defense of the Broadman Bible Commentary," *Western Recorder* 144 (11 April 1970): 4. Daley identified the issue between Davies and his critics as that of "literalism versus nonliteralism" and asserted that the "*Broadman Bible Commentary* is not intended to be *the* Southern Baptist interpretation of every Biblical passage."

Did Abraham's conviction or the writer's account of that conviction correspond to a real divine request? Did God make, would God in fact have made, such a demand upon Abraham or anybody else, except himself? There are those who would accept the command literally.

Our answer however is no. Indeed what Christian or humane conscience could regard such a command as coming from God? How then did this conviction arise in the mind of Abraham, since we believe that God did not put it there? The question can only be answered in part. Abraham's conviction that his son must be sacrificed is the climax of the psychology of his life. . . .

The theme of Abraham's life after Isaac's birth must have been, "What if I should lose him?" Such a question is the raw material of the resultant conviction: "I am called upon to give him: God wants me to do it."[105]

The issue in Davies's interpretation, however poorly it may have been identified or described by some of his critics, was not historical versus symbolic interpretation but rather the authenticity (or) unauthenticity of the divine command.

In its 1970 session, preceded by an Affirming the Bible Conference, the Southern Baptist Convention approved a motion by Gwin Terrell Turner (1931-), pastor, First Baptist Church, Mar Vista, California, to "request the Sunday School Board to withdraw Volume 1 from further distribution" and to request "that it be rewritten with due consideration of the conservative viewpoint."[106] In August 1970 the Sunday School Board voted to withdraw volume one "from distribution and sale" and named "a special committee to make suggestions for re-writing the commentary from a conservative viewpoint." That committee recommended to the board in January 1971 "that the authors of the Genesis and Exodus sections . . . be asked to rewrite their material." An amendment to the committee's report asking the authors to undertake the task "with due consideration of the conservative viewpoint" was approved, as was the

---

[105]*The Broadman Bible Commentary; Volume 1: General Articles; Genesis-Exodus*, pp. 196-99.

[106]SBC, *Annual*, 1970, pp. 63, 76, 77-78.

entire recommendation.[107] Such a plan for retention of authors was not destined to be executed, however, for the convention in 1971 by a narrow margin passed a motion by Kenneth Barnett of Lawton, Oklahoma, which advised the Sunday School Board "that the vote of the 1970 Convention regarding the rewriting of Volume 1 of *The Broadman Bible Commentary* has not been followed and that the Sunday School Board obtain another writer and proceed with the Commentary according to the vote of the 1970 Convention in Denver."[108] Interpreting "another writer" to refer only to the Genesis portion, the members of the Sunday School Board in July 1971 by a vote of thirty-four to twenty-one instructed the board's administration to obtain another author for the commentary on Genesis.[109] Clyde T. Francisco (1916-1981), John R. Sampey professor of Old Testament, Southern Baptist Theological Seminary, was obtained, and his commentary on Genesis appeared in the revised volume one, which was published in 1973.[110] The second Hermeneutical Controversy had come to an end.

The preceding study of the results of the principal theological controversies in which Southern Baptists have been engaged as they affect the present nature and self-understanding of Southern Baptists has recognizable limits. No attempt has been made to deal with essentially ethical or moral issues. No effort has been made to assess the total cultural environment in which Southern Baptists have lived. No specific investigation has been attempted concerning the increasing geographical and ethnic diversity of Southern Baptists. What has been sought is an interpretation of the major Southern Baptist theological controversies and their consequences which will contribute to the answer to the question, "Are Southern Baptists 'Evangelicals'?"

---

[107]Shurden, *Not a Silent People: Controversies That Have Shaped Southern Baptists,* pp. 115-16.

[108]SBC, *Annual,* 1971, pp. 71, 76, 80. On Barnett's motion there were 2,672 for and 2,290 against.

[109]Shurden, *Not a Silent People: Controversies That Have Shaped Southern Baptists,* pp. 116-17.

[110]*The Broadman Bible Commentary; Volume 1: Revised: General Articles; Genesis-Exodus* (Nashville: Broadman Press, 1973). Francisco, in reference to Gen. 22, stated: "Although Abraham might well have asked himself such a soul-searching question [i.e., "whether he loved his God as much as his heathen neighbors loved theirs when they offered up their children"], a man so signally led and blessed by God would have had to hear from God himself the actual imperative to make the sacrifice" (p. 188).

From an examination of the Calvinist-Arminian and the Missionary-Antimissionary controversies it has been possible to confirm the basic evangelistic and missionary belief and practice of Southern Baptists within the context of the eternal purpose of the God of grace and forgiveness who freely has provided the needed way of redemption in His Son and who through His Spirit utilizes the witness of believers, which is indeed a divine mandate, for the announcing and demonstrating of this good news and the drawing of many human beings in many cultures and nations to Christian faith and discipleship. Such evangelistic and missionary commitment of Southern Baptists is parallel to the evangelistic and missionary commitment of contemporary Evangelical Protestants.[111]

From an interpretation of the Modernist-Liberal-Conservative-Fundamentalist and the Hermeneutical controversies it has been possible to identify the basically conservative theological stance of the majority of Southern Baptists, who regard the Christian gospel as essentially other than and often quite contrary to the contemporary culture and as derived from the Bible, the inspired record of God's self-disclosure, which centers in Jesus Christ and his holy history—from preexistence and virginal conception to ascension and *parousia*—and which is rightly to be interpreted in the light of its language, grammar, syntax, literary forms, and historical context without the intrusion of alien or modern ideology. The appropriate and necessary response of human beings to the Christ of the Bible and of the gospel is repenting and believing. Such an understanding of the gospel, of the Bible, and of Jesus Christ the divine-human Savior and Lord is, at least in its basics, shared by Southern Baptists and contemporary Evangelical Protestants.[112]

From an investigation of the Landmark and the Ecumenical controversies it has been possible to detect the basic denominationalism of Southern Baptists which has refused to embrace either the "we only" exclusivism of Landmarkism or the goal of organic church union of Conciliar Ecumenism and has reckoned that Baptists continue to have a *raison d'être* within the larger context of Christianity. This dimension of Southern Baptist life is parallel to some, but by no means to all, contemporary Evangelical Protestants.

---

[111]This is the third of the three tests as to who is an Evangelical given by Quebedeaux. See above, ch. 1, quotation preceding fn. 109.

[112]These are the first and second tests as to who is an Evangelical given by Quebedeaux. See above, ch. 1, quotation preceding fn. 109.

Are Southern Baptists Evangelicals?
The Contemporary Question

The accumulation of significant evidence that Southern Baptists, both in the past and in the present, share much in common with those who today may be described as Evangelical Protestants does not, of course, mean that present-day Southern Baptists are eagerly and unanimously ready to be identified more formally as "Evangelicals."

The Negative Answer. Two Southern Baptist leaders have specifically disavowed the idea that Southern Baptists are Evangelicals. On the eve of the 1976 U.S. presidential election, Foy Dan Valentine (1923-), executive secretary of the Christian Life Commission of the Southern Baptist Convention, issued a public denial that Southern Baptists were in any sense to be reckoned as Evangelicals. In an interview reported in *Newsweek*, Valentine declared concerning Southern Baptists:

> We are *not* evangelicals. That's a Yankee word. They want to claim us because we are big and successful and growing every year. But we have our own traditions, our own hymns and more students in our seminaries than they have in all of theirs put together. We don't share their politics or their fussy fundamentalism, and we don't want to get involved in their theological witch-hunts.[113]

Valentine's statement, admittedly issued amid the tension of a political campaign, however, calls for careful analysis. First, it fails to differentiate Evangelicals and Fundamentalists in any sense and thus implies that the two terms are synonymous. Second, it does not explain why and in what sense "Evangelical" is a "Yankee word." Third, it seems to rest the truth or validity of Southern Baptist teachings on the statistics of Southern Baptist numerical growth. Fourth, it seems to attribute an unwarranted uniqueness to the hymnody used by Southern Baptist churches. Fifth, it fails to take sufficient note of the significant increases in enrollment during the 1970s in such institutions as Fuller Theological Seminary, Trinity Evangelical Divinity School, Gordon-Conwell Theological Seminary, and Asbury Theological Seminary—increases that parallel increases in enrollment in the six seminaries of the Southern Baptist

---

[113]Kenneth L. Woodward, John Barnes, and Laurie Lisle, "Born Again! The Year of the Evangelicals," *Newsweek* 88 (25 October 1976): 76.

Convention. Sixth, it fails to recall and reckon with the involuntary resignations of Crawford Howell Toy (1836-1919) and William Heth Whitsitt (1841-1911) from the faculty of Southern Baptist Theological Seminary in 1879 and 1898, the dismissal of thirteen professors after controversy with the president of the same institution in 1959, the dismissal of Theodore Roscoe Clark (1912-   ) from the faculty of New Orleans Baptist Theological Seminary in 1960, and the dismissal of Ralph Harrison Elliott from the faculty of Midwestern Baptist Theological Seminary in 1962. Seventh, it implies that virtually all Evangelicals have the same political views and loyalties and that virtually all Southern Baptists have the same political views and loyalties. It would seem, therefore, that Valentine, at least in his published statement, did not offer sufficient evidence to warrant his comprehensive and negative conclusion that Southern Baptists are not Evangelicals. He did make it clear that he himself did not wish to bear the identification "Evangelical," even though he had participated in and spoken to the 1973 Thanksgiving Workshop on Evangelicals and Social Concern in Chicago which drafted "A Declaration of Evangelical Social Concern."[114]

At the end of the 1980 U.S. presidential campaign, Edward Glenn Hinson (1931-   ), David T. Porter professor of church history, Southern Baptist Theological Seminary, contended firmly in an address to the South Carolina Baptist Historical Society that Baptists are not Evangelicals.[115] Deploring the frequent confusion of Baptists with Evangelicals, Hinson asserted that the proper differentiation of Southern Baptists from Evangelicals was essential "for Southern Baptists if they wish to retain anything of their Baptist heritage." He allowed for commonalities between the two movements but differentiated the two as to origins:

> Both of us go back to the Protestant Reformers. Both of us
> commit ourselves to the scriptures. Both of us have inherited a
> zeal for evangelical conversion. But make no mistake about it,
> we come from different wombs. Evangelicals are the descend-

---

[114]Sider, ed., *The Chicago Declaration*, pp. 23, 57-77. Valentine's presentation was entitled "Engagement—The Christian's Agenda." Also participating was James M. Dunn (1932-   ), executive secretary, Christian Life Commission, Baptist General Convention of Texas (p. 24, fn. 13). See above, ch. 2, quotation preceding fn. 33.

[115]E. Glenn Hinson, "Baptists and Evangelicals: What Is the Difference?" unpublished typescript of address delivered to the South Carolina Baptist Historical Society in Columbia on 10 November 1980.

ants of the late sixteenth and early seventeenth century Protestant scholastics. They are the children of English and American millenialists [sic] and fundamentalists of the late nineteenth and early twentieth centuries. As such, they let nothing stand above what they consider the objective Word of God found in the scriptures.

Baptists, by contrast, are the descendants of the persecuted and harassed dissenters of the seventeenth century who came forth from the womb crying for liberty. They are the children of the refugees who fled from the European continent to these shores to found here a society in which there would be no restriction of conscience and no religious test for public office. As such, they have insisted that faith must be free and voluntary if it is to be genuine faith, that there is no objective word apart from uncoerced human response.[116]

Hinson recognizes but does not major on the distinctions between "neo-evangelicalism" and the older Evangelicalism or Fundamentalism. Instead he takes Bernard Ramm's *The Evangelical Heritage* as a representative and acceptable norm for identifying what is Evangelicalism and analyzes Ramm's approach to the definition and description of Evangelicalism. Hinson then, taking Ramm's characterization of Evangelicals, places over against these characteristics that which he reckons as the characteristics of Baptists so as to identify negatively what it means to be Baptists.[117] According to Ramm, "evangelical Christianity refers to that version of Christianity which places the priority of the Word and Act of God over the faith, response, or experiences of men."[118] According to Hinson, the term "Baptist" "refers to *that version of Christianity which places the priority on voluntary and uncoerced faith or response to the Word and Act of God* over any supposed objective Word and Act of God." Hinson concludes that "Baptists assign priority to the response of believers to the Word of God over against scriptures and creeds presented as an objective Word of God."[119]

116Ibid., pp. 2-3.

117Ibid., pp. 7-14.

118Ramm, *The Evangelical Heritage*, p. 13.

119Hinson, "Baptists and Evangelicals," p. 14.

Believer's baptism, according to Hinson, embodies the Baptist concern for "voluntarism," "*and it was voluntarism which most set Baptists apart from those groups from which they sprang.*" Moreover, the differences between the article, "Of Christian Liberty, and Liberty of Conscience," as found in the Westminster Confession of Faith and as found in the Second London Confession of Particular Baptists and the new article in the latter, "Of the Gospel, and of the extent of the Grace thereof," are evidence, for Hinson, that Baptists and Evangelicals are fundamentally different.[120]

Hinson adds to his arguments from the seventeenth century two drawn from the later history of Baptists and Evangelicals. First, whereas Evangelicals "*regarded the Enlightenment as an enemy, Baptists came to know it as in many respects a friend.*" That friendship was due chiefly to the Enlightenment's "emphasis upon experience in religion" and its support for "the struggle for religious liberty." Second, whereas Evangelicals "*counted Schleiermacher*, whom they regard as the father of Protestant liberalism, *the bane of orthodoxy, Baptists*" in the person of Edgar Young Mullins "*could respond warmly to his emphasis upon 'feeling' and his accentuation of soul competency.*"[121]

Although Hinson's argument has nuances and implications that cannot be fully probed within a brief analysis, several questions ought to be raised concerning his presentation. First, is it possible that Hinson has underemphasized the common roots which both Evangelicals and Baptists have in Puritanism? Second, has Hinson set in an antithesis unwarranted by Baptist history itself the Baptist understanding of the authority of the Bible and the role of confessions of faith and the Baptist commitment to religious freedom? Third, is it possible that by failing to differentiate between "voluntaristic" (a philosophical term for human volition) and "voluntaryistic" (a term used to describe the "free" churches in contrast to the "established" churches) Hinson has inadvertently contributed to the confusion of the issue which he discusses? Fourth, how does Hinson explain the fact that Bernard Ramm has been a lifelong Baptist if indeed Evangelicals and Baptists are so antithetical? Fifth, can one afford to forget that Tom Paine's *The Age of Reason* was an aspect of the Enlightenment strongly resisted by Baptists of Paine's day? Sixth, was

---

[120]Ibid., pp. 15-20.

[121]Ibid., pp. 20-23.

E.Y. Mullins's emphasis on religious experience characteristic of most Baptists prior to, during, or since the day of Mullins?

The Constricted Answer. A second option relative to present-day Southern Baptists has been set forth by Harold Lindsell (1913-   ), former professor in Columbia Bible College, Northern Baptist Theological Seminary, and Fuller Theological Seminary, former editor of *Christianity Today*, and a member of Southern Baptist churches from 1942 to 1944 and since 1964, in his books, *The Battle for the Bible* (1976) and *The Bible in the Balance* (1979).[122] Lindsell would grant that Southern Baptists in the past have been Evangelicals and that the majority of present-day Southern Baptists are Evangelicals.[123] But he sees a contemporary danger for Southern Baptists, which he variously describes as a spread of "infection," an opening of "the floodgates to disbelief," the leavening of "the whole lump," and denominational shipwreck.[124] The danger, according to Lindsell, derives from the fact "that the Southern Baptist Convention has numbers of people in it who deny biblical infallibility."[125] Lindsell has pressed his argument to the ultimate conclusion: "No one who is truly a Southern Baptist has a right to insist that others *must* believe that the Bible is the inerrant Word of God, but it is consistent to argue that those who do not have really ceased to be Southern Baptists."[126] A critical assessment of Lindsell's perspective is in order.

First, whereas Lindsell presses the doctrine of biblical inerrancy on two levels, that is, both the level of doctrine and ethics and the level of history, geography, and science,[127] the 1925 and 1963 SBC statements of the Baptist Faith and Message, based in this respect on the New Hampshire Confession of Faith, put the emphasis on the inerrancy of saving truth and on the Bible as "the supreme standard by which all human

---

[122]See above, ch. 2, text embraced by fns. 7-17.

[123]According to Lindsell, *The Battle for the Bible*, pp. 89, 104, who equates holding to the Turretin-Hodge-Warfield doctrine of biblical inerrancy with being Evangelicals: "Through the years, the Southern Baptist Convention . . . has been numbered among the large denominations that have remained faithful to the Scriptures. . . . At this moment in history the great bulk of the Southern Baptists are theologically orthodox and do believe that the Word of God is inerrant."

[124]Ibid., pp. 104, 142.

[125]Ibid., p. 91. What Lindsell finds to be alarming among Southern Baptists he also finds to be alarming in all Evangelical Christianity, ibid., p. 70.

[126]Ibid., p. 91.

[127]Ibid., pp. 18-19, and Harold J. Ockenga's "Foreword," p. 9.

conduct, creeds and religious opinions should be tried."[128] Second, the inerrancy issue as delineated by Lindsell is clearly to be distinguished from the basic Christian doctrines of Trinity, Christology, justification, man and sin, etc., which were the central content of the ancient Christian creeds and the Reformation confessions of faith and from those doctrines of the church, baptism, the Lord's Supper, and religious liberty which were often the distinctive emphases in Baptist confessions of faith. Hence Lindsell's charges of doctrinal heresy against any Southern Baptist who holds to the supreme authority or the doctrinal and moral inerrancy of the Bible are unsupportable on the basis of the undisputed orthodoxy of Lindsell's own doctrine of the historical, geographical, and scientific inerrancy of the Bible. Third, whereas the majority of the questions or problems which seem to challenge the historical, geographical, and scientific inerrancy of the Bible have derived from the Enlightenment, modern science, and modern critical study of the Bible, Lindsell has insisted upon trying to trace the doctrine of biblical inerrancy on such matters back through the centuries to the New Testament era.[129] Accordingly, the remedy would have been applied for many centuries to a malady which had yet to appear. Fourth, the doctrine of biblical inerrancy which Lindsell demands necessitates, if the research by Jack Bartlett Rogers can be validated, the exclusion from the ranks of Evangelicals of such Evangelical theologians as James Orr (1844-1913), Abraham Kuyper (1837-1920), Herman Bavinck (1854-1921), and Gerrit Cornelis Berkouwer (1903-   )[130] and, one may be inclined to add, the Southern Baptist theologian, E. Y. Mullins. Fifth, Lindsell in defending the two-level doctrine of biblical inerrancy has declared war on the historical-critical method of biblical interpretation and has demanded its total rejection[131] but has not made clear what method of interpretation should be put in its place. The historical-critical method, Lindsell affirmed, "has in it all the seeds that lead to apostasy"[132] and "is indeed the great enemy of evangelical faith."[133] Although he has discussed Gerhard Maier's *The End of the*

---

[128]Art. 1, in Lumpkin, *Baptist Confessions of Faith*, p. 393, and Lumpkin, *Baptist Confessions of Faith*, rev. ed., p. 393.

[129]See above, ch. 2, fn. 8.

[130]See above, ch. 2, fn. 7; also Lindsell, *The Bible in the Balance*, p. 312.

[131]*The Battle for the Bible*, pp. 204-205; *The Bible in the Balance*, pp. 275-302.

[132]*The Battle for the Bible*, p. 204.

[133]*The Bible in the Balance*, p. 301.

Historical-Critical Method,[134] Lindsell has not made it clear whether he wishes to endorse Maier's "historical-biblical method."[135] Or would Lindsell have present-day biblical scholars adopt the abandoned allegorical, dogmatic, or mystical methods of earlier Christian history? He seems to allow for no possibility of the reform or alteration of the historical-critical method. Finally, Lindsell's suggestion that he and those who agree with him should abandon as a term of self-identification "Evangelical" because it "has been so debased that it has lost its usefulness" and either readopt the term "Fundamentalist" despite "all of the pejoratives attached to it by its detractors" or adopt the term "Orthodox Protestant"[136] can be productive for Southern Baptists in that they can more clearly decide whether they are willing to march under the banner of "Fundamentalism."

Whereas Valentine and Hinson would deny the validity of any classification of Southern Baptists as "Evangelicals" and would accentuate the differences between Southern Baptists and Evangelicals, Lindsell would constrict or confine the label "Evangelical" to those Southern Baptists who accept the Turretin-Hodge-Warfield-Lindsell doctrine of biblical inerrancy in all historical, geographical, and scientific matters and deny the label to any other Southern Baptists.

Is there any other alternative to these negative and constricted answers?

The Affirmative Answer. Chapter one of this study was designed to show the diversity of usages of the term "Evangelical" by Christians in various regions of the Western world, especially the United States, and the increasingly comprehensive, yet definable, usage of the term in the United States. From Quebedeaux's writings it was possible to derive a threefold test of what it means to be an Evangelical: the reliability and authority of the Scriptures, the necessity of personal faith in and commitment to Jesus Christ as Savior and Lord, and the urgency of evangelistic witness.[137] Chapter two was intended to identify briefly the basic doctrines, the personal and social ethics, and the missionary endeavor of contemporary Evangelicals. From the doctrines of those groups which

---

[134]Trans. Edwin W. Leverenz and Rudolph F. Norden (St. Louis: Concordia Publishing House, 1977).

[135]Ibid., ch. 3.

[136]*The Bible in the Balance*, pp. 315-16, 319-21.

[137]See above, ch. 1, quotation preceding fn. 109.

had been identified in chapter one as "Evangelicals" it was possible to identify three areas of doctrinal emphasis or agreement among Evangelicals: justification by grace through faith or regeneration by the Holy Spirit, the supreme authority of the Scriptures, and the deity of Jesus Christ together with the events of His "holy history."[138] Part of chapter three was an effort to interpret the consequences of the major theological controversies in which Southern Baptists have been involved in reference to the present-day identity of Southern Baptists. That study led to the conclusion that Southern Baptist doctrinal affirmations give evidence of much common ground with Evangelicals but that Southern Baptists are unmistakably and intentionally denominationalists.[139]

The final question posed vis-a-vis the answers by Valentine and Hinson and by Lindsell, is this: Can one accurately and properly affirm today that Southern Baptists are Evangelicals? The writer believes that the evidence, as set forth above, warrants a clear and affirmative answer: *Southern Baptists are denominational Evangelicals.* They belong to and exemplify the great heritage of Scriptural authority, Christocentric doctrine, gospel proclamation, experience of grace, and evangelistic endeavor which is Evangelicalism. Some will doubtless have reservations about this conclusion. Is there not a very tiny minority of Southern Baptists that would somewhat identify with Liberal Protestantism? Is there not a somewhat larger minority segment that would identify rather fully with Fundamentalism? One should not deny that these questions may prove to need an affirmative answer. A third question may prove to be even more crucial: Are not many Southern Baptist individuals and churches in danger of succumbing to a cultural or socioeconomic or ecclesiastical captivity in which they are formally evangelical but not actively evangelistic and lose touch with and care not for those outside their class, neighborhood, or ethnic identity?

It is beyond the scope of this study to investigate, on the basis of the conclusion that Southern Baptists are Evangelicals, how and to what extent Southern Baptists and other Evangelicals should and could relate more effectively to each other and how each might profit from such relationships. Admittedly the contacts have been rather limited, and the alternation of admiration and suspicion may have prevailed in the past.

---

[138]See above, ch. 2, paragraph 4.

[139]See above, ch. 3, esp. paragraphs preceding fns. 111 and 112.

These questions of relationships should be taken up in a responsible manner, if indeed Southern Baptists are Evangelicals.

It is likewise beyond the scope of this study to propose specifically how Southern Baptists, if indeed they are Evangelicals, ought to clarify, intensify, and extend their own self-consciousness as Evangelical Christians or to declare whether Southern Baptists ought to seek to evaluate their proclamation, teachings, outreach, ministries, and practices in the light of what it should mean to be Evangelical Christians during the closing decades of the twentieth century. Some deeper awareness, some penetrating analysis, and some specific actions would seem to be needed.

Part Two

Baptists and "Evangelicals"
—There Is a Difference

by E. Glenn Hinson

Chapter One

In Search of Our
Baptist Identity

The focus of this study will be the discovery or *re*discovery of our identity as Baptists. The topic grows out of a strongly felt conviction that we are in the midst of an identity crisis, one which bears especially on our relation to those Christians who call themselves "Evangelicals." The crisis has not pounced upon us suddenly and unexpectedly. Rather, it has crept up stealthily, quietly, and almost imperceptibly. Now it has sprung with full force.[1]

These pages will have a strong existential flavor, for my own identity as a Christian and even as a person is tied inseparably to my identity as a Southern Baptist. Consequently, the identity crisis Southern Baptists are wrestling with is also my identity crisis. Thence, I may inject more passion into what I say than a historian's objectivity should allow. Nonetheless, I will speak without apology, for, though passion can get out of hand, it can also drive us closer to the truth, as I hope it does here.

As most of you will know, the current crisis has been triggered by the effort of some to equate the term "Baptist," particularly Southern Baptist, with "Fundamentalist" or "Evangelical." Belief in biblical inerrancy,

---

[1]W. R. Estep, "Southern Baptists in Search of an Identity," in *The Lord's Free People in a Free Land*, ed. W. R. Estep (Fort Worth, Texas: Faculty of the School of Theology, Southwestern Baptist Theological Seminary, 1976), pp. 145-70, reviewed earlier efforts to establish identity. However, he proposed no solution to the current crisis.

according to this group, is the chief test point. What inerrancy means, of course, is a bit unclear. For some it applies to the current translations, especially the King James Version. For others it refers only to the original autographs. In the last analysis, as we will see later, it has less to do with defense of the Bible than with the effort of certain persons to set themselves up as the inerrant and infallible interpreters of the Bible and guides to Baptist orthodoxy.

Such periods of soul searching as this are probably quite healthy so long as we are willing to go through the process with an open agenda. Whether Fundamentalism will permit this kind of openness is debatable, for it is by nature a closed system. As James Barr has said, "Fundamentalism never sought or intended to preserve something which it would thus make available for the church as a whole: on the contrary, its distinctive and continual insistence was that the acceptance of the fundamentalist position was the one and exclusive way by which the essentials of Christian faith could be preserved."[2] Fundamentalists want to hear or talk only to those who agree with them already on the fundamentals, as they define them. I would point out, however, that there is a vast difference between persons who believe in fundamentals, as all of us probably do, and Fundamentalism. Fundamentalism is a mentality which says, "I am right and only those who agree with me can be right or Christian or Baptist!" Where such an attitude prevails, we have little hope of discovering who we are as Southern Baptists.

In this discussion, however, I am proceeding on the assumption that Baptists are inherently open to discussion. As I have prepared this essay, I have had to ponder the implications of our Baptist diversity. In America we have produced more than fifty denominations or sects, plus an untold multitude of independent churches, and the end does not appear to be in sight. Does this say: "We agree to disagree, and we will tolerate other views"? Or, does it say: "We will not tolerate those with whom we disagree"? Rather than going through the pain of dealing with conflict, we go our separate ways and associate only with "our kind."

If this latter, essentially negative, reading is the proper one, the Southern Baptist Convention has gloomy prospects for survival as the entity we now know. It has experienced some divisions: a Landmark one in the early twentieth century, and a Fundamentalist one in the 1920s. Moreover, it has spun off many churches along the way. On the brighter

---

[2]*Fundamentalism* (Philadelphia: Westminster Press, 1977), p. 344.

side, however, it has tiptoed through several mine fields without losing much of its constituency, saved more often than not by an unwillingness to divert too much attention from its principal purpose. We can be modest enough to admit that God will carry on his work even if such a rift occurs, but we ought also to have enough pride in what we have been doing to believe that a split will strike a serious blow at what God can do through a united people. I offer this study in the hope that a clearer understanding of who we are may help us to avoid the worst and possibly to achieve a common ground for working together in spite of our disagreements.

In this first chapter I will deal with the question: How do we Baptists, specifically Southern Baptists, go about determining our identity? For persons who like to "get on with it," this may seem superfluous. "Just do it!" you may exclaim. "Don't bother me with your method!" Though I am sensitive to the fact that I will be going along a sidepath, I will keep to this path anyway out of the conviction that proper method is critical for determining who we are with any degree of accuracy. If our approach is wrong, our conclusions also will likely be wrong.

Earlier Efforts

Southern Baptists have had two major efforts to define who they are. One was the Baptist high churchism of J. R. Graves; the other E. Y. Mullins's *Axioms of Religion*. It will help us to note how they went about this task.

J. R. Graves's Baptist Primitivism and Successionism. James Robinson Graves disenfranchised every denomination except Baptists by way of a Baptist high churchism. His argument ran as follows: The local church is the kingdom of God on earth. The only true church is that which follows the New Testament to the letter. This would mean Baptist churches, for they alone practice scriptural baptism. Pedobaptist churches cannot be New Testament churches. Consequently they cannot perform valid baptisms, administer the Lord's Supper, ordain, or do other things mandated by the Scriptures. Moreover, their ministers are not gospel ministers. Baptists, therefore, must not recognize their baptism, even if by immersion. They must not take communion with them. They must not let Pedobaptist ministers preach in Baptist pulpits.

Graves supposed that he founded his argument squarely upon the assumption that Baptists, and Baptists alone, truly hold to the New Testament as "the supreme authority" as "the distinguishing doctrine of our denomination."[3] Speaking against open communion, he declared that tradition or denominational precedent "weigh not a feather's weight with me:" Centuries of observance by Baptists makes no difference. If there is not direct, and presumably explicit, scriptural warrant, it should not be done. Thus,

> though it can be proved that Baptists, since the days of Paul, and that by the very churches he planted and instructed, have practiced inter-communion, the question is, "What were the instructions *he* gave?" These must constitute the "Old Landmarks" to guide us in the observance of this ordinance, and not "denominational usage," or the mistakes and errors of our fathers, if our ancestors did, indeed, err from the "old paths."[4]

Over and over, Graves would reiterate his reliance wholly on the New Testament. "The instructions given to the New Testament churches must be our 'Landmarks'."[5]

His protestations notwithstanding, the father of Landmarkism did invoke "tradition" when it suited his purposes. In 1855, he published J. H. Orchard's *A Concise History of Foreign Baptists: Taken from the New Testament, the First Fathers, Early Writers, and Historians of All Ages.* Historical evidence, he wrote in the preface to the Orchard history, substantiates which denomination truly represents the company of faithful and true witnesses to the gospel of Christ. Will not knowing this history, he asked, "add unmeasurably to their boldness and the faithfulness of their testimony, to their zeal and sacrificing in the kingdom and patience of the Saints?" His answer was an emphatic yes.[6] To admit continuity from the medieval church would put Baptists in the same position as Pedobaptists vis-à-vis the church of Rome. That is, they would have to admit the validity of Roman baptisms and ordinations. Per contra,

> To decide that the Romish apostasy is not the true Church of Christ, is to decide that all her ordinances are invalid, and

---

[3] J. R. Graves, *Old Landmarkism: What is it?* (Ashland, KY: Calvary Baptist Church Book Shop, 1880, reprinted), p. 93.

[4] Ibid., pp. 58-59.

[5] Ibid., p. 77.

[6] J. H. Orchard, *A Concise History of Foreign Baptists* (Nashville: Graves & Marks, 1855), p. vi.

consequently that all Protestant societies are bodies of unbaptized persons, and therefore not churches of Christ, and all Protestant ministers are both unbaptized and unordained, and consequently unauthorized either to preach or administer the ordinances.[7]

Graves professed a lack of confidence that other Protestants would tell the truth here. "If the world is ever favored with a faithful history of Christian Churches, it will receive it from Baptists."[8] Baptists needed such a history to reply to Pedobaptist taunts, "Where were you before the days of Roger Williams, or before the days of Muncer?"[9] Enemies, Graves charged, had denigrated Baptists long enough, especially in connecting them with the Anabaptist revolt at Münster. History must reply.

Still, Graves would not concede the demands of those whom he labeled "Liberals" that he demonstrate an uninterrupted church succession. "We point to the Word of God, and, until the Infidel can destroy *its* authenticity, our hope is unshaken."[10] He didn't have to demonstrate complete continuity. People would know this from the correspondence of the beginning and the end of the story just as they would know the Atlantic cable existed though they could not trace it for thousands of miles.

> All that any candid man could desire—and it is from Catholic and Protestant sources—frankly admitting that churches, substantially like the Baptists of this age have existed, and suffered the bitterest persecution from the earliest age until now; and, indeed, they have been the only religious organizations that have stood since the days of the apostles, and are older than the Roman Catholic Church itself.[11]

Nevertheless, in support of his views Graves frequently invoked "eminent Baptists" and repudiated those who cited Baptist history to oppose Landmark views. And when it came time to summarize his argument for "Old Landmarkism," he resorted to his succession theory.[12]

---

[7]Ibid., pp. x-xi.
[8]Ibid., p. xi.
[9]Ibid., p. xi.
[10]*Old Landmarkism*, p. 80.
[11]Ibid., p. 81.
[12]See ibid., pp. 140-41.

J. R. Graves's method seems to have combined primitivism and successionism. Baptists do only those things which Scriptures warrant more or less literally. There is no room for development or adaptation. History is important only if it offers documentation or support for what you are doing.

E. Y. Mullins's Axiomatism. E. Y. Mullins held his own denomination in high esteem, too, but, unlike Graves, he made no effort to disenfranchise all others. Roman Catholicism alone among the major denominations came in for severe censure by Mullins, chiefly because it stood at variance with what he regarded as the principal tenet of the Christian religion, namely, soul competency. Indeed, Mullins charged, "the Roman Catholic system is the direct antithesis to the doctrine of the soul's competency."[13] Where Graves wrote to establish an absolute Baptist franchise, Mullins sought to supply "a new cohesive principle" strong enough to give unity and purpose to his denomination. Several contemporary currents prompted him in this: the Liberal-Fundamentalist debates, questions of Christian unity, the social gospel movement, and Christian successes on foreign mission fields. "Denominational self-respect, a sense of divine calling and mission," Mullins wrote, "must possess any religious body which counts for much in the world."[14]

Mullins, too, posited his position on the Scriptures. "The authority of the Scriptures lies at the basis of our plea," he wrote. Then he added:

> We do not believe any form of Christianity which breaks with the Scripture as the revealed and authoritative word of God can long serve the interests of God's kingdom on earth in any thoroughgoing way. Every position, therefore, which we assume in the following pages is either directly or indirectly grounded upon the revelation of God in Christ as recorded in the Old and New Testament Scriptures.[15]

Elsewhere, Mullins noted the Baptist belief in the sufficiency, certainty, and authoritativeness of the Scriptures as based on inspiration. Yet, at the same time, he cautioned against overextending their application. "The Bible is the book of religion," he admonished. "It is a mistake to think of it

---

[13]E. Y. Mullins, *The Axioms of Religion* (Philadelphia: The Griffith & Rowland Press, 1908), p. 60.

[14]Ibid., pp. 19-20.

[15]Ibid., p. 26.

as a text-book on science or any other subject except religion."[16] It must be interpreted, and we can count on the same Spirit who inspired the writing to help us in interpreting.

In the actual framing of his understanding of the Baptist tradition, however, Mullins was no biblicist. Indeed, he seldom cited scriptures directly. His method actually was more philosophical and historical than proof-textual and for that reason perhaps more truly biblical. Philosophically Mullins moved from the New Testament ideal of the kingdom of God to a statement of "axioms." He did not cite proof-texts. Rather, lifting out characteristics of the kingdom, he drove in a beeline to the Baptist principle of voluntarism or soul competency as the essence of biblical religion. The religion of the New Testament is intensely personal. God relates to us as a father to his children. Not only so, he discloses himself to us through Jesus Christ. Our response is one of faith, a voluntary and uncoerced response. Faith is not merely "interrupted and occasional" but "the permanent attitude of the soul."[17] Such faith is in Christ, the Son of God, and thus "excludes meritorious works, the acceptance of a formal creed, or entrance merely into a visible church organization, or grace through humanly administered sacraments, as conditions of salvation."[18] It requires "Freedom of intercourse between the Father in heaven and the child" and excludes "the limiting of acceptable worship to particular places, or through human mediators, or by means of physical appliances."[19] It necessitates filial service in voluntary societies and excludes hierarchical or oligarchical forms. It assures the freedom of the individual soul, an idea inherent in the idea of grace, "which means that God comes into the soul to raise it into a state of moral power, and transform it into his own image."[20] However, freedom does not mean pure individualism but freedom for interdependence and brotherhood. Further, growth occurs through voluntary means. "Truth apprehended and obeyed is the way of God's kingdom in making men holy."[21] Finally, "all the means adopted in the church must be adjusted to the ends of personal and social righteousness."[22]

---

[16]E. Y. Mullins, *Baptist Beliefs* (Valley Forge, Pa.: Judson Press, 1912), pp. 13-14.
[17]*The Axioms of Religion*, p. 34.
[18]Ibid., p. 38.
[19]Ibid., pp. 38-39.
[20]Ibid., p. 40.
[21]Ibid.
[22]Ibid., p. 41.

Historically Mullins proceeded to show how Baptists articulated the very principles he drew from the New Testament. He summed up his historical treatment as follows:

> The biblical significance of the Baptists is the right of private interpretation and obedience to the scriptures. The significance of the Baptists in relation to the individual is soul freedom. The ecclesiastical significance of the Baptists is a regenerated church-membership and the equality and priesthood of believers. The political significance of the Baptists is the separation of Church and State. But as comprehending all the above particulars, as a great and aggressive force in Christian history, as distinguished from all others and standing entirely alone, the doctrine of the soul's competency in religion under God is the distinctive historical significance of the Baptists.[23]

From this basic premise about the competency of the soul in religion under God, which he believed would accord with the teachings of the New Testament and gain the consensus of Methodists, Presbyterians, and Episcopalians, Mullins set forth his famous axioms:

- The theological axiom: The holy and loving God has a right to be sovereign.
- The religious axiom: All souls have an equal right to direct access to God.
- The ecclesiastical axiom: All believers have a right to equal privileges in the church.
- The moral axiom: To be responsible man must be free.
- The religio-civic axiom: A free Church in a free State.
- The social axiom: Love your neighbor as yourself.[24]

By contrast with Graves, Mullins held his Baptist heritage in high regard, not to score points against opponents but for its notable contributions to humankind. He concluded the *Axioms* with a ringing affirmation of the Baptist contribution to American civilization and to the world's religious and intellectual progress.

---

[23]Ibid., p. 57.
[24]Ibid., pp. 73-74.

Discovering Our Identity in a New Day

Both Graves and Mullins made contributions to Southern Baptist efforts to define who they were in particular times and circumstances. Mullins's work, of course, was better informed, more balanced, and based on a more reliable methodology than Graves's, but both have produced many children. Yet neither could suffice forever. Different times and circumstances necessitate doing afresh what they tried to do and, with the redoing, the application of a new methodology.

Scripture and Tradition. Our effort to say who we are must take as its point of departure the commitment of our Baptist forebears to the Scriptures alone as their rule of faith and practice. Both Graves and Mullins began here, and I would judge that we cannot move far from that position.

A rigid *scriptura sola* stance, however, does run into difficulties, as we have recognized in part in looking at Graves's methods. One problem is that *tradition colors the way we interpret and apply the Scriptures*. It fits us, as it were, with denominational glasses through which we "see" evidence only for our ideas or practices. Thus in the Scriptures we will "find" *our* view of baptism or the Lord's Supper, *our* polity, and *our* concept of church-state relations. Other denominational apologists do the same.

Another problem is that *the Scriptures-alone position fails to recognize the legitimate role of tradition*. Modern historical studies have shown us that the Scriptures contain tradition. Indeed, it is in the Scriptures of the New Testament that we find the earliest and most essential tradition about God's act on our behalf in Jesus of Nazareth. The Apostle Paul, for instance, told the Corinthians: "For I delivered to you as of first importance what I also received, that Christ died . . . was buried . . . was raised on the third day . . . and appeared to Cephas, then to the twelve . . . " (1 Cor. 15:3-5). This "tradition" belongs to the very essence of Christianity.

A third problem is that *this stance leaves no room for development if adhered to too strictly*. You will know the consequence of J. R. Graves's selective literalism. Using his method, his children could oppose not only open communion, alien immersion, and pulpit affiliation but also the "high salaried Board system" for doing missions. By focusing on scriptural principles and not taking the literalist route, Mullins did not encounter as much difficulty. Nevertheless, he too strained biblical evidence to find support for the most vital of Baptist principles. Religious liberty, for instance, is not a highly developed plant—indeed, it is scarcely even a sprout—in the New Testament. Yet no group of Christians has cherished it more nor paid a higher price to attain it than Baptists. Recognition of the legitimacy of development would ease the hermeneutics here somewhat.

This is not to denigrate the centrality of the Scriptures. The "eyewitnesses and ministers of the word" (Luke 1:1-4) who recorded their testimonies in them stood closest to the events which they attested. Later generations cannot reproduce their experience; they can only repeat the story. Therefore, they must return to these ever again to check their own handling of the tradition. The tradition found in the Scriptures and that found in later writings may be viewed as a historian views primary and secondary sources. Primary sources are firsthand accounts; secondary sources rely on primary sources. Scriptures contain both primary and secondary sources, but later accounts consist only of secondary sources in the sense that they obtain *primary* sources from the Scriptures and not from a firsthand experience. Thus we are compelled to return always to the Scriptures in which primary sources are embedded.[25]

The Baptist Tradition. What I am trying to steer us toward here is "the Baptist tradition." In doing so, I recognize fully the aversion Baptists have had toward tradition—"tradition," however, understood as convention, rote repetition of meaningless rites, or ascription to creeds. Tradition may be understood in another way, as the *essence or the spirit of a movement.* Defining the word in this way, Baptists may reveal their "tradition" precisely in their opposition to tradition. We came into this world kicking and screaming against Anglican and Puritan efforts to impose uniformity either in worship or in faith and practice. Consequently, as E. Y. Mullins intuited, the essence of our tradition lies in the conviction that faith must be free, a voluntary response to God.

In his massive history of the development of doctrine entitled *The Christian Tradition,* Jaroslav Pelikan has supplied a definition of tradition or doctrine which will be helpful to us in determining our self-understanding. The Christian tradition, Pelikan says, is "what the church of Jesus Christ believes, teaches, and confesses on the basis of the word of God."[26] This statement, I think, leaves plenty of room for recognition of

---

[25]For more detailed discussion of the above see my article on "The Authority of the Christian Heritage for Baptist Faith and Practice," *Search* 8 (Spring 1978): 6-24.

[26]Jaroslav Pelikan, *The Christian Tradition,* vol. 1, *The Emergence of the Catholic*

the intense commitment of Baptists, along with other Protestants, to the Scriptures as the record of divine revelation and yet takes into account also the multiple ways in which they have sought to act upon and interact with this revelation. To discover what the church "believes," Pelikan examines its devotion, spirituality, and worship. To learn what it "teaches," he looks at its proclamation, instruction, and churchly theology. To find what it "confesses," he considers its polemics and apologetics, its creeds and dogmas. The central issue, however, is always how, in all of these areas, the church has responded in its context to the Word of God as found in the Scriptures. What do Christians, in our case Baptists, think the Scriptures mandate for them in their age and context? Why have they acted as they have?

What this approach will mean is that we will recognize our traditional commitment to the scriptures as the heart of our tradition while searching for what this commitment has produced and preserved over nearly four centuries of history. One thing which I have increasingly realized as a result of participation in ecumenical dialogue is that I plug into the larger Christian tradition, the "catholic" tradition with a little "c," by way of the Baptist tradition. Roman Catholics, similarly, plug in by way of the Roman Catholic tradition, Presbyterians by way of the Presbyterian, Methodists by way of the Methodist, and so forth. This larger tradition may be viewed as a conduit containing numerous wires, each wrapped in its own insulation. Each of these wires carries the central current of the divine revelation. Though not exactly alike, each hands on what is essential.[27] Without a clear understanding of our distinctive tradition, we will not appropriate the Christian tradition as we should.

Depth and Persistence. There remains still another issue in our search for an appropriate method to determine who we are: How do we sort out the essential elements from the superficial or peripheral or ephemeral? How do we find the *real* Baptist character? Many outside observers, for instance, have thought of the practice of immersion as a central tenet of Baptists, and Landmarkists have made much of mode. Most Baptists, however, have emphasized believers' baptism rather than immersion, on sound historical grounds. Moreover, faced with difficulties

---

Tradition (100-600) (Chicago & London: University of Chicago Press, 1971), p. 1. See also *Development of Christian Doctrine: Some Historical Prolegomena* (New Haven & London: Yale University Press, 1969), pp. 9-36.

[27]For this model see Yves Congar, O.P., *Tradition and Traditions* (New York: Macmillan Co., 1967). Congar has dealt fully with the patristic understanding of tradition.

in their relations with other Christians, some have looked behind believers' baptism to the intention of their founding fathers and, as is true of Mullins, discerned the voluntarist principle in religion. As a second example, Fundamentalists have recently argued that Baptists have always been proponents of the inerrantist theory of scriptures. In support they have cited a few of the many Baptist confessions and some noted theologians of an earlier day.[28] Other Baptists, however, have disputed this contention.[29] What criteria do we use in disputed cases? I would cite two: depth and persistence.

Depth is admittedly a subjective idea. I mean by it the principles and practices which *serve as the core* of the Baptist tradition and give it vitality. This core is obviously not easy to uncover: How will we do so with confidence? To some extent, such characteristics can be measured by the *frequency* with which they appear in the sources: confessions, hymns, biographies, sermons, and so forth. In the long run, however, they will have to be uncovered by dialectical digging in highly diversified Baptist minds to see why Baptists have behaved as they have. E. Y. Mullins, for instance, correctly discerned that voluntarism or soul competency underlay the other axioms of religion despite the fact that Baptists may not often have alluded to it.

On a more practical level, we may find the "soul" of early Baptists by asking, "For what were they willing to go to prison or to die?" In our free land it is easy to forget the price some paid for "soul liberty." John Bunyan, for instance, left a wife and four children, one a blind daughter who "lay nearer my heart than all I had beside," he said, rather than stop preaching.[30] Any father will know how deeply he ached and how agonizingly he weighed his decision. "I say in this condition," he confessed, "I was as a man who was pulling down his house upon the head of his wife and children; yet thought I, I must do it."[31] For all he knew, he might end up on the gallows. Still he persisted. "If God doth not come in, thought I, 'I will leap off the ladder, even blindfold into eternity; sink or swim, come heaven, come hell. Lord Jesus, if thou wilt catch me, do; if not, I will

---

[28]See especially Russ Bush and Tom J. Nettles, *Baptists and the Bible* (Chicago: Moody Press, 1980).

[29]See the critique of the Bush-Nettles book by Dale Moody in *Review and Expositor* 77 (Fall 1980): 565-66.

[30]*Grace Abounding*, in *Doubleday Devotional Classics*, ed. E. Glenn Hinson (Garden City, N.Y.: Doubleday & Co., Inc., 1978), 1:302.

[31]*Grace Abounding*, 324; in *Doubleday Devotional Classics*, 1:302.

venture for thy name.' "[32] Somewhere in John Bunyan's agonizing words
you will find the "depths" of the Baptist tradition. In his *Prison Medita-*
tions he explained what sent him there—a desire to obey God:

They were no fables that I taught
　　Devis'd by cunning men,
But God's own word, by which were caught
　　Some sinners now and then.

Whose souls by it were made to see
　　The evil of their sin;
And need of Christ to make them free
　　From death, which they were in.

And now those very hearts, that then
　　Were foes unto the Lord,
Embrace his Christ and truth like men
　　Conquer'd by his word.

I hear them sigh, and groan, and cry,
　　For grace to God above:
They loathe their sin, and to it die,
　　'Tis holiness they love.

This was the work I was about,
　　When hands on me were laid,
'Twas this from which they pluck'd me out,
　　And vilely to me said:

You heretic, deceiver, come,
　　To prison you must go,
You preach abroad, and keep not home,
　　You are the church's foe.

But having peace within my soul,
　　And truth on every side,
I could with comfort them control,
　　And at their charge deride.

Wherefore to prison they me sent,
　　Where to this day I lie;
And can with very much content
　　For my profession die.

---

[32]*Grace Abounding*, 333; in *Doubleday Devotional Classics*, 1:305.

Persistence is easier to establish than *depth*. By persistence I mean continuity of influence and effect. I use the word persistence rather than continuity, however, for there may be times when Baptists have left gaps in representation of their tradition. Our own is one of those, surely, wherein persons calling themselves Baptists have joined forces with those who would circumscribe first amendment prohibitions of an establishment of religion and guarantees of its free exercise, a clause which few religious groups have labored more assiduously than Baptists to see implemented and conserved. Along similar lines, some would restrict the religious freedom of denominational employees by imposing narrow confessional statements, all the while, ironically, professing to subscribe fully to the Baptist principle of soul liberty. The reasoning is: "Denominational employees must represent the beliefs of the majority in the denomination and not hold individual opinions. Anyone can believe what he or she wishes but not if employed by the denomination."

Conclusion

Over nearly four centuries Baptist consciousness has been subjected to many influences and undergone many changes. It has taken on new aspects and sloughed off old ones as Baptists have sought to respond to the Spirit's guidance as they have acted upon the word of God which they found in the Scriptures. As a consequence of interaction with many contexts, this consciousness has been multifaceted. Like the different sides of a complex personality, these different facets of the Baptist consciousness place a strain on it. They may fracture it.

One of the most serious challenges to Baptist identity is the one which now faces the Southern Baptist Convention. In the South—East of Texas to the Atlantic coast and South of the Mason-Dixon line to Mexico—Baptists have attained a status they have never enjoyed in any culture, a status similar to that which Constantine handed early Christianity. Intensely motivated to discharge one aspect of the Baptist tradition—evangelism and missions—they have begun to neglect another aspect—voluntarism in religion. Claiming more than half of the constituency of most counties in the South, they exhibit many features of "catholic" Christianity of the fourth century in the Roman Empire. As in the latter, so also in the South many favor an "alliance" between church and state and argue for uniformity of faith and practice. Under the circumstances, it is appropriate to ask whether there will be an abandonment of enough facets of the Baptist tradition that Southern Baptists will cease to be Baptists, or whether the vital elements will remain strong enough to avert this danger. In either case, we would do well to ferret out the essential elements of the Baptist tradition.

Chapter Two

The Battle of Baptist Selves
—Evangelical and Voluntarist

Denominations, like people, have diverse selves. Such selves, like personal ones, are due in part to inheritance and in part to experience. Baptists, for instance, inherited some of their characteristics from the medieval Church of England and some from the Protestant Reformers. Yet through the centuries they have acquired others which have added other touches to their corporate personality.

Also like persons, denominations pass through many phases in their self-understanding and ability to function. Sometimes they, as it were, "put it all together." At other times they are immobilized by split personalities and unable to get their multifaceted selves to operate in a coordinated way. The tensions between different facets are too great.

In this chapter I want to talk about two facets of our Baptist personality which have stood in tension with one another and frequently have done battle. I am speaking of our evangelical and our voluntarist strains. These two are, I believe, the dominant aspects of the Southern Baptist personality. From the evangelical comes an intense commitment to the Great Commission, from the voluntarist a vigilance on behalf of religious liberty and the separation of church and state. If the two are not held in balance, and integrated in some way, our personality may split. If, for example, the evangelical note crowds out the voluntarist, "zeal for souls" may lead to total disregard for individual and corporate liberty to the point of employing physical or psychological coercion. Any "means" is permissible, some may reason, so long as it achieves the main goal. On the other hand, if voluntarism is carried to an extreme, it may generate indifference toward the divine claim upon human life and our responsibility for announcing that claim. How have Baptists, specifically Southern Baptists, brought these together? How can they integrate them today?

Since time will prevent me from telling the whole Baptist story, my approach here will be to highlight some key phases in this struggle. My chief thesis will be that a balance between voluntarist and evangelical strains must be maintained if we are to remain true to our vocation as Baptists. Not only so, voluntarism has served the Baptist evangelical cause well, at least in the United States, where 30 out of 34 million Baptists now reside. Since the voluntarist side is currently being subjected to the greater perils, in the third chapter I will sound a warning about a very real and present danger from the evangelical side.

Puritan-Separatist Baptists

The voluntarist-evangelical tension is evident, first of all, in Baptist origins out of English and American Puritanism. Though a case can be made for Anabaptist and even earlier[1] connections, I would see all of these as secondary rather than primary. All three of the major strands which figured in Baptist beginnings were first Puritan and then Baptist.

The first strand is the group called General Baptists because they believed in a general atonement, that is, that Christ died for all and not just the "elect." The roots of this strand can be traced to a Separatist congregation meeting at Gainesborough. The Separatists differed from other Puritans in that they counted congregationalism the only form of

---

[1] Actually there are three theories of Baptist origins. One—called variously the "Succession," "Jerusalem-John-Jordan," or "Trail of Blood" Theory—traces Baptist history from Jesus' baptism by John the Baptist by way of a succession of sects (Montanists, Novatianists, Donatists, Petrobrusians and Henricians, Waldenses, Cathari, Lollards, and so forth) to the emergence of Baptists in the seventeenth century in England. A second, the Anabaptist Spiritual Kinship Theory, argues for a "spiritual kinship" with earlier groups but attempts only to make a historical linkage of Baptists with Anabaptists (now Mennonites). The third, which I follow here, places primary emphasis on the emergence of Baptist churches out of left wing Puritanism in England. Theologically Puritans were heirs of John Calvin who sought "further reform" of the Church of England. They differed among themselves, however, on the way the reform should be effected. Some were content to retain the episcopal structure and thus to wait for official action. Others tied reform efforts to adoption of a presbyterial polity such as the Scottish churches had adopted. Radicals refused to wait and formed "separate" or "independent" congregations, seeing in these the only way to obtain "Reformation without Tarrying for Any."

church government which would lead to genuine and speedy reform. In the words of the "father" of Separatism, Robert Browne, they wanted "Reformation without Tarrying for Any"—the title of one of Browne's treatises. This congregation had experienced a split, the other group meeting at the Manor House of Scrooby. In 1608 the latter group fled to Holland under the leadership of John Robinson; in 1620 they came to America on the Mayflower.

The Gainesborough congregation also fled to Holland, led by John Smyth, a Cambridge graduate, and funded by Thomas Helwys, a prosperous merchant. In Amsterdam they lived in a building owned by a Dutch Mennonite named Jan Munter. Possibly under Anabaptist influence[2] Smyth concluded in 1608 that the Scriptures teach believers' baptism only. He then proceeded to baptize himself and other members of his congregation. Subsequently, however, he did a retake on his *se*-baptism and sought baptism at the hands of the Waterlander Mennonites.[3] This caused a split between Smyth and Helwys. Helwys then led a group of ten back to England in 1612 to found the first Baptist church on English soil. Smyth's followers eventually joined the Mennonites after his death in 1612.

The second strand of Baptists is called Particular Baptists because of their belief that Christ died only for the "elect." The first of this strand originated several years later out of an Independent or Separatist congregation[4] which we identify by the names of its first three pastors: Jacob-Lathrop-Jessey. Henry Jacob served from 1616-1622; John Lathrop, from 1625-1634; and Henry Jessey, after 1637. The story of this congregation is

---

[2]This is a matter of debate. Goki Saito, "An Investigation into the Relationships between the Early English General Baptists and the Dutch Anabaptists" (unpublished Th.D Thesis, Southern Seminary, 1974), has shown clearly the difficulties in assuming that Mennonites directly influenced the Smyth/Helwys congregation. Munter did not speak English; the English people did not speak Dutch. Smyth's treatises, moreover, did not acknowledge Anabaptist works. Separatist congregations were known to have debated various issues relative to baptism from an early date. Re-examination of theology and practice was a natural consequence of the effort to achieve a reformation of the church along scriptural lines as proposed by all of the major reformers.

[3]Smyth seems definitely to have come under Mennonite influence here. What troubled him most was the issue of succession. See Saito, "An Investigation," p. 175.

[4]Sources dating from this period usually distinguish "separate" and "independent," but the distinction is by no means clear-cut. Normally "independent" would refer to a congregation not seeking to establish interconnection with others. "Separate," on the other hand, would designate those which tended to establish associational ties with other congregations when they "separated" from the Church of England.

a complex one. Actually it debated various baptismal issues over a number of years and eventually begot several Baptist congregations. A Mr. Dupper seceded with others in 1630, declaring baptism by the parish clergy invalid. In 1633 Samuel Eaton and others received "a further baptism." It is uncertain, however, whether either of these had anything to do with infant baptism. It was in 1638 that a group of six people definitely rejected infant baptism and "joined with Mr. Spilsbury." Spilsbury apparently had become pastor of an antipedobaptist church between 1633 and 1638. What is important is, of course, the Puritan and Separatist connections.[5] It seems probable that about 1641 Spilsbury's group was led by a certain Richard Blunt to adopt immersion as practiced by a certain group of Mennonites called Collegiants, whom Blunt visited that year. This custom was obviously subordinate to the concern of early Baptists about baptism of believers only, but after 1644, when included in the First London Confession, it became the commonly accepted custom of baptizing.

The third strand of Baptists originated more or less independently of the other two in the American colonies through Roger Williams, who, curiously, did not remain a Baptist long. Williams, then about thirty years old, came to the colonies in 1631 to escape the wrath of Charles I and William Laud against the Puritans. Educated at Charter House in London and at Cambridge, he was ordained to the Anglican priesthood. He took a job first in Salem, Massachusetts, but he soon ran afoul of authorities over his view that the magistrate should not punish breaches of the first "table," that is, the first part of the decalogue. Subsequently, he welcomed an invitation to teach among the more tolerant pilgrims of Plymouth. There, too, however, he ran into trouble, evidently stirred up by some persons from the Massachusetts Bay Colony. At any rate, in 1633 he returned to Salem. Summoned twice to Boston to answer charges, in April and in July of 1635, he was sentenced to be banished. Due to ill health, he received a brief reprieve until the spring of 1636. At that time he purchased land from the Indians and established Providence Planta-

---

[5]Glen H. Stassen, "Anabaptist Influence in the Origin of the Particular Baptists," *Mennonite Quarterly Review* 36 (1962): 322-48, has demonstrated probable Anabaptist influence reflected in the First London Confession by examining ways in which it differed from the True Confession written in 1596 by Francis Johnson, on which it was based. However, I would again insist that this shows secondary rather than primary influence. The major determinants in Baptist thought and practice were already present in the Puritan/Separatist tradition.

tion, later Rhode Island, which he desired to be "a shelter for persons distressed of conscience." In 1637 or 1639 Williams received baptism from Ezekiel Holliman, a former member of his Salem congregation. He then baptized Holliman and ten others to form what was probably the first Baptist church in the American colonies. Shortly afterward, possibly as early as 1639, a physician and lay preacher named John Clarke established a second church at Newport.[6]

The Puritan connections, therefore, are clear. What did this mean in terms of Baptist self-understanding? The Puritans, as most of you will be aware, wanted further reformation of the church of England along lines of Calvin's reform in Geneva. They had a two-sided concern which they bequeathed to all their descendents: heartfelt religion, and authentic application in reformed lifestyle and transformation of society. For them, as Bunyan's *Pilgrim's Progress* makes crystal clear, religion could not be a matter of words or mere formality. "The soul of religion is the practical part," Christian told Talkative.[7] In this two-sided perception lay the aniconic and antiliturgical bent of the Puritans. Sometimes, as most heirs of the Puritans would readily admit, these children of John Calvin got very petty in their critique of the religious practice of others. Many of their particular viewpoints represented a lower socioeconomic outlook, and we have to remember that the Puritans were part of a vast social revolution. If we would understand Southern Baptists, however, we must pay close attention to this Puritan root. In it lay their "zeal for conversion." It is this root which supplies a central feature of the Southern Baptist outlook.

In connecting Baptists with Puritans, however, I do not want to obscure the way in which they differed radically from the Puritan mainstream. In their case historical circumstances aroused an intense concern for voluntarism in the exercise of religion which counterbalanced zeal for conversion. Emerging from the womb during a period of religious wars and persecution, Baptists, both in England and in America, issued eloquent pleas for unrestricted freedom guaranteed by the separation of Church and State. In England Thomas Helwys, who was incarcerated after his return and later died there, addressed King James I in 1612 with the admonition that:

---

[6]The date for the founding of the Newport church may be as late as 1644. Church records date back no earlier than 1648.

[7]*Pilgrim's Progress; Doubleday Devotional Classics,* ed. E. Glenn Hinson (Garden City, N.Y.: Doubleday & Co., 1978), 1:384.

our lord the king is but an earthly king, and he hath no
authority as a king but in earthly causes, and if the king's
people be obedient and true subjects, obeying all humane lawes
made by the king, our lord the king can require no more: for
men's religion to God, is betwixt God and themselves; the king
shall not answer for it, neither may the king be judge between
God and man. Let them be heretikes, Turcks, Jewes or what-
soever, it apperteynes not to the earthly power to punish them
in the least measure.[8]

In America Roger Williams echoed these sentiments in his famous
ship metaphor:

There goes many a ship to sea, with many hundred souls in one
ship, whose weal and woe is common, and is a true picture of a
commonwealth, or a human combination or society. It hath
fallen out sometimes, that both papists and protestants, Jews
and Turks, may be embarked in one ship; upon which supposal
I affirm, that all the liberty of conscience, that ever I pleaded
for, turns upon these two hinges—that none of the papists,
protestants, Jews, or Turks, be forced to come to the ship's
prayers or worship, nor compelled from their own particular
prayers or worship, if they practice any. I further add, that I
never denied, that notwithstanding this liberty, the com-
mander of this ship ought to command the ship's course, yea,
and also command that justice, peace and sobriety, be kept and
practiced, both among the seamen and all the passengers.[9]

Williams showed in *The Bloudy Tenet of Persecution* how far he would
press the voluntary principle.

It is the will and command of God that, since the coming of his
Son the Lord Jesus, a permission of the most Paganish, Jewish,
Turkish, or antichristian consciences and worships be granted
to all men in all nations and countries: and they are only to be
fought against with that sword which is only, in soul matters,

[8]*A Short Declaration of the Mistery of Iniquity* (1612) (London: Kingsgate Press,
1935), p. 69.

[9]Letter "To the Town of Providence," cited by Anson Phelps Stokes, *Church and State
in the United States* (New York: Harper & Bros., 1950), 1:197.

able to conquer: to wit, the sword of God's Spirit, the word of God.[10]

Strong as these statements are, they are less revealing of early Baptist commitment to voluntariness in religion than the position they took on prayer. In *A paterne of true Prayer*, John Smyth urged prayer without ceasing (1 Thess. 5:17) and berated canonical hours set by the Church of England:

> The false Church of Antichrist hath devised certaine houres which they call Canonicall; which are in number eight, as Father *Robert* rehearseth them: which must be observed every day, and cannot be omitted without deadly sinne, as he teacheth: but we do know that Christians must stand fast in that libertie wherewith Christ has made us free: and seeing that we are redeemed with a price, we must not be the servants of men, much lesse of times:[11]

So also regarding form. Although Smyth allowed recitation of the Lord's prayer, he insisted that "It is safer to conceive a prayer, than to reade a prayer: . . ." for this will prevent wandering thoughts.[12] Better stumbling public prayers than rote repetition, for such prayers come from the heart, and God looks only upon the heart. The same Spirit who taught the Lord's prayer also helps us.

John Bunyan, writing early in his first imprisonment (1662 or 1663), took a still stronger stance. He forbade use even of the Lord's prayer. Prayer is, Bunyan said,

> a sincere, sensible, affectionate pouring out of the heart or soul to God through Christ, in the strength and assistance of the Holy Spirit, for such things as God hath promised, or, according to the Word, for the good of the Church, with submission, in Faith, to the will of God.[13]

Such prayer can be offered only in the Spirit. Set prayers are "like the Sons

---

[10]*The Bloudy Tenent of Persecution*, ed. Edward Bean Underhill (London: J. Haddon, 1848), p. 2.

[11]In *The Works of John Smyth*, ed. W. T. Whitley (Cambridge: The University Press, 1915), 1:77-78.

[12]Ibid., p. 81.

[13]*I Will Pray with the Spirit*, ed. Richard L. Greaves (Oxford: Clarendon Press, 1976), p. 235.

of Aaron, offering with strange fire."[14] The main thing is not the mouth, "but whether the heart be so full of affection and earnestness in Prayer with God, that it is impossible to express their sense and desire."[15]

Awakened Baptists

The voluntarist-evangelical balance was tested a second time in the Great Awakening. A critical twist in Baptist self-consciousness in the direction of experiential conversion occurred in America during this period. It should be noted, of course, that many Baptists around the world show few signs of this change and that it affected chiefly Baptists in the South. Since most early Baptists migrated to the American colonies from England, this is a curious development which needs careful attention.

Baptist immigration to the American colonies and Baptist growth from 1639 to 1735 proceeded at a slow pace. In the New England colonies Baptists received little encouragement to grow because of the Puritan establishment. In the Middle colonies—New York, New Jersey, Pennsylvania, and Delaware—they had virtually complete freedom, but there were only a handful of Baptist churches there before 1735. In the Southern colonies—Virginia, North Carolina, South Carolina—they also met solid resistance from the Anglican establishment. We know of few Baptist churches there before 1735.

The Great Awakening, an outburst of renewal, changed Baptist status as markedly as it added to Baptist numbers. Beginning in New Jersey about 1726 with the preaching of Theodore Frelinghuysen, a Dutch Reformed minister, it spread quickly to other colonies. About 1735 it took on major proportions in the Northampton, Massachusetts, parish of Jonathan Edwards, who became the chief theologian of the Great Awakening. Subsequently it touched the Middle and Southern colonies as well. Baptists benefited as much or more than others from the Awakening. Many converts from other denominations adopted Baptist views.

Significative of the tension between their evangelical and voluntarist strains, however, Baptists split over the use of "means" to effect conversions. "Regular" Baptists opposed such methods, "Separate" Baptists favored them. The moot point was whether human beings were now stepping in to usurp the role of the Spirit in conversion. Late in the century, William Carey still had to argue the point with Hyper-Calvinists in England. Baptists, he contended, should not only pray for the conver-

---

[14]Ibid., p. 242.
[15]Ibid., p. 257.

sion of the heathen but exert themselves "in the use of means for the obtaining of those things we pray for."[16] Among other things, it would be a way to spread their voluntarism.

The most significant fact to relate here, as W. L. Lumpkin has ably demonstrated, is that large numbers of "New Light" or "Separate" Baptists migrated southwards.[17] The group usually pointed to by Southern Baptists as their forebears was one led by Shubal Stearns and Daniel Marshall to Sandy Creek, North Carolina, in 1755. This particular congregation expanded rapidly, adding over 600 members in ten years. It immediately began to start other churches. Within three years there were three churches with a combined membership of more than 900. Other sources of Baptist life in the South would have been diverse, but none as important as this one.

In the Separate Baptist tradition we can see clearly the two strains of our Baptist heritage. On one side, the Separate Baptists placed heavy emphasis on experiential faith and its correlate, the winning of converts. They insisted on an identifiable conversion experience to which one could give testimony, and they employed revivalism as their chief instrument for effecting conversions. On the other side, Separate Baptists emphatically rejected confessions of faith as unnecessary because of the Bible and restrictive of the Spirit. As James O. Renault has demonstrated, they acknowledged three sources of authority: the inspiration of the Holy Spirit, the Bible and Separate Baptist preachers. "By far, the most important source," Renault concluded, "was the inspiration of the Holy Spirit."[18] Alongside the Spirit, however, stood the Bible, interpreted literally. Separate Baptists were more biblicist than their New England counterparts,[19] and thence objected more strongly than they to the use of confessions of faith. This attitude helps to explain why Southern Baptists adopted no confession until 1925 even if subscribing to some established ones long before at a congregational level and then added a "king's X" with the Preamble.

---

[16]William Carey, *An Enquiry into the Obligations of Christians, to use means for the Conversion of the Heathens* (Leicester: Ann Ireland, 1792), p. 81.

[17]William L. Lumpkin, *Baptist Foundations in the South* (Nashville: Broadman Press, 1961), pp. 1-71.

[18]James Owen Renault, "The Development of Separate Baptist Ecclesiology in the South, 1755-1976," unpublished Ph.D. thesis, The Southern Baptist Theological Seminary, 1978, p. 85.

[19]Ibid., pp. 85-87.

Revolutionary Baptists

The voluntarist-evangelical balance was tested again in the era of the American Revolution with the voluntarist note sounding the loudest. Riding the crest from the Great Awakening, Baptists experienced a second boom between 1770 and 1800. Whereas in 1740 they had only 96 churches and in 1780 only 457, by 1820 they had 2,700. They emerged from relative obscurity to become the largest denomination in America. Why?

Winthrop S. Hudson has ascribed this success to several factors. One was their "whole-hearted support of the American Revolution."[20] They quickly realized that the greater threat to their liberties came from England and Anglican bishops than from Congregationalists in America. Meantime, competing groups such as Anglicans and Quakers suffered setbacks as a result of the Revolution. Anglicans did so because of their identification with the royal cause, Quakers because of their pacifism. Thirdly, Baptists benefited from the influx of aggressive new leadership. Most of these were converts from Congregational churches during the Awakening. Whereas other churches suffered a shortage of able leaders, Baptists had an ample supply. Finally, Baptists were more in tune than any other denomination with popular concern for religious liberty. Their concern for "individual rights, lay control, and local autonomy typified the American spirit," says Hudson. They "were so closely in tune with the temper of the time that they had no difficulty in regarding themselves and being regarded by others as a truly American church."[21]

The efforts of Isaac Backus in New England and John Leland or James Ireland in Virginia on behalf of religious liberty typify the voluntarist spirit of Baptists. In 1772 the Warren Association employed Backus as its agent. He pled their case against the Congregational establishment in New England before the Continental Congress assembled in Philadelphia in 1774. Though these pleas fell, for the most part, on deaf ears, Baptists did not slacken in their zeal. Instead, they intensified their efforts. Even as the Congress debated the articles of the Bill of Rights, Baptists were going to prison and suffering seizure of property for refusal to pay taxes in support of the established religion. Backus himself suffered reviling and abuse in the press for his efforts in behalf of disestab-

---

[20]Winthrop S. Hudson, *Baptists in Transition* (Valley Forge, PA: Judson Press, 1979), p. 76.
[21]Ibid., p. 79.

lishment and religious liberty. Greatly bouyed by a new respect gained for their efforts in the war and by increased membership in their churches, however, Baptists eventually succeeded in making their point: "True religion is a voluntary obedience to God."[22]

In Virginia beleaguered Baptists gained the ear of political leaders such as Thomas Jefferson and James Madison. At the urging of Jefferson, in 1776 the Virginia legislature passed a compromise bill repealing the laws punishing heresy and absence from worship and those requiring dissenters to contribute to the establishment. In 1785 James Madison's "Memorial and Remonstrance on the Religious Rights of Man," which laid down both practical and ideological reasons why government could not interfere in religious affairs, cleared the way for adoption of Jefferson's "An Act for Establishing Religious Freedom," introduced first in 1779 but passed finally in 1786. In 1789, shortly after his election to the House of Representatives, James Madison introduced the articles for a proposed bill of rights. Passed in that year by both the House and the Senate, the Bill of Rights was ratified by the required number of states in 1791.[23]

Frontier Baptists

A fourth testing of the balance between voluntarist and evangelical strains occurred as Baptists sought, in the frontier era, to institutionalize their concern for the Great Commission. From the American Revolution onward the formation of Baptists in the South involved an expansion westward with the American frontier. To a great extent this expansion depended on farmer preachers who were responsible for planting churches wherever they went. Not to be overlooked, however, is the fact that these Baptists retained their forebears' strong concern for evangelical conversion and quickly developed institutions which could implement evangelistic goals—associations, conventions, Sunday schools, and schools for training ministers. A casual approach worked all right so long as there were few people on the frontier, but the growth of the population there soon necessitated a more highly organized approach. Institutionalization, however, put a new strain on the balance between the voluntarist and the evangelical inheritances.

---

[22]Pamphlet published by the Warren Association, September 9, 1781; cited by Isaac Backus, *History of the Baptists in New England,* ed. David Weston, 2nd ed. (Newton, Mass.: Backus Historical Society, 1891).

[23]For more details see E. Glenn Hinson, *Soul Liberty* (Nashville: Convention Press, 1975), pp. 99-103.

Baptists in America, of course, inherited associational structures from England, where Baptists almost immediately developed them. Between 1624 and 1630 five or six General Baptist churches acted jointly to petition the Waterlander Mennonites for union with them. In 1644 seven Particular Baptist churches adopted a confession of faith. In 1650 three Welsh churches met together for common action. In 1651 thirty General Baptist churches of the midlands established the pattern for future associational organizations by sending two messengers each for a territory of one hundred by twenty-four miles. The first Baptist association in the American colonies, the Philadelphia Association, came into existence in 1707. Subsequently, associations were formed in many areas as small and scattered congregations joined hands for fellowship, inspiration, education of ministers, discipline, and missionary endeavors.

In the Southern states two purposes tended to dominate as associations came into existence: evangelism or missions and education.[24] Now one and now the other of these assumed a primary place, but it was evangelism or missions, especially foreign, which usually received first place after formation of the SBC. If any others moved into prominence at times, it was in order to serve evangelism better. The most revealing confirmation of this is the way Southern Baptists interpreted and applied all programs—Sunday schools, training of ministers, and the rest—to the one great goal—the evangelization of the world. It would probably be impossible to overemphasize this point.

The first state convention in the South, South Carolina's, was formed in 1821. Subsequently other states followed the lead of South Carolina: Georgia in 1822, Virginia and Alabama in 1823, North Carolina in 1830, Missouri in 1834, Maryland and Mississippi in 1836, Kentucky in 1837, Louisiana, Texas and Arkansas in 1848, and Florida in 1854. Such conventions coordinated and assisted the associations and churches in their common work.

Until 1845 Baptists in America promoted foreign and later home mission work through two societies. The Foreign Mission Society, called the Triennial Convention because it met every three years, was formed in 1814; the American Baptist Home Mission Society in 1832. The word "society" is indicative of the character of these organizations. Both were very loose knit. Members could be churches, associations, or individual

---

[24]For a fuller exposition of this process of growth see E. Glenn Hinson, *A History of Baptists in Arkansas* (Little Rock: Arkansas Baptist State Convention, 1978).

subscribers. The purpose was chiefly solicitation of funds for a single purpose—either foreign or home missions respectively—which the societies used to hire missionaries and sustain their work. The inspiring figure behind the Baptist Foreign Mission Society was Luther Rice, a Congregational missionary who adopted Baptist views while en route to Burma along with Adoniram Judson and his wife. Rice returned home to work for the Judsons' support.

When tensions over the question of slavery mounted to a high level, Baptists in the South began to criticize the efforts of the American Baptist Home Mission Society. There were numerous calls for separate conventions dating back to the 1830s, usually charging neglect of the Southern states in their mission efforts. When the split actually occurred in 1845, it centered around the refusal of the ABHMS to appoint a slaveholder, James E. Reeve, as a missionary, which, in the eyes of a Southerner, of course, indicated abolition sentiment in the Society.

The most significant thing to notice about the Southern Baptist Convention was that it differed markedly from the earlier structures developed by Baptists to pursue mission interests. It was more centralized. The word "convention," of course, designated only the annual gatherings. But this convention decided to follow the pattern of South Carolina in appointing Boards to carry out its mission aims. At the beginning it organized a Foreign Mission Board and a Domestic and Indian Mission Board. In 1891 it added a Sunday School Board. Subsequently the missionary drive has impelled the Convention down the institutional route at a high rate of speed, a matter to which we must return later.

Once again, however, we can see the Baptist evangelical urgency checked by Baptist concern for voluntarism. The organizing of Baptist mission effort aroused considerable dissent, especially on the American frontier. Baptists came by their distrust of church organizations naturally. In England they had suffered persecution under an established church. In America they experienced similar restrictions in New England and in the Southern colonies. As a result, early Baptist leaders such as Isaac Backus, the apostle of religious liberty in New England, feared associations and dragged their heels to hold back developments in organization beyond the local congregation. On the frontier, where a strongly individualistic spirit prevailed, suspicion of organization, as well as education, led to criticism and an effort to interrupt the work of the Foreign and Home Mission Societies. The three most articulate spokesmen were John Taylor

of Kentucky, Daniel Parker of Illinois, and Alexander Campbell, founder
of the Disciples and Christian churches. Their opposition disrupted the
development of organizations throughout the Midwest and South.

Baptist suspicions of organization beyond the local congregation
crested in Landmarkism, a Baptist high churchism devised by J. R. Graves
in the mid-nineteenth century, largely against Campbell's "reform"
movement. Graves did not challenge the powerful commitment of Baptists to missions. He applauded it. But he insisted that, since the local
church is the only true expression of the kingdom of God on earth, it
alone has a right to support mission work, whether at home or abroad.
Combined with the "Hardshellism" of Taylor and Parker, Graves's teachings fostered a major split among Baptists in Arkansas and led to the
Missionary Baptist Association, in 1901. The central issue in this split
was what leaders of the latter group called "the high salaried Board
system" used by Southern Baptists. To many, it looked like a form of
"episcopacy" of the worst sort. Being mostly farmers, they could not
understand or appreciate the business model which was beginning to
impose itself on church life in their day.[25]

Business Baptists

A sixth challenge to the voluntarist-evangelical balance in the Baptist
personality has emerged more recently, this time from a shift in the social
model for church institutions. From the late nineteenth century on, the
Southern Baptist Convention and its churches have steadily taken on the
business model as a pattern for church life. Evangelism and missions have
become a "business." Church structures and programs have all been
geared to the one great end, the "salvation of souls" or "soul winning."
Southern Baptists have gotten caught up in this enterprise with ever-
heightening fervor, sometimes to the point of obscuring and threatening
characteristic Baptist concern for voluntarism. I would envision the
following scenario for this.

World War I opened an era of optimism which was reflected in the
churches as well as in the society as a whole. In 1919 Southern Baptists,
heretofore struggling financially but now embued with vigor in the world
mission drive, began a campaign to raise $75,000,000 within a five-year
period. This proved to be a crucial step along the path toward a huge
forward thrust in the work of evangelism and missions. They pledged

---

[25]See ibid., pp. 176-79.

$92,000,000, but, because of the depression, collected only $56,000,000. That failure mattered little, however, for the important thing was that the campaign gave them an idea. The idea resulted in 1925 in the Cooperative Program, which is, more than any other factor, the key to the huge programming effort of the SBC. The Cooperative Program has been important for more than the program, however; it also has united the diverse constituency of the SBC in a tangible way.

During this same period, the business model, which was becoming so powerful in American society, increasingly gripped the imagination of Southern Baptists as a model for church life. Most Southern Baptists, of course, are not self-conscious of the impact of this model. Actually it may not obtrude noticeably into their worship or some other aspects of their life, but it dominates the overall pattern nonetheless, and it brings in its train some dangers for voluntarism, above all, in forcing both persons and programs to fit snugly the corporate pattern.

First, *the model affected the SBC superstructure.* In 1917 Southern Baptists created an Executive Committee, which was responsible for the coordination of the programming effort of the convention. They employed an executive secretary to implement the decisions of this committee as their concern for efficiency grew. Following World War II, as American enterprise flourished, Southern Baptists developed their programs more and more on business lines. In the fifties they hired Booz, Allen and Hamilton, a consultative firm on business operations, to study the operation of various boards and agencies. This resulted in further structuring along corporation lines. Southern Seminary, for instance, employed Booz, Allen and Hamilton in 1956 and again in 1966. The result has been several restructurings to bring the Seminary from the school model where the president functioned as chairman of the faculty to the small university model where he presides over a corporation. The operation is now divided into four areas: academic, business, development, and student affairs. Heading these departments are vice presidents. Below them are a number of supervisors, and below them an elaborate network of "employees."

The adoption of the business model at the national level was paralleled by its adoption, often more slowly, at the state, associational, and congregational levels. I will not elaborate on the development of state or associational organization because it paralleled SBC development so closely. *At the congregational level* the process moved forward somewhat haltingly because more Southern Baptist churches were and are in rural areas or small towns. Many small rural congregations still operate very much as they did in the mid-nineteenth century. As Southern Baptists have concentrated increasingly in the cities, however, this reluctance to opt for the business model has weakened. Now ninety percent of the churches use it with considerable effectiveness.

A rationale for the application of the business model came from Gaines S. Dobbins, onetime professor of Sunday School Pedagogy and later Dean of the School of Religious Education at Southern Seminary. In 1923 Dobbins published a book entitled *The Efficient Church*. Subsequently he pushed the adoption of business techniques in other writings, for example, *The Church Book* and *Building Better Churches*, always updating them as the business model changed.

Among other practices which came out of this was an exacting system of record keeping. For the Sunday school, for example, an eight-point record-system was developed, checking key items emphasized: being present, bringing Bibles, reading assigned lessons, giving to the Church systematically, staying for worship, and so forth. For Training Union a six-point system was developed—attending, reading the Bible daily, staying for evening worship, participating in the program, and so forth. For the overall organization of the Church an emphasis was placed on recording data about attendance, participation, contributions, decisions, and other matters. The net result was, as Dobbins learned in early experiments in Louisville, an improvement in all these categories. Keeping records primed the pump, as it were, and got many church programs flowing in a steady stream.

Since Dobbins's heyday, the business model has become the generally accepted model in most urban situations. The function of larger churches may be caricatured as follows: The members form a corporation. They elect a Board (of deacons) and entrust them with the direction of the corporation. The Board seeks an executive (the pastor). They offer him $30,000 a year plus a housing allowance, car allowance, book allowance, retirement, and various other benefits. If other corporations (churches) compete, the Board may raise the salary and/or benefits to assure that they keep a good executive. The Board puts pressure on the executive to produce documentable results—X-baptisms, Y-additions by letter, Z-contributions. If the latter fails to meet expectations, they put pressure on him. If he cannot improve, they bring the matter to the attention of the stockholders, and he may get fired or eased out in some way. Usually some effort is made to reduce the amount of embarrassment, often by offering continued salary for a time. To assure success, the executive puts on a major advertising campaign. He starts a busing program to increase attendance, sending buses in a fifty-mile radius around the church. He gives incentives to bus drivers for securing the most riders. The bus drivers give candy bars and balloons to the kiddies and place five-dollar bills under certain seats. The executive advertises on radio and TV. He promises money-back satisfaction: "Jesus will meet every need." Thus flourishes the corporation.

The use of this model naturally poses serious questions.[26] In terms of goals and objectives set by Southern Baptists, however, it has proven successful. Admittedly it might not have worked so well in the industrialized North as it did in the rural South, but the pragmatic character of it has probably made it adaptable in most American settings. This can be seen in Southern Baptist growth since about 1900. The following chart should help to illustrate the actual progress of the corporation during these years.

Year	Churches	Members	Offering	Sunday School Enrollment	Foreign Mission-aries	Home Mission-aries
1900	19,558	1,657,996	3,456,014	670,569	102	811
1910	23,248	2,332,464	10,424,486	1,248,116	273	1,047
1920	27,444	3,149,346	34,882,082	1,926,610	417	1,656
1930	23,731	3,850,278	37,489,021	2,839,183	423	116
1940	25,259	5,104,327	40,359,038	3,590,374	446	391
1950	27,788	7,079,889	197,242,154	5,024,553	803	754
1960	32,251	9,731,591	480,608,972	7,383,550	1,480	2,035
1970	34,360	11,629,880	892,255,918	7,290,447	2,634	2,222
1980	35,831	13,606,808	2,315,149,038	7,433,405	3,057	2,970

The remarkable success of Southern Baptists in this century has not happened without cost, especially in the way of erosion of their concern for voluntarism. In the traditional Southern states, from Texas eastwards to the Atlantic coast, Southern Baptists have staked out a clear claim,

---

[26]I have discussed potential problems in several writings. See "Southern Baptists: A Concern for Experiential Conversion," in *Where the Spirit Leads*, ed. Martin E. Marty (Atlanta: John Knox Press, 1980), pp. 137-48.

what Martin Marty calls an "Empire,"[27] county by county. They no longer exhibit strong minority perceptions about religious liberty or the separation of church and state. To be sure, they give occasional lip service to these in conventions and participate in the Baptist Joint Committee on Public Affairs or other organizations devoted to the preservation of religious freedoms. Many, however, take this part of their heritage very lightly. At best Southern Baptists find themselves caught in compromises and contradictions vis-á-vis their heritage. Voluntarism and evangelicalism *are again* under stress.

---

[27]Jackson W. Carroll, Douglas W. Johnson, and Martin E. Marty, *Religion in America: 1950 to the Present* (New York: and so forth: Harper & Row, 1979), p. 53.

Chapter Three

Baptists and Evangelicals
—What Is the Difference?

Those who know me and my ecumenical outlook will recognize that I have experienced considerable pain in preparing this chapter. Among Southern Baptists you will find few who come closer to meriting the title of "ecumaniac" than I. For many years I have worked hard to open up ecumenical dialogue and to lead Southern Baptists toward responsible participation in world Christianity.

In this chapter, however, I may appear to be working at cross purposes with myself, for I am calling for a sharpening of the distinction between Baptists and other Christians. Stated another way, I am saying, we must *think* Baptist. By that I mean we must become so conscious of our self-identity that we can differentiate ourselves with conviction and clarity from those who call themselves "evangelical" Christians.

Why focus on Evangelicals? Why not other Christian groups which have appealed for great ecumenical involvement of Southern Baptists? The answer to that is, because we are in grave danger of letting our association with Evangelicals and Evangelicalism of a particular type obscure and even obliterate voluntarist perceptions which stand most at the center of our life together as Baptists, and those are the perceptions which best represent our *raison d'être* and our contribution to world Christianity and to modern civilization. It is self-evident, I think, that we do not face the same challenge from other denominations. They have well-established identities which we will not likely confuse with our own. The more they diverge from us in ethos and outlook, the easier it is for us to say, "We are not that." We face no danger, for instance, of confusing ourselves with Roman Catholics, Episcopalians, or Orthodox. We don't even run much risk with Protestants who are fairly close to us in history, theology, and polity—Disciples, other Baptists, and so forth. No—we confront a danger chiefly with this nebulous and ill-defined group called Evangelicals with whom we are often classified by non-Baptist observers. They are too much like us in too many ways, or, conversely, we are too like them in too many ways. Many, perhaps most, Southern Baptists can't tell the difference. Meantime, Evangelicals are infusing their outlook deeper and deeper into Southern Baptist life.

The point I want to make emphatically is that being able to tell the difference is absolutely critical for Southern Baptists if they wish to retain one of the two major strains in their Baptist heritage. Maybe we should not try. Maybe we should say that we have made our contribution and can now immolate ourselves on the pyre of evangelical success. Some Southern Baptists seem to be saying that, or, if not saying it, to believe it. If you are among those, do not count me in your camp. I and my house still see a mission for Baptists quite distinct from and at critical points set over against the mission Evangelicals set for themselves.

Baptists and Evangelicals: What is the difference? Both of us go back to the Protestant Reformers. Both of us commit ourselves to the Scriptures. Both of us have inherited a zeal for evangelical conversion. But make no mistake about it, we come from different wombs. Evangelicals are the descendants of the late sixteenth and early seventeenth century Protestant Scholastics. They are the children of English and American Millenarians and Fundamentalists of the late nineteenth and early twentieth centuries. As such, they let nothing stand above what they consider the objective Word of God found in the Scriptures.

Baptists, by contrast, are the descendants of the persecuted and harassed dissenters of the seventeenth century who came forth from the womb crying for liberty. They are the children of refugees who fled from the European continent to these shores to found here a society in which there would be no restriction to conscience, no stiffling of freedom to propagate their faith, no circumscribing of faith or practice, and no religious test for public office. As such, they have insisted that faith must be free and voluntary if it is to be genuine and responsible faith, that there is no objective word apart from uncoerced human response.

Old Evangelicals and New Evangelicals

In demonstrating my point in a conclusive way, my first challenge is to define who Evangelicals are, and this is not an easy assignment. Today one may hear three general nuances. The term is applied (1) to Lutherans, especially in Europe; (2) to Protestants who emphasize personal conversion or "heart religion" (a broad view); and (3) to those preoccupied with orthodoxy. The third group, however, has laid special claim to the word, as evidenced by the way the public media use it, and that is the group I will focus on in this paper. At one time the name was used more or less interchangeably with the name Fundamentalist, but that is not accurate any longer. Evangelicals have split. One group still retains the essential identity of the Fundamentalists of the 1920s and 1930s. The other group has chosen to call themselves Neo-Evangelicals. Many who belonged to the fundamentalist movement mediate between these two groups, being sympathetic with some points made by the new Evangelicals but not wanting to cut their ties with the "old" ones.

What is the difference between the new and the old in Evangelicalism? The term "new evangelicalism" was first coined by Harold J. Ockenga, President of Gordon-Conwell Seminary, in an address delivered at Fuller Seminary in 1948. Ockenga defined it in terms of a break with three movements.

> The new evangelicalism breaks first with neo-orthodoxy because it accepts the authority of the Bible as a plenarily inspired Bible which is historically trustworthy and authentic. The new evangelical breaks also with the modernist because he embraces the full orthodox system as opposed to that which the modernist accepts. He breaks with the fundamentalist in that he believes the Biblical teaching must apply to the social scene as well as to the individual man.[1]

For obvious reasons it is Fundamentalism which comes in for the closest attention, for Neo-Evangelicalism is an outgrowth of it. John F. Walvoord posited four points of opposition of Neo-Evangelicalism to Fundamentalism: (1) to its separationism, (2) to its anti-intellectualism, (3) to its anti-social character and its indifference to contemporary issues, and

---

[1] "The New Evangelicalism," *The Park Street Spire*, February 1948, pp. 4-5. Summary of Robert P. Lightner, *Neo-Evangelicalism* (Findlay, Ohio: Dunham Publishing Co., n.d.), pp. 4-5.

(4) to its controversial character.[2]

The most thoroughgoing case for the new Evangelicalism was made by Edward John Carnell, late professor and president of Fuller Seminary, in his book *The Case for Orthodox Theology*. Carnell contended that Fundamentalism had become a mentality—rigid, intolerant, doctrinaire—and not a movement. He accused it of not keeping true to the classic creeds. He criticized its substitution of dispensationalism for the creeds, its intellectual stagnation, and its negative ethic. Further, he said, it elevates evangelism too much at the expense of charity and social concern. As a solution to the problems of Fundamentalism, Carnell proposed: (1) disowning both Modernism and Fundamentalism; (2) applying orthodox Christianity to the theological confusion of the world by realignment with the biblical theology movement and penetration of the ecumenical movement; (3) embracing creedal Christianity (that is, the historic creeds); (4) returning to positive preaching; (5) overcoming minority group attitudes; (6) bearing the marks of a true disciple— especially love (thus reducing negativism); (7) returning to the classical view of the Church, that is, a non-separatist one—(a) remaining in the fellowship which gave one birth, (b) judging the claims of a church by official creeds or confessions and not by the lives of its members, (c) separating only for *eviction or apostasy* by departing from the gospel in confession and doctrinal statements; (8) developing a fresh and pervasive concept of the Christian life; (9) broadening concern for individuals to include social implications (war, racial hatred, liquor traffic, exploitation of labor and management); (10) creating a Christian university to go beyond the existing evangelical educational facilities, a "supradenominational" school—to penetrate American Christianity and regain a place for young people searching for a Christ-centered college, to prepare missionary workers, to equip teachers and leaders to uphold and defend the faith, and to compete with secular universities.[3]

In these comments we need to pay particular attention to the non-separating character of the new Evangelicalism, for in that lies a clue to its penetration into mainline denominations such as the Southern Baptist Convention. In most other points the new Evangelicalism is not radically different from the old. What is more problematic for us, it has given birth

---

[2]Preface to Lightner, *Neo-Evangelicalism.*

[3]Edward John Carnell, *The Case for Orthodox Theology* (Philadelphia: Westminster Press, 1959), pp. 113-38.

to the church growth movement, on which many Southern Baptists have seized with élan, which relies on a highly authoritarian model standing at cross purposes with Baptist voluntarism and threatening to destroy it. To this I will return later.

The Nature and Roots of Evangelicalism

What I want to do now is to let a respected Evangelical, Bernard Ramm, define "Evangelical" and indicate its historical rootage. From there we can proceed to differentiate Baptist from Evangelical with reference both to nature and roots.

Ramm uses the word Evangelical to refer both to Fundamentalists and to Evangelicals. Though confessing the difficulty of giving a neat definition, he emerges with the following:

> In the most general sense evangelical Christianity refers to that version of Christianity which places the priority of the Word and Act of God over the faith, response, or experiences of men. Concretely this means the supremacy and authority of the Word of God (as a synonym for all the revelations of God, written or unwritten) *over* all human philosophies or religions. Truth in the garments of theology is prior to, and more fundamental than, faith or experience.[4]

Stated in terms of classical theology, evangelicals assign priority to scriptures and creeds as the objective Word of God over against the response of believers as a subjective Word. They place *fides quae creditur* ("the faith which one believes") above *fides qua creditur* ("the faith by which one believes").

Ramm discerns the literary heritage of Evangelicals in the writings of the Protestant Reformers (especially Luther and Calvin), in the great creedal statements of their time, and especially in the major works of seventeenth century Protestant scholastics. Against charges of dated theology and deadening orthodoxy he defends the third period as one of "great Protestant orthodoxy" (p. 53). He makes special mention of Francis Turretin, whose *Institutio Theologiae Elencticae* (1688-1700) was employed for a long time at Princeton as the standard textbook of Protestant theology. From this period, Ramm adds, Evangelicals get: (1)

---

[4]Bernard Ramm, *The Evangelical Heritage* (Waco, Texas: Word Books, 1973), p. 13. A more elaborate review of definitions of the word may be found in Robert E. Webber, *Common Roots* (Grand Rapids: Zondervan Publishing House, 1978), pp. 25-38.

"the theological continuity of Protestant orthodoxy" (all the early and Protestant creeds); (2) "the passion to be biblical"; and (3) "the goal of precision in theology." In summary, he concludes that "the modern Evangelical is the distant heir of Protestant Orthodoxy." He observes further that Evangelicals desire "to preserve the best of this tradition and add all the modern correctives necessary" (p. 63).

Protestant orthodoxy emerged again in the twentieth century in Fundamentalism. In the meantime, however, it suffered a severe blow in the Enlightenment of the seventeenth century. The Enlightenment brought direct attacks on orthodoxy. These included: (1) severe critical treatment of biblical history; (2) literary criticism of Scriptures; (3) substitution of science for Scriptures; (4) suspicion of the supernatural; (5) replacement of revelation by reason and philosophy; (6) erosion or rejection of the doctrines of original sin and human depravity; (7) rejection of the orthodox explanation of evil; (8) repudiation of the idea of dogma; and (9) ethical critique of the Scriptures.

Ramm, whose position would lean toward the neo-evangelical end of the spectrum, would make room in Evangelicalism for a cautious response to the critique of orthodoxy by the Enlightenment. He proposes: (1) coming to terms with scientific history; (2) dealing with science; (3) not ignoring biblical criticism; (4) following the standards of research and scholarship set by the Enlightenment; (5) taking seriously the intrusion of false cultural assumptions in theology (for example, leaving out hell); and (6) responding to the Enlightenment claim that Christian faith has to be restated for each generation if we are to communicate with it. "To be modern and yet biblical; to be biblical and yet contemporary;" he concludes, "that's the rub" (p. 73).

Protestant orthodoxy received a second blow from Liberalism, defined chiefly by F. D. E. Schleiermacher, and it was against this that Fundamentalists and Evangelicals have set themselves. Schleiermacher's chief contention, according to Ramm, was that "*all of the dogmas of orthodox Lutheranism can be restated in a modern acceptable way, and what cannot be restated can be discarded*" (p. 78). As defined by Kenneth Cauthen, Protestant Liberalism emphasized three themes which raised doubts about the older orthodoxy—continuity, autonomy, and dynamism. Emphasis on *continuity* between God, humanity, and creation precipitated questions about: (1) the dichotomy between natural and supernatural; (2) miracles; (3) special revelation; (4) depravity of humankind; (5) the incarnation, conception of the Holy Spirit and virgin birth, sacrificial death, bodily resurrection, and ascension into heaven; (6) the fatherhood of God and the brotherhood of man; (7) eschatology; (8) the dichotomy between saved and lost; and (9) the dichotomy between the Church and the world. Emphasis on *human autonomy* introduced skepticism about special revelation and accentuated human experience (à la Schleiermacher). This shift had other consequences: (1) seeing scripture as normative only in context, (2) reducing dogma to a secondary place, (3) placing reason and intuition above revelation, (4) admitting only theological statements capable of experiential response, and (5) shoving dogma out to the edge of the Church's life and replacing it with service. Emphasis on *dynamism* led to: (1) relativizing of theological systems; (2) emphasis on a social gospel gradually transforming society; (3) belief in an "upward fall" of humankind by way of evolution; (4) emphasis on the immanence of God; (5) questioning of the uniqueness and finality of the Christian faith; (6) belief in progressive revelation; (7) belief in progressive eschatology and doubts about the second coming, millenium, and so forth; and (8) belief in the natural origins of Christianity.

Ramm notes that fundamentalist response to Liberalism surfaced at two different levels. One was that of fundamentalist ministers, the other that of learned theologians such as Kuyper, Lecerf, Orr, Warfield, and Machen. Fundamentalists, above all, resented ridiculing and discarding of fundamental doctrines by historical criticism, and extension of the doctrine of evolution to biblical religion.

Ramm cannot be viewed as a right wing Evangelical or Fundamentalist. Though critical of neo-orthodoxy, he can express appreciation for several facets: (1) its attack on Liberalism for neglect of the Bible, empty preaching, oversimplification of christology, rank individual sin, failure to advance theology beyond the Reformation, and inadequate ethics based on philosophy rather than the Bible; (2) its summons to the Scriptures as the source and authority for Christian theology (*scriptura sola*); (3) its appreciation for the reformers—not merely Luther and Calvin but lesser ones as well; (4) its interaction with the whole history of theology; (5) its (especially Barth's) detailed critique of Catholic theology; and (6) its enrichment of theology. Ramm is unhappy, however, with (1) the antipathy of Barth and Brunner to Protestant orthodoxy and evangelical theology; (2) an imbalance of emphasis on revelation rather than on inspiration; (3) too much attention to making scriptures relevant with consequent danger to doctrine; (4) Barth's overemphasis on christology;

(5) overemphasis on love and a corresponding de-emphasis on the wrath of God; (6) subjective rather than objective view of the atonement; and (7) situation ethics.

Ramm concludes his effort to define Evangelicalism with a statement of its character from both a negative and a positive perspective. Contrary to popular impressions, he contends, it is: (1) "not obscurantistic" with reference to biblical criticism or science; (2) "not a literalism" holding "a flat view of the Scriptures" (pp. 125, 126); (3) not "reactionary or quietistic or exclusively personal or conservative in ethics" (p. 126); (4) not convinced "that the final or near-final statement of Christian theology has been achieved" (p. 128) but allows for development; (5) not essentially committed to a propositional view of revelation; and (6) "not anti-cultural, world-denying, or inherently pessimistic" (p. 132). He admits that some Evangelicals or Fundamentalists may hold such views, but these do not belong to the essence of evangelical faith. He notes numerous divisions among Evangelicals: (1) Calvinists and Arminians; (2) pre-, post-, and a-millennialists; (3) those who make inerrancy and those who make inspiration the biggest issue; (4) differences over which issues are not critical (*adiaphora*); (5) differences of strategy for combatting modernism; (6) varied views on the Bible and science; (7) different assessments of the charismatic movement; and (8) variety caused by the generation gap.

In conclusion, Ramm lists the following guiding convictions for Evangelicalism: (1) *"that Christianity is one and not many and is not capable of continuous radical reinterpretation"* (p. 140); (2) *"Christological and incarnational"* (p. 143); (3) *"that faith is the fundamental response of the sinner to the gospel and is the foundation of Christian experience"* (p. 144) with corresponding wariness regarding a church state and social involvement; (4) *"that theology will have genuine dignity if it retains an important and non-negotiable element of the objective of its doctrine of revelation"* (p. 146); (5) *"that the real touchstone of a theology is its spiritual power not necessarily its intellectual shrewdness, or sophistication, or learning"* (p. 146); and (6) *"the absolute distinction between saved and lost"* as a governing principle (p. 148). The future of evangelical theology, Ramm suggests, will depend on: (1) thorough knowledge of the Scriptures; (2) mastery of the "inner structure of evangelical theology;" (3) knowledge of the cultural climate; (4) diligent study of the linguistics and communications, rethinking the theory of inspiration and revelation; and (5) rethinking the manner in which the church is related to the world.

Baptists Differentiated from Evangelicals

I have taken great care to let one of the most perceptive representatives of Evangelicalism define its nature, so that it might be presented in the best light. It would have been easy to have caricatured the movement by selecting a spokesperson from the fundamentalist fringe. By hearing a respected theologian, we will not expose the worst features, but we can see the main tenets clearly enough outlined to allow us to differentiate Baptists from Evangelicals.

From the historical study of the second chapter, you will recognize that we Baptists have about as much difficulty defining who we are as do the Evangelicals. We possess some advantage in having denominational structures and certain official statements which give us loose definitions. But we too can find about as many definitions as there are Baptists, which means that we have no way to establish our identity except through study of our history. And even expert historical study ends up being my interpretation versus somebody else's interpretation. Some people obviously possess better credentials for doing an interpretation than others, but, among Baptists, such credentials are not always recognized.

For the purpose of this paper I will approach the task of defining who we are by the negative route, namely, casting ourselves and our history as Baptists against Ramm's definition of Evangelicals and their history. Thus I will not again attempt to give a full definition or to narrate the main parts of our story. Here, in other words, I am simply trying to put Baptists in relief against the evangelical/fundamentalist movement and mentality.

Let me begin by trying a definition of Baptists which will distinguish us from Evangelicals as defined by Ramm. Counterpointing as closely as possible the points which he has made vis-à-vis Evangelicals, I would say that the name Baptist refers to *that version of Christianity which places the priority of voluntary and uncoerced faith or response to the Word and Act of God* over any supposed "objective" Word and Act of God. Concretely this means that faith or response can be considered authentic and responsible only if free and uncoerced. Authentic faith or experience is thus more fundamental than ecclesiastical dogmas to which are attached claims of ultimate authority. Stated in terms of classical theology, Baptists assign priority to the response of believers to the word of God over against the Scriptures and creeds presented as an objective Word of God. In other words, they question whether *fides quae creditur* means anything unless held in tension with *fides qua creditur*.

The difference between Baptists and Evangelicals at this critical juncture stems from their diverse heritages in the seventeenth century. Like Evangelicals, of course, Baptists have consistently claimed to go back to the Protestant Reformers—Calvin perhaps more than Luther. Unlike Evangelicals, however, they have not put a lot of stock into "the great creedal statements" of the Reformation or the major works of the seventeenth century Protestant scholastics. Quite to the contrary, they have frequently repudiated creeds as human contrivances and consistently insisted on the Scriptures alone as their "sole rule of faith and practice." While Evangelicals were drawing from the seventeenth century "the theological continuity of protestant orthodoxy," "the passion to be biblical," and "the goal of precision in theology," Baptists were extracting from it a suspicion of orthodoxy, a penchant for dissent and nonconformity, and a passion for voluntarism in religion. No two religious movements could have differed more from one another at this juncture than these—the Baptist and the Evangelical.

Some may be wondering where baptism, which would usually be cited in an identification of Baptists, comes in. Does it have anything to do with the items I have cited? I would answer: much in every way. Our Baptist emphasis on baptism of believers only (which I take to be our *key* concern and not mode) grows out of and epitomizes our forebears' deep dual but inseparable convictions about the singular authority of the scriptures and about voluntarism.

However many points of doctrine or practice Baptists disputed among themselves, they spoke with one voice in their conviction that they *followed* the scriptures in the practice of baptizing believers. To do otherwise, they said, would mean substitution of human traditions for "the divine and true witness of our Lord Christ and his apostles."[5] We can see in the way they interpreted the scriptures, however, that their religious and cultural situation markedly affected the way they viewed baptism in relation to salvation. As children of the Enlightenment, they interpreted salvation in a highly individualistic way and not in the corporatistic fashion characteristic of Anglicans, Roman Catholics, or

---

[5]Thomas Helwys, *The Mistery of Iniquity*, in *A Baptist Treasury*, ed. Sydnor L. Stealey (New York: Thomas Y. Crowell Co., 1958), p. 15.

even Reformed Protestants. The covenant, as Baptists conceived it, was one which necessitated individual decision. "Doth our Savior Christ say," Helwys asked, "that those with whome he hath made the new Covenant are they in whose mynds and harts he hath written his Law, whome he declares to be those, that believe and are baptized? And will you add unto the covenant of the Lord and say, it is made with the faithful, and their seed before they can beleeve?"[6]

Voluntarism was of the essence in such an understanding of covenant, and it was voluntarism which most set Baptists apart from those groups from which they sprang. We must remember that Baptists came forth from the womb suffering all the birth pangs of the late sixteenth and early seventeenth centuries. This period was one wracked by religious wars and persecution. In France there were eight religious wars—1562 to 1594. In Germany was the Thirty Years' War—1618 to 1648. In England there was the Civil War—1642 to 1646. Only Holland and the American colonies offered refuge for persons distressed of conscience for religious reasons, but even in America dissenters soon faced disappointment. Like many others, therefore, Baptists were born crying for liberty. It should come as no surprise that they penned some of the most far-reaching and eloquent statements calling for freedom. They had more to lose from constriction and more to gain from freedom than any other group save Quakers.

Many of the pleas of early Baptists for liberty of conscience have been cited already so that I do not need to go over that ground here. I would like, however, to point up the contrast between Baptists and Evangelicals by remarking on the way the authors of the second London Confession handled the Westminster Confession's article "Of Christian Liberty, and Liberty of Conscience," for what they did in their revision indicates in an unmistakable way what differentiates the two vis-à-vis orthodoxy. What Baptists added to or deleted from the Westminster Confession separates them by miles from Evangelicals, who would see the Confession as one of their mainstays.

First of all, the Second London Confession inserted a new chapter "Of the Gospel, and of the extent of the Grace thereof" just before the one on religious liberty. The last article of this chapter plugged the Baptist emphasis upon experience.

---

[6]Ibid.

4. Although the Gospel be the only outward means, of revealing *Christ*, and saving Grace; and is, as such, abundantly sufficient thereunto; yet that men who are dead in Trespasses, may be born again, Quickened or Regenerated; there is moreover necessary, an effectual, insuperable work of the Holy *Spirit*, upon the whole Soul, for the producing in them a new spiritual Life; without which no other means will effect their Conversion unto God.[7]

Is this article not saying, "Coercion will not produce conversion, but only the Spirit acting freely?"

As to the chapter "Of Christian Liberty, and Liberty of Conscience," the Second London Confession introduced only one significant alteration in the first three sections. It repeated verbatim the strong affirmation of liberty of conscience contained in Article 1:

God alone is Lord of the Conscience, and hath left it free from the Doctrines and Commandments of men which are in any thing contrary to his Word, or not contained in it. So that to believe such Doctrines, or obey such Commands out of Conscience, is to betray true liberty of Conscience; and the requiring of an implicit Faith, and absolute and blind Obedience, is to destroy Liberty of Conscience, and Reason also.[8]

In Article 3, however, there was introduced a twist which reflects again the Baptist preoccupation with voluntarism. Where the Westminster Confession read "They who, upon pretense of Christian liberty, do practice any sin, or cherish any lust, do thereby destroy the end of Christian liberty; . . . ," the Second London Confession read: "They who upon pretense of Christian Liberty do practice any sin, or cherish any sinful lust; *as they do thereby pervert the main design of the Grace of the Gospel to their own Destruction; so* they wholly destroy the end of *Christian* Liberty."[9] What is the implication of the addition? Does it not mean that we err to think of ourselves as the ultimate judges of our fellow mortals?

---

[7]W. L. Lumpkin, *Baptist Confessions of Faith* (Philadelphia: Judson Press, 1959), p. 278-79.

[8]*Creeds of the Churches*, ed. John H. Leith (Garden City, N. Y.: Doubleday Anchor Books, 1963), pp. 215 ff.

[9]Lumpkin, *Baptist Confessions*, p. 280; my italics.

Though additions require considerable interpretation to establish how the Baptist perspective varies from the evangelical one, the Baptist deletion of Article 4 leaves no doubt. The deleted article stated:

> IV. And because the power which God had ordained, and the liberty which Christ hath purchased, are not intended by God to destroy, but mutually to uphold and preserve one another; they who, upon pretense of Christian liberty, shall oppose any lawful power, or the lawful exercise of it, whether it be civil or ecclesiastical, resist the ordinance of God. And for their publishing of such opinions, or maintaining of such practices, as are contrary to the light of nature, or to the known principles of Christianity, whether concerning faith, worship, or conversation; or to the power of godliness; or such erroneous opinions or practices, as either in their own nature, or in the manner of publishing or maintaining them, are destructive to the external peace and order which Christ hath established in the Church; they may lawfully be called to account, and proceeded against by the censures of the Church, and by the power of the Civil Magistrate.[10]

To catch the full impact of this deletion, we need quote again only a couple of Baptist statements about liberty. One is Thomas Helwys's preface to *The Mistery of Iniquity* addressed to King James I in 1612:

> The King is a mortall man, and not God[;] therefore hath no power over ye immortall soules of his subjects, to make lawes and ordinances for them, and to set spirituall Lords over them.

The other is Roger Williams's contention that

> . . . It is the will and command of God, that (since the coming of his Sonne the Lord Jesus) a permission of the most Paganish, Jewish, Turkish, or Antichristian consciences and worships, bee granted to all mean in all Nations and Countries: and they are onely to bee fought against with that Sword which is only (in Soule matters) able to conquer, to wit, the Sword of Gods Spirit, The Word of God.[11]

---

[10]Leith, *Creeds*, p. 216.

[11]List of propositions discussed in *The Bloudy Tenent of Persecution for Cause of Conscience*, in *A Baptist Treasury*, p. 17.

Since the Seventeenth Century

All of us will recognize that Baptists, like Evangelicals, have evolved a lot since the seventeenth century. At times our paths have crossed. However, we have not been in danger of confusing our identities until at least the twentieth century. The fact is, the high points of our two stories have not meshed any more closely than our beginnings. Let me call attention to two major divergencies.

(1) *Where Evangelicals regarded the Enlightenment as an enemy, Baptists came to know it as in many respects a friend.* They appreciated two things in particular. One was the Enlightenment emphasis upon experience in religion. In America especially the Enlightenment and the Great Awakening went hand in hand. Jonathan Edwards, the theologian of the Awakening, borrowed much from John Locke in his interpretation of religious affections.[12] Baptists had much reason to appreciate the Awakening, for, while they had barely gotten started prior to it, now they suddenly shot forward. By 1820, as we have seen, they had become the largest Protestant denomination in America.

Baptists appreciated the Enlightenment also because it was a major ally in the struggle for religious liberty. By the end of the English Civil War and the Thirty Years' War in Europe many persons could no longer see justification for the dogmatism in religion which produced religious wars and persecutions. Baptists, a persecuted minority themselves, could scarcely do anything but welcome voices such as that of Locke calling for toleration. In the American colonies they cast their lot with the colonial cause in the hope they would gain by independence. They were not disappointed. Their service in the colonial army gained them new respect in the eyes of their countrymen and new allies in their search for liberty. Consequently the pleas of Baptist apostles of freedom such as Isaac Backus and John Leland were heard in a way they would not have been heard before the Revolution.

(2) *Where Evangelicals counted Schleiermacher,* whom they regard as the father of Protestant Liberalism, *the bane of orthodoxy, Baptists could respond warmly to his emphasis upon "feeling" and his accentuation of soul competency.* The most significant witness here is E. Y. Mullins. Mullins is often cited these days by Southern Baptist Fundamentalists as one of the conservators of their heritage, but they fail to reveal

---

[12]See Harold Simonson, *Jonathan Edwards: Theologian of the Heart* (Grand Rapids: William B. Eerdmans, 1974), pp. 23-29.

the heart of Mullins. He did write an essay for *The Fundamentals*, a collection of papers published in four volumes in 1917. His topic, however, did little to undergird the fundamentalist position; it was on "The Testimony of Christian Experience." Where other Fundamentalists were throwing science and philosophy out the window, Mullins was saying, "Science and philosophy are beginning to recognize the evidential value of Christian experience though they are very slow about it and very reluctant about it even yet, apparently because it is not as obvious to the sense as the facts of the physical world." Mullins proceeded to argue that "Christian experience, the experience of regeneration and conversion, of moral transformation through Christian agencies, has evidential value in several directions," in effect, reconciling Christianity and philosophy.[13] A few years later he steered a committee commissioned to frame *The Baptist Faith and Message* away from any explicit statement opposing evolution.

Much more importantly, Mullins reinterpreted the Baptist heritage along Schleiermacherian lines in *The Axioms of Religion* published in 1908. In doing so, he attempted quietly to lay to one side the Princeton theology which had governed the thinking of his predecessors at Southern Seminary. You will not need to be reminded that he made "soul competency" a key article. In *The Christian Religion in Its Doctrinal Expression*, published in 1917, Mullins again gave Schleiermacher a major role in his interpretation of Christian theology in experiential terms. He ranked Schleiermacher alongside Clement of Alexandria and Augustine precisely because of this emphasis. Though he could register mild disagreement with his mentor, Mullins was deeply indebted to him for his entire theological perspective.

The Sources of Confusion

Until the twentieth century, Baptists have had little difficulty distinguishing themselves from persons or groups whom Evangelicals claim as their forebears. In the past several decades, however, the situation has changed. During the 1920s and 1930s, Baptists in the North passed through a period of crisis which eventuated in two splits in the Northern Baptist Convention, now known as the American Baptist Churches. During the past two decades, Southern Baptists have encountered similar difficulty. What are the sources of the confusion?

---

[13]E. Y. Mullins, "The Testimony of Christian Experience," in *The Fundamentals* (Los Angeles: The Bible Institute, 1917), IV: 314.

One source is the *overt, organized effort of some to spread "Evangelicalism."* No such effort existed until the development of the fundamentalist reaction to modern biblical criticism, the teaching of evolution, and the social gospel movement. Rooted in the dispensationalist theology of J. N. Darby,[14] Fundamentalism took wing in the 1920s. It was disseminated through Bible conferences, evangelism conferences, Bible institutes, publishing houses, fellowships, radio preaching, faith missions, specialized evangelism, and the Scofield Reference Bible. Since it did not have the support of denominational structure, it depended especially on the Bible institutes—for instance, Moody Bible Institute—for coordination. Development of the Bible institute, Ernest Sandeen has observed, allowed the Fundamentalists to break away from denominational ties without cutting themselves off from some base of operations.[15]

Southern Baptists should be quite conscious of the continuation of this same pattern. Two such institutes—Criswell Center for Biblical Studies and Mid-America Seminary—are the headquarters for the effort to disseminate Fundamentalism and eventually to take control of the Southern Baptist Convention. Many other activities supplement what is done by these institutes. For a long time, for instance, state and southwide evangelism conferences have served as a platform for Fundamentalists to plant in the minds of Southern Baptists the seeds of suspicion on which they now capitalize to take control of Convention institutions. Frequently Southern Baptist agencies and institutions have supplied other platforms.

There is surely considerable irony in the way Evangelicals have succeeded in confusing Baptist identity. They have trumpeted their main line—about the "objective Word of God" as contained in an inerrant Bible—loud enough and long enough to gain many converts. As they have gained some following, they have turned around to accuse Baptists of teaching, preaching, or acting contrary to our "historic Baptist position." Surely it is curious to hear those same "Baptists" arguing for an amendment to the United States Constitution which would prohibit the Supreme Court from deciding whether certain types of prayer in public

---

[14]See Ernest R. Sandeen, *The Roots of Fundamentalism: British and American Millenarianism, 1800-1930* (Chicago: University of Chicago Press, 1970).

[15]Ibid., p. 241. See also George M. Marsden, *Fundamentalism and American Culture: The Shaping of Twentieth Century Evangelicalism, 1870-1925* (New York: Oxford University Press, 1980), pp. 127-32 passim.

schools violate our first amendment guarantees of separation of church and state.

A second source of the confusion is *the electronic church*. By some estimates the major TV churches reach 47% of the adult viewing public on Sundays. By contrast, only about 42% attend public worship.[16] "There is virtually no home in the United States into which the electronic church cannot send its songs, sermons, and appeals in generous measure," Jeffrey K. Hadden and Charles E. Swann have observed. "Merely to contemplate its potential power is staggering."[17] Exactly what effect the electronic evangelists such as Jerry Falwell have is difficult to measure. The jury is still deliberating, for instance, the Moral Majority's impact in the recent election. However, no one can dispute that Fundamentalists or Evangelicals have a firm grip on the media. "Even the most casual observer," Hadden has said, "can note that the airwaves are dominated by evangelicals. . . ."[18] And one thing is sure: their theology leans decidedly toward Fundamentalism. "If you find anyone to the right of me," Falwell once remarked, "tell me and I'll move over."

A third source of confusion between Baptists and Evangelicals is *the church growth movement*. The father of this movement is Donald McGavran, a professor at Fuller Seminary. Now twenty-five years old, the movement has gotten much attention in denominations such as the SBC. Burning as they do to make converts, some Southern Baptists have swallowed the church growth approach hook, line, and sinker. The obvious attraction of this approach is that, on the short term, it gets evangelistic results, and results are what please Southern Baptists. The key to its effectiveness, however, is centralization of authority.[19] At the Southern Baptist Convention in Houston in 1979, a succession of pastors of large churches repeated the refrain: the pastor has to have the last word in everything.

This authoritarian model is now being put forth as the Baptist model. The quasi-independents who use it in their own local congregations are trying their best to expand it to associations, state conventions, and the

---

[16]William F. Fore, "There Is No Such Thing as a TV Pastor," in *TV Guide* (19 July 1980): 15.

[17]*Prime Time Preachers* (Reading, MA: Addison-Wesley Publishing Co., Inc., 1981), p. 8.

[18]Jeffrey K. Hadden, "Soul-Saving via Video," *Christian Century* (28 May 1980): 610.

[19]See Larry McSwain, "A Critical Appraisal of the Church Growth Movement," *Review and Expositor* 77 (Fall 1980): 532-33.

Southern Baptist Convention. They are using a contrived issue, "the battle for the Bible" (to use Harold Lindsell's phrase), to effect this goal. Inerrancy or infallibility of the Bible, however, is not the real issue. The real issue is whether pastors of a few jumbo-size churches can establish themselves as inerrant and infallible teachers and thus qualify for the kind of authority they want to exercise in the Southern Baptist Convention. The bottom line argument is neither theological nor historical but pragmatic: "Observe how we succeed? You can't argue with our success. If you follow the *other* model or models, you won't have this kind of success."

A fourth source of confusion lies in *the success of the Southern Baptist Convention itself*. By this time, as I noted earlier, Southern Baptists represent a Southern establishment. Concern about liberty has always been a *minority* concern. Small, oppressed groups are the ones who know and appreciate liberty. Groups which gain a plurality may easily forget pleas they once made. They take advantage of their circumstances to gain further advantage. Southern Baptists have joined the Moral Majority, rightly observing that separation of church and state should not mean separation of Christians from government but forgetting their heritage in some issues this group pushes. Thus, for instance, they may be found pressing for prayer in public schools. Would they want the same in Utah, a state which is 96% Mormon? Shades of the Puritan establishment in New England before the American Revolution!

Conclusion

Much could be added to fill out the picture I have sketched. It will not be difficult to see from what has been given how Evangelicalism threatens our most central and basic concerns as Baptists. It is quite clear that we are talking about an *essential* difference between the Baptist and the evangelical traditions. This difference boils down to an entirely different attitude toward human response to the Word of God. For Evangelicals the Word has such an objective character that human beings can impose it by force, if necessary, on other human beings. For Baptists this cannot be so. Nothing handled by human beings can have such an objective character that we, fallible human beings, can presume to impose it on others. To be valid, our response must be voluntary. It can never be coerced. The Word itself will win us. But it will never coerce.

Our Baptist commitment to this underlying principle has manifested itself in several ways. One is in efforts to guarantee the liberty of the individual. We have worked to insure liberty of conscience for every person—even liberty not to believe. But liberty of conscience is only a beginning. In the past tyrants have affirmed that principle and still persecuted. Consequently Baptists have labored also to guarantee freedom to organize and to propagate one's faith, however erroneous. Within their own congregations they have taken the view that no individual, pastor or any other, has any more authority than any other. Baptists have extended this thinking outwards toward society. They have adjudged the separation of church and state the best means for perserving liberty for all. None strove more mightily than Baptists to incorporate the First Amendment into the U. S. Constitution, saying that "Congress shall make no law respecting an establishment of religion, or prohibiting the free exercise thereof." No group has kept a more vigilant eye on possible violations.

Have we reached the point in our history when, filled with our visions of success, we no longer want to be Baptists? Have we reached the point where, fired by zeal for conversions, we will deny liberty to the individual? Have we reached the point where, wanting more effective means to achieve our goal, we will replace our egalitarian church model with an authoritarian one because the latter works better? Have we reached the point where, dominant in a geographical area, we will repudiate the separation of church and state as a way of conserving liberty for all? Some have. Do not number me among them.

Chapter Four

The Future of the Baptist Tradition

What is the future of the Baptist tradition in the Southern Baptist Convention? Prior to the annual meeting of the Convention in Los Angeles in June 1981, I would have given a more cautious and qualified answer to this question. This convention seemed to say, "We will be Baptists after all, and not Fundamentalists." Not that we can breathe easily even now, for those who have tried to turn the Southern Baptist Convention into a fundamentalist body will persist in their efforts. My personal hunch is that they will do so at least two or three years longer. Then, if they do not succeed in taking control, they will spin off or else be assimilated into the Convention's structures. Assimilation, however, is less likely than separation because of the extensive degree to which fundamentalist leaders have institutionalized their movement. When in the 1920s J. Frank Norris went so far in this direction, he chose about the only option he had, namely, the formation of his own organization, the Baptist Bible Fellowship International, to which Thomas Road Baptist Church in Lynchburg belongs.

Looking at the Baptist tradition from our present vantage point, I am cautiously optimistic. We may yet balance our Evangelicalism with our voluntarism sufficiently to deserve the name of Baptist. To do so, however, will require vigilance and effort on our part, for many forces threaten this balance. We must be dead sure we ourselves understand how central voluntarism is to our tradition and develop some means through which we involve the bulk of our constituency with it.

The Centrality of Voluntarism to the Baptist Tradition

How central has voluntarism been in our approach to the mission to which God has called us as Christians, particularly in the way we go about fulfilling the Great Commission? How essential is it for us in the future? Can it be accommodated in some way after these nearly four centuries of our history? Or must it remain as it is if we are to be and to go on being Baptists? Allow me first to define voluntarism.

What is Voluntarism? As a philosophical theory, voluntarism places the will above the intellect or reason. For Baptists, however, it has been more than an idea. It concerns the way we perceive God, the Holy Spirit, to work through the individual will in the development of the faith and life of believers. If you range denominations across a spectrum from voluntarist to its opposite, involuntarist, or as I prefer to designate it, intentionalist, you will find Baptists near the extreme voluntarist end alongside Quakers, and Roman Catholics on the extreme intentionalist end. Intentionalism considers the Spirit to work through composite structures—clergy and sacraments—and thus the Church assumes primary responsibility for the faith and life of believers.

The contrasting profiles for these approaches can be seen in a number of areas:

- Intentionalists are *pedobaptists*; voluntarists are *believer-baptists* or *just believers.*
- Intentionalists are *sacramentalists*; voluntarists are *non-* or *anti-sacramentalists.*
- Intentionalists are *liturgical*; voluntarists are *non-* or *anti-liturgical.*
- Intentionalists are *iconic*; voluntarists are *aniconic* or even *iconoclastic.*
- Intentionalists are *sacerdotalists*; voluntarists are *non-* or *anti-sacerdotalists.*
- Intentionalists are *institutionalists*; voluntarists are *experientialists.*
- Intentionalists are *creedalists*; voluntarists are *non-* or *anti-creedalists.*
- Intentionalists are *authoritarian*; voluntarists are *non-* or *anti-authoritarian.*
- Intentionalists favor *church-state alliance*; voluntarists, *church-state separation.*

That is the theory, and in their origins Baptists fitted the profile pretty well. With their emphasis on the Spirit they could be called "charismatics" in the broad sense of the term. Over several centuries, however, Baptists, especially Southern Baptists, have moved a long way from their voluntarist ancestors. Note these shifts among Southern Baptists on virtually every point of the profile:

- The average age for baptism is now eight years, whereas it was once eighteen or twenty, as a consequence of a better program of nurture.
- Though retaining the name ordinance and denying even symbolic importance to them, landmark Southern Baptists elevate baptism and the Lord's Supper to the level of sacraments by refusing to recognize those administered in other denominations.
- A Roman Catholic friend tells me that worship in many Southern Baptist churches is more formal than that in Roman Catholic counterparts.
- Even the most conservative now allow paintings or other images in their churches.
- Southern Baptists are highly institutionalized along modern corporate lines.
- All observers of Southern Baptist life can discern a radical tilt from an anti-creedal toward a creedal stance in theological matters.
- Finally, Southern Baptists frequently join those who step far over lines of separation between church and state.

What does this shift mean for us? Is it merely the inevitable consequence of a passing of time? Or does it mean we really question the viability of the voluntarist approach itself as a way of doing the calling of God? Does it mean we doubt whether God can work directly through the will of individuals to effect his purposes or whether, as the Catholic tradition has insisted through many centuries, the corporate body has to assume a dominant role? I ask these questions with a good deal of urgency, for many Southern Baptists seem now to answer them in the affirmative. An affirmative answer raises for me the still more urgent question: Has our voluntarist tradition a future?

Why Were Our Forebears Voluntarists? Before answering these important questions it will be helpful to discover why our forebears took the voluntarist route in their quest to do the will of God. Why did John Smyth, Thomas Helwys, John Bunyan, Roger Williams, and others repudiate the intentionalism of the medieval and protestant churches and opt for the voluntarism of their day at great cost to themselves?

One reason, perhaps the most self-evident, is that they were simply swimming with a powerful stream bubbling up out of the Renaissance in which individual self-consciousness again assumed a significant place. By the seventeenth century this stream had widened out to become a roaring river.

Our Baptist forefathers also stood in a better place than many of their contemporaries to see and to appreciate what was happening. Those who belonged to the lower socioeconomic strata as they did sensed its vibrations in their bones. They popped out of the womb kicking and screaming for liberty, and they were willing to pay any price—even life itself—to obtain this precious gift. None of those in the first generation, to be sure, lived to see the permanent establishment of religious liberty, but, Abraham-like, they looked longingly towards it and saluted it from afar.

Religious wars and persecutions which wracked Europe in those days sharpened all the more the already flaming hopes of the deprived and oppressed for freedom. Traumas such as these often generate heroic recklessness for a cause, and the sufferings of the seventeenth century do nothing to alter the general pattern.

In the last analysis, however, it was not external motives—the Enlightenment, class struggle, or wars and persecutions—but an internal one which had the most to do with the selection of the voluntary way as the way to effect holy obedience. It was a matter of obeying God rather than human beings!

In the first chapter, I cited the readiness of Bunyan to leave his family to fend for themselves and endure twelve and a half years in prison rather than place obedience to human beings before obedience to God. The more closely I examine the records of the period, the more I am driven to the conclusion that it was an outgrowth of this conviction: *to be authentic and responsible, faith must be free.* Coercion of any form (and remember that the first Baptists saw baptism of infants as a form of coercion), they concluded, takes away the element which most authenticates faith, namely, the spontaneous assent of the human will to God. *However ardently our forebear's hearts burned to win adherents, they knew that only those whom the Holy Spirit wooed came as wholly obedient children of God.* Chains and tongs and racks and water tortures do not produce saints.

This perspective peppers John Bunyan's writings. In his famous treatise *I Will Pray with the Spirit*, published a year or two after he first went to jail for refusal to stop preaching, Bunyan rejected all set forms of prayer, even the Lord's Prayer. According to Bunyan, prayer is "a sincere, sensible, affectionate pouring out of the heart or soul to God through Christ, in the strength and assistance of the Holy Spirit, . . . with submission, in Faith, to the will of God."[1] Set forms, he said, represented only "a little lip-labour and bodily exercise, mumbling over a few imaginary Prayers."[2] These would produce nothing. Only the Spirit acting on the individual will assure the proper *matter* or *manner* of prayer. Bunyan listed ten reasons for this, which together add up to the point that the Spirit alone can account for "a sincere, sensible, affectionate pouring out of their souls to God."[3] The Spirit alone can lift the heart up and keep it up before God. The Spirit alone can generate sensitivity to God's will. The Spirit alone can change and transform the human will.

The Viability of Voluntarism. Let us at this point return again to the question of the current viability of voluntarism. Is it still a workable approach to the goal of fulfilling the Great Commission? Or have we come to a new and radically different social setting which brings it seriously into question? Have we Southern Baptists been right in scooting over toward the intentionalist end of the scale, thus in effect opting for the Catholic tradition? In brief, shall we go on believing that the Holy Spirit moves principally through the individual will or shall we shift our confidence to the corporate and institutional?

Even though I am inclined by instinct, heritage, and present circumstances to shout, "On with voluntarism!" I am forced by lengthy reflection and study to reply with considerable caution. There are both theological and sociological aspects of this caution.

● *First, the theological caution.* While it is true that God communicates himself and his purpose through individuals, perhaps especially through individuals, this does not preclude his acting through corporate experience. To deny the corporate channel would be to shut our eyes to centuries of religious experience, especially that of the Jewish people. God is revealed as the One who makes a covenant with them as a people: "You have seen what I did to the Egyptians, and how I bore you on eagles' wings and brought you to myself. Now therefore, if you will obey my voice

---

[1] John Bunyan, *I Will Pray with the Spirit*, ed. Richard L. Greaves (Oxford: Clarendon Press, 1976), p. 235.
[2] Ibid., p. 239.
[3] Ibid., pp. 251-52.

and keep my covenant, you shall be my own possession among all peoples; for all the earth is mine, and you shall be to me a kingdom of priests and a holy nation" (Exod. 19:4-6, RSV).

Our forebears drew their perceptions of their relationship with God from the concept of a *new* covenant, a concept much more highly interiorized and individualized. They cited Jeremiah's version: "I will put my law within them, and I will write it upon their hearts; and I will be their God, and they shall be my people. And no longer shall each man teach his neighbor and each his brother, saying, 'Know the Lord,' for they shall all know me, from the least of them to the greatest, says the Lord;..." (Jer. 31:33-34, RSV). In their Enlightenment context the early Baptists could not grasp communal nuances of faith which Roman Catholics, Anglicans, and other Protestants may have legitimately claimed on the basis of the Scriptures, even of the New Testament. Today, I think, we have reached the stage in ecumenical dialogue where we do not have to fear we have abandoned everything if we concede some place to the corporate as well as to the individual channel of God's action.

• *Second, the sociological caution.* The movement which gave birth to Baptists was part of a great sociological revolution with far more than religious implications. Like most revolutions, this one too went to extremes, specifically in singling out the individual. It represented a further giant step beyond the individualism of the Renaissance. In the Enlightenment, Bacon and Descartes concluded that the individual alone could arrive at whatever certainty one could achieve by way of use of human physical senses and rational powers. The most precious product of this revolution was the western concept of liberty, which places the individual's freedom at the center. Here is the spawning pool of the American Declaration of Independence and Bill of Rights.

Having witnessed the continued advance of a self-serving kind of individualism, however, we Baptists, despite our love for individual freedom of the will, cannot be insensitive to the danger here. The voluntarism of our forebears in the Enlightenment stood only a step or two away from the autonomism of secular persons of the same era. For the latter the concern was not submission of the individual will to God, a theonomy, but the rule of life by the individual self.

The advance of the autonomous mode has led toward what Charles Reich has labeled "Consciousness III." Whereas earlier there was acceptance of society, the public interest, and institutions as the primary reality, Consciousness III "declares that the individual self is the only true reality." Postulating the absolute worth of every individual, it "rejects relationships of authority and subservience" and concludes that "coercive relations between people are wholly unacceptable." This means that it "will neither give commands nor follow them" and offers a radical critique of society.[4]

Much in Consciousness III resonates with what our forebears longed to see and gave their lives to attain. Nevertheless, it falls short of that which they envisioned when they spoke of voluntarism in religion. As all of you would know, their voluntarism led to voluntary association and produced remarkable selflessness in social service and social action, an outlook far removed from "Consciousness III."

The lesson which I judge we must draw from the preceding discussion is this: if we persist in our commitment to voluntarism, we must be dead sure we differentiate it from Consciousness III. Voluntarism should not lead to autonomism and selfish privatism but to holy obedience and selfless social concern. The crucial issue is: Is there such great danger that it will lead to autonomy that we dare not risk it any longer? Or can we moderate it in such a way as to lesson the risk?

I am inclined to reply that we have no choice. True obedience to God will come by the voluntarist route or not at all. Here we can learn from recent Roman Catholic experience.

In a recent issue of the *Concilium* series devoted to the subject of *Christian Obedience*, Roman Catholic scholars have come out remarkably close to the position which our forebears articulated, save for fuller attention given to the corporate. Edward Schillebeeckx, O. P., distinguished professor of theology at the University of Nijmegen, has offered a critique both of the heteronomous concept of the Christian middle ages and the autonomous and privatized concept of the Enlightenment. For him "Christian obedience is above all listening and watching out for the *kairos*, the opportune moment and especially listening obediently to the cry of two-thirds of the world's population for liberation and redemption and then acting in a concrete way in accordance with the voice of God."[5] Pierre de Locht, a marriage and family counselor, has ventured to express himself more boldly still in a voluntarist vein. Asking whom the Chris-

---

[4]Charles A. Reich, *The Greening of America* (New York: Bantam Books, 1971), pp. 241-45.

[5]Edward Schillebeeckx, "Secular Criticism of Christian Obedience and the Christian Reaction to that Criticism," *Obedience*, ed. Christian Duquoc and Casiano Floristan, "Concilium" (Edinburgh: T. & T. Clark Ltd.; New York: Seabury Press, 1980), p. 20.

tian is to obey in the Church, he steers a course between the individual will
and ecclesiastical law, observing, "Jesus Christ came into this dialectic of
individual freedom and the commandment of authority, in order to
establish or confirm a third pole of obedience: loyalty to the Spirit."
Citing Galatians 5:13-18, a text often quoted by our forebears, he adds,
"Loyalty to the Spirit of Jesus which is the ultimate court of appeal both
for authority and for those subordinate to it, introduces a specific dimension into Christian behavior."[6] Obedience to the Spirit leads to an "indis-
pensable contestation," a healthy element in any society, including the
Church. If one undertakes to challenge the Church, he or she "to some
extent experiences the solitude of Jesus . . . a solitude beyond all human
guarantees."[7]

Such reflections as these confirm the wisdom of our Baptist forebears
vis-à-vis voluntarism. In the last analysis, our concern should be as theirs:
to obey God rather than other human beings. Like them, we will continue
to affirm that the Spirit effects obedience, above all, through voluntary
assent. Yet in retrospect we may see better than they a danger which is
ever near: that voluntarism may veer into an autonomous privatism, a
self-centeredness of the worst sort. The autonomous outlook has taken
control of many minds in the Western world. To avert it, we would do
well to make more room for the Spirit to work through our corporate
experience than our forefathers did. Our quest is to be responsive to the
Spirit's promptings in both corporate and individual experiences so that
we may put ourselves at God's disposal for the overcoming of evil and the
effecting of justice and peace and hope and love for all humankind.

The Challenge of Conserving Identity

Before closing I want to say a word about the conservation of our
identity in the future. At one period in our history this posed less of a
problem, for we had several natural preservatives which no longer exist.
One was a minority status, a situation which tends to heighten consciousness. A second was a natural rivalry with competing denominations.
Unhappy as such rivalry was, it served to clarify and highlight Baptist
self-understanding. A third was a vigorous church training program
devoted to teaching the Baptist heritage and fostering the denominational program.

---

[6]Pierre de Locht, "Freedom of Obedience to the Spirit in the Church," in ibid., p. 38.
[7]Ibid., p. 40.

If Southern Baptists recover some semblance of identity as Baptists, they will have to make a determined effort to do so, for those external factors which, in the past, helped to foster a Baptist consciousness no longer do so. In the South, Baptists are no longer a minority. Moreover, as they become more urban, ecumenism will grow, not diminish, and evening training programs have slim prospects for revival.

I for one have no wish at all to turn the calendar back, even if we could. Surely our size and influence are more advantageous than disadvantageous. Cooperation with other Christians is preferable to acrimonious debate; and urban strength is better than rural weakness. Instead of a return to yesteryear, let me enumerate some possible approaches to the problem.

● First, *the current conflict may help*. As disruptive and irritating as the "inerrancy debate" is, it may force us once again to define who we are as Baptists, or perhaps whether we will continue to be Baptists. Other controversies have served in this way.

● Second, *it would be wise for us to hold some Baptist heritage rallies*. We cannot stand by passively and let our self-consciousness trickle away. In heritage rallies we could highlight again our traditional commitment to the Scriptures as our sole rule of faith and practice, to the Great Commission, to voluntarism, to religious liberty, to the separation of church and state. If some spark of Baptist-consciousness still burns within our breasts, such themes should set it aflame again. Southern Baptists have been rallying for all kinds of causes—the Bible, evangelism, missions; it is high time they rallied to recover their own identity.

● Third, *we must find ways to inculcate the Baptist idea as church training once did*. Rallies may suffice for the short run; a more persistent program is needed for the long one. We cannot be content with education of the few here. We must reach the majority.

Some churches crowd extra programs into Wednesday evenings. Often, however, these attract the few. The only time we reach a majority is on Sunday morning or perhaps in periods of specialized study. One approach which seems to me to be viable would be *a two-track Sunday morning school*. The first period would consist, as it does now, of Bible study, the second of training in Baptist heritage, theology, ethics and spirituality. Each period might last approximately forty-five minutes separated by a fifteen minute break. If properly organized, the entire school would require no more than thirty minutes longer than the present Bible school. An alternative approach would be *concentrated study periods* devoted to Baptist heritage, perhaps in lieu of Bible study on Sunday but at least arranged so as to reach a majority of our active members.

• Fourth, *much effort should be expended in the informing of new members about our Baptist tradition.* Southern Baptist success has not been without problems. The older generation of Southern Baptists know and love their heritage. A younger generation has arisen, however, who "know not Joseph" and may not care. The typical Southern Baptist congregation is a mix of Methodists, Presbyterians, Episcopalians, Roman Catholics, Pentecostals, and others as well as Baptists. Unless a concerted effort is made to educate them in the Baptist idea, they will not know.

The night is far spent as regards the recovery of our self-consciousness as Baptists. It is time for all of us to look deep into the past and into our selves to see whether we can again find the vision which has guided us through nearly four centuries. Not to do so at this time will be costly.

A Response
to Professor Hinson

by James Leo Garrett, Jr.

The debate contained within the pages of this volume is a fraternal one. Its purpose is not to foster antagonisms or encourage separations but to probe and clarify the identity and destiny of Southern Baptists in a spirit of humility and love. With some reluctance I accepted my assignment to prepare a reply or rebuttal to my friend and long-time colleague, Professor E. Glenn Hinson. My reluctance, due partly at least to the fact that it is more satisfying to state one's agreements than one's disagreements with a fellow Christian, has been transcended by a willingness and inner constraint to write further about what I regard as a basic issue in the self-understanding of Southern Baptists at the present time. It is my hope that this debate will indeed clarify the issue under discussion, as did the Ernest A. Payne-Winthrop S. Hudson debate during the 1950s about the Continental Anabaptist and/or English Puritan origins of Baptists.[1]

I shall deal with four basic issues specifically arising from Professor Hinson's four chapters and then conclude by treating a fifth issue.

---

[1]Ernest A. Payne, *The Anabaptists of the 16th Century and Their Influence in the Modern World* (London: Carey Kingsgate Press, 1949); Winthrop S. Hudson, "Baptists Were Not Anabaptists," *Baptist Quarterly* 16 (July 1956): 303-12; Payne, "Who Were the Baptists?" *Baptist Quarterly* 16 (October 1956): 339-42; Hudson, "Who Were the Baptists?" *Baptist Quarterly* 17 (April 1957): 53-55; Gunnar Westin, "Who Were the Baptists?" *Baptist Quarterly* 17 (April 1957): 55-60.

Misunderstanding Spawned by the
Confusion of "Voluntarism" and "Voluntaryism"

Hinson has repeatedly ascribed to Baptists in general and to Southern Baptists in particular what he calls "voluntarism." According to Hinson, "voluntarism" is to be equated with E. Y. Mullins's concept of "soul competency"; is both "intensely personal" religion and "the essence of biblical religion"; and is to involve "faith" in the sense of "a voluntary and uncoerced response" of a human being to the revelation of God in Jesus Christ. Such uncoerced faith, for Mullins, brings individual freedom, but not what Hinson calls "pure individualism." The Southern Baptist emphasis on "evangelism and missions," according to Hinson, has caused Southern Baptists to "neglect . . . voluntarism in religion." Voluntarism, moreover, is one of two basic "strains" or "facets" of "the Southern Baptist personality," the other being evangelicalism, and "voluntarism" leads to the Baptist stress on religious liberty and the separation of church and state. Tensions between these two strains characterized the Baptist rise out of Puritanism, Baptists during and after the Great Awakening, Baptists during the American Revolution, Baptists on the American frontier, and twentieth-century Baptists as influenced in their churches and their denominational structures by the model of the business corporation. Hinson also insists that "voluntarism" was essential to participation in the New Covenant and was the distinctive that most clearly differentiated Baptists *"from those groups from which they sprang."* Veritably central to the Baptist heritage, "voluntarism" is the opposite of "intentionalism" or involuntarism. The early Baptists became "voluntarists," Hinson contends, not merely because of the "individual self-consciousness" of the Renaissance or the Enlightenment or class struggle or "religious wars and persecutions" but indeed because they wanted to obey God rather than men. This same "voluntarism," Hinson concludes, is viable for today's Southern Baptists.[2]

Hinson's use of "voluntarism" rather than "voluntaryism" serves to complicate his exposition of the theme rather than to clarify it. Admittedly *Webster's Third New International Dictionary* (1966) has removed the last vestige of a differentiation between these two terms by defining "voluntarism" in terms of philosophical, free-church, and labor-management meanings.[3] But the *Random House Dictionary of the Eng-*

---

[2]Hinson, supra, pp. 137, 144, 147-64, 175, 186-92.

[3]Accordingly "voluntarism" is (1) "a theory that conceives will to be the dominant factor in experience or in the constitution of the world"; (2) "the principle of supporting a

lish Language (1966), as indeed Webster's second edition (1939) had done, has preserved the differentiation by defining "voluntarism" as a philosophical term which refers to "any theory that regards the will rather than the intellect as the fundamental agency or principle" and by defining "voluntaryism" as "the principle or system of supporting churches, schools, etc., by voluntary contributions or aid, independently of the state." Franklin Hamlin Littell has preserved the older meaning of "voluntaryism" in his writings on the Anabaptists and the free church tradition. The Anabaptist congregations, according to Littell, were "voluntary religious associations" gathered "by a freely and comprehensively conceived evangel, sealed by believers' baptism."[4]

> "Freiwilligkeitskirche" was a term used by their [the Anabaptists'] enemies, in part justified by their championing of Erasmus against Luther in the controversy about the Free Will. . . . Pilgram Marpeck and Peter Ridemann were Augustinian, Hubmaier and Denck and Menno more Erasmian. "Freiwilligkeitskirche" also conveys their significance as voluntary religious associations in lands controlled by Roman Catholic and Protestant state churches. . . .[5]

This dual meaning of *Freiwilligkeitskirche* is comparable to the multiple definitions of "voluntarism" in *Webster's Third*. In another book Littell preferred to use "voluntaryism," referring to it as "the positive side of opposition to state interference in affairs of the Church" and a "positive principle" in which "voluntary" is used "in the legal sense, not in the theological."[6] Hence when one wishes to refer to the pattern of financial support of churches by their members without governmental financial assistance, one would do well to use "voluntaryism."

These semantic considerations lead to the question as to whether Hinson by his use of "voluntarism" intends to mean the primacy of the will over the intellect (the philosophical usage) or the capability of human persons freely to initiate their appropriation of God's saving

---

religious system and its institutions by voluntary association and effort rather than by state aid or patronage"; and (3) "a principle calling for development of union labor relations with employees by free choice of the workers and without outside influence, assistance, or interference."

[4]*The Anabaptist View of the Church: A Study in the Origins of Sectarian Protestantism*, 2d ed., rev. (Boston: Starr King Press, 1958), p. 118; see also p. 46.

[5]Ibid., p. 199, fn. 44.

[6]*The Free Church* (Boston: Starr King Press, 1957), pp. 61, 67.

grace in Christ (the theological usage). He seems to suggest the latter, but not the former, in his various allusions to "voluntarism." The question as to the propriety of the theological usage goes back at least to Augustine's controversies with the Manichees and with the Pelagians and to his distinction between *liberum arbitrium* (the capacity to choose between alternatives) and *libertas* (the capacity consistently to choose the right or good). Only the latter, for Augustine, was lost by sinning, and genuine faith was necessarily the gift of God.[7] Erasmus and Luther debated the freedom or bondage of the will in regard to the initiation of conversion to Christ.[8] Moreover, this same theological issue as to free will claimed the attention of seventeenth-century English Baptists. General Baptists tended to affirm free will and Particular Baptists to deny it in favor of prevenient grace, but Thomas Helwys as a General Baptist could deny free will.[9] Both groups of Baptists espoused religious liberty despite their differences on free will.

Hinson should inform his readers as to the extent to which his own use of "voluntarism" has reference to this centuries-old debate on free will. If his usage does, as it seems to do, impinge upon that historic debate, Hinsonian "voluntarism" can never be confined to religious liberty and the separation of church and state. Until Hinson's meaning or meanings of "voluntarism" should be further delineated, the antithetical relation which he sees between "voluntarism" and "evangelicalism" will remain somewhat obscure and not clearly validated.

Hinson's less than clear usage of "voluntarism" is coupled with his own identification of such "voluntarism" with the concept of "soul competency" which was set forth by E. Y. Mullins in *The Axioms of Religion: A New Interpretation of the Baptist Faith* (1908). But, one may

---

[7]J. N. D. Kelly, *Early Christian Doctrines* (New York: Harper & Brothers, 1958), pp. 365-68; Gerald Bonner, *St. Augustine of Hippo: Life and Controversies* (Philadelphia: Westminster Press, 1963), pp. 211-14.

[8]*Luther and Erasmus: Free Will and Salvation:* Erasmus, *De Libero Arbitrio*, trans. and ed. E. Gordon Rupp in collab. with A. N. Marlow; and Luther, *De Servo Arbitrio*, trans. and ed. Philip S. Watson in collab. with B. Drewery, Library of Christian Classics, vol. 17 (Philadelphia: Westminster Press, 1969).

[9]On General Baptists, see John Smyth et al., "A Short Confession of Faith" (1610), art. 5, and "Propositions and Conclusions concerning True Christian Religion" (1612-1614), art. 17, in Lumpkin, *Baptist Confessions of Faith*, pp. 103, 126-27. On Particular Baptists, see "Second London Confession" (1677), art. 9, in Lumpkin, *Baptist Confessions of Faith*, pp. 263-64. On Thomas Helwys, see "A Declaration of Faith of English People Remaining at Amsterdam in Holland" (1611), art. 4, in Lumpkin, *Baptist Confessions of Faith*, pp. 117-18.

ask, is Hinson correct in identifying the two? Mullins, in defining soul competency as "the historic significance of the Baptists" and as "the distinguishing Baptist principle," clearly stated:

> The competency of the soul in religion . . . means a competency under God, not a competency in the sense of human self-sufficiency. There is no reference here to the question of sin and human ability in the moral and theological sense, nor in the sense of independence of the Scriptures.[10]

Inasmuch as Mullins clearly separated soul competency from the historic theological issue of free will, we must conclude that Hinson's identification of his own concept of "voluntarism" with Mullins's concept of soul competency is inaccurate to the extent that his "voluntarism" embraces the old question of free will.

Is Hinson's Hypothesis on Baptist History Valid?

Recent controversy within the Southern Baptist Convention has, it seems, evoked new typologies concerning Baptist history or new configurations of the streams of Baptist life that have flowed together to form present-day Southern Baptists. Walter B. Shurden in his Carver-Barnes Lectures (1980) set forth the view that "at least *four* distinct traditions among Baptists of the South" during the nineteenth and twentieth centuries "helped shape the Southern Baptist synthesis." These were the Charleston tradition, the Sandy Creek tradition, the Georgia tradition, and the Tennessee or Landmark tradition.[11] Hinson has provided another typology of epochs with the purpose of utilizing that typology to exhibit his central hypothesis, namely, that Baptists throughout their history have contained two antithetical streams, the evangelical and the voluntarist. In each epoch, Hinson contends, the two streams have been in tension, if not conflict.

First, concerning the Puritan and Separatist origins of the early Baptists, Hinson asserts: "The voluntarist-evangelical tension is evident . . . in Baptist origins out of English and American Puritanism." In his subsequent discussion, Hinson offers not a single example or instance of

---

[10](Philadelphia: American Baptist Publication Society), p. 53.

[11]*Outlook* 30 (March-April 1981, insert): 5-10. Shurden's identification of the Charleston, the Sandy Creek, and the Landmark traditions is indisputable. Whether his "Georgia tradition," based largely on the lives and work of W. B. Johnson and I. T. Tichenor, can be clearly established will depend, partly at least, on the work of other scholars.

evangelical-voluntarist tension within early Baptist history. Instead he attempts to establish his point by an abstract definition of Puritans in terms of their "zeal for conversion" and by reviewing the fact that early Baptists strongly advocated religious freedom for all human beings. But such statements are in no sense clear evidence of *tensions* among early seventeenth-century Baptists between their evangelical zeal and their espousal of religious freedom vis-à-vis the civil state. Hinson's contention regarding the earliest Baptists, therefore, is by no means established.

Second, Hinson asserts that the "voluntarist-evangelical balance was tested [among Baptists] a second time in the Great Awakening." Then bypassing the important Charleston heritage of Southern Baptists and somewhat erroneously stating that Regular Baptists and Separate Baptists "split over the use of 'means' to effect conversions," he finds that the Separate Baptists that stemmed from Sandy Creek Church in North Carolina embraced in balanced fashion the evangelical and the voluntarist strands. How, then, was the "balance" "tested" if the Separate Baptists, a product of the Great Awakening, were so balanced and Hinson has offered no evidence of imbalance among the Regular Baptists?

Third, Hinson declares that the "voluntarist-evangelical balance was tested again in the era of the American Revolution with the voluntarist note sounding the loudest." Baptist advocacy of and struggle for the attainment of religious freedom during this era is rightly emphasized. Can the demise of Baptist Evangelicalism during wartime, however, not be attributed more to Deism and religious indifference than to the dominance of "voluntarism"? Moreover, if the Revolutionary era can be extended to the first decade and a half of the nineteenth century, does not the Second Great Awakening afford evidence of the resurgence of Evangelicalism among Baptists?

Fourth, Hinson finds another instance of the "testing of the balance between voluntarist and evangelical strains" among Baptists during the extension of the American frontier and the development of Baptist denominational structures on the associational and the convention levels. Such an epoch extended from about 1814 to the Civil War. Especially noteworthy, according to Hinson, was the centralizing tendency inherent in the very nature of the Southern Baptist Convention. Hinson's evidence that Baptist Evangelicalism during this period was "checked by Baptist concern for voluntarism" is twofold: the antimissionary leaders (Daniel Parker, John Taylor, Alexander Campbell) and the Landmarkism of

James Robinson Graves and his associates. But, one must ask, in what ways were these leaders "voluntarists" that contemporary Baptists were not? Surely the founders of the "Triennial Convention" were "voluntaryistic" in the best sense of that term. The missionary leaders and the antimissionary leaders did not differ on religious freedom; they differed on the propriety of societies for the sending out and supporting of foreign and home missionaries. Furthermore, Landmarkism did not rest its case on a peculiar claim respecting religious freedom or on the Erasmian concept of free will in salvation. Rather it rested its case on Baptist local church ecclesiology and Baptist historical succession. Landmarkers were localists and denominationalists, but in no sense do they seem to have been peculiarly "voluntarists."

Fifth, Hinson finds that in the twentieth century Southern Baptists have adopted the model of the business corporation both in the local churches in urban settings and in denominational agencies, and this he deplores as a "challenge to the voluntarist-evangelical balance." The business model, he alleges, constitutes a danger by "forcing both persons and programs to fit snugly the corporate pattern." But Hinson has changed his subject matter without telling his readers. Formerly he has been treating civil or governmental coercion in denial of religious freedom; now he deals with some alleged administrative coercion within church and/or denominational life. It is surely by now evident that the term "voluntarism" in his argument suffers from a lack of precise definition.[12]

Whether Hinson's identification of the major epochs within Baptist history and with special reference to Southern Baptist history is valid is a question that is not central to the present discussion and can be bypassed. Rather the central issue is whether the major epochs so chosen yield clear evidence in support of Hinson's hypothesis about evangelical-voluntarist tensions. The preceding analysis fails to discern such evidence in Hinson's review of the epochs. At best, therefore, Hinson's hypothesis remains an unverified hypothesis. It may have grown out of Hinson's personal fear that the "evangelical" stream in Baptist life may become coercive, but it should not be admitted to the canon of commonly held insights about Baptist history.

---

[12]Supra, pp. 147-64.

Faith and Experience above Scripture,
or Scripture above Faith and Experience?

It is somewhat ironical that Hinson has employed the writings of Bernard Ramm as the representative antithesis to Baptist beliefs. I use the term "ironical" inasmuch as Ramm has been a member of Baptist churches for many years.[13] How indeed can the theology of this lifelong Baptist be rightly taken as the antithesis of Baptist beliefs? It is possible because Hinson has imputed to Baptists his own view that places religious experience above the Bible as a source of religious truth.

Although in chapter one Hinson asserts that Baptists have held to *sola Scriptura*,[14] in chapter three he identifies the term "Baptist" with *"that version of Christianity which places the priority of voluntary and uncoerced faith or response to the Word and Act of God* over any supposed 'objective Word' and Act of God." He then clarifies this statement by asserting that "Baptists assign priority to the response of believers to the word of God over against scriptures and creeds presented as an objective Word of God."[15]

Hinson attempts to sustain such a view of the Baptist conception of authority by reckoning E. Y. Mullins the supreme Baptist theologian, by assuming that all Baptists have shared what Hinson finds to have been Mullins's sympathetic appropriation of the experience-oriented theology of Friedrich Daniel Ernst Schleiermacher (1768-1834), and by positing a rather cozy friendliness of Baptists toward the men of the Enlightenment.[16] Hinson follows an unsafe, if not dangerous trend in allowing one Baptist theologian, however eminent and representative, to speak for all Baptists. On that basis, to elevate John Gill would mean that Baptists offer no gospel invitations to unbelievers; and, with that approach, to

---

[13]Ramm since 1938 has been continuously a member of a Baptist church, affiliated either with the Baptist General Conference, the American Baptist Churches (U. S. A.), or the Southern Baptist Convention. Bernard L. Ramm to James Leo Garrett, Jr., 19 January 1982.

[14]Hinson, supra, p. 139. Hinson, although critical (supra, p. 142 and fn. 28) of L. Russ Bush and Tom J. Nettles, *Baptists and the Bible* (Chicago: Moody Press, 1980), does not acknowledge, as Bush and Nettles do not (pp. 393, 397-99), that *suprema Scriptura* has had its advocates among Baptists as well as *sola Scriptura*. The term "supreme standard," used in art. 1 of the New Hampshire Confession, needs to be taken more seriously, as should the evidence from popular monographs on Baptist beliefs. Concerning the latter, see James Leo Garrett, Jr., "Sources of Authority in Baptist Thought," *Baptist History and Heritage* 13 (July 1978): 47-49.

[15]Hinson, supra, pp. 173-74.

[16]Hinson, supra, pp. 178-79.

elevate J. R. Graves would mean that all Baptists teach an unbroken historical succession of Baptist churches from the first century A.D. Furthermore, one must ask whether Mullins utilized Christian experience primarily as a source of Christian truth or as an apologetic tool[17] in an era when pragmatism and personalism were prevalent. Once again, one needs to inquire as to whether Baptists such as Isaac Backus (1724-1806) and John Leland (1755-1841) cooperated with the American Deists on the issue of the source or sources of religious truth or only in the securing of religious freedom and the separation of church and state.

Baptists, both those who have affirmed *suprema Scriptura* and those who have declared for *sola Scriptura*, have consistently placed the authority of the Bible above that of faith or religious experience. The confessions of faith make this clear, and so do the writings of Baptist systematic theologians and the authors of popular monographs on what Baptists believe.[18] In four representative Baptist theological journals during the last half-century, only in one article did the author contend for the "finality" of "personal Christian experience."[19] Among Baptists experience is to be tested by Scripture, but Scripture is not to be tested by experience, though it may indeed be confirmed in experience. Baptists therefore share some common ground with other Christians who hold the Scriptures in such an exalted place of authority.

Baptists as Advocates of Religious Freedom and as Evangelicals

Hinson's identification of two strains within Baptist life, the "evangelical" and the "voluntarist," although these are intended according to Hinson's statement[20] to be complementary, or at least balancing, serves rather to posit the two as antitheses, or as an either/or alternative for today's Southern Baptists.

Baptists in the past, however, have taught and championed religious freedom in the civic sphere and have upheld the supreme authority of the Bible, made Jesus Christ the center of their message, and called for

---

[17]Mullins wrote five chapters on "The Evidence of Christian Experience" in *Why Is Christianity True?* (Philadelphia: American Baptist Publication Society, 1905), which was published twelve years prior to *The Christian Religion in Its Doctrinal Expression* (1917). See Russell Hooper Dilday, Jr., "The Apologetic Method of E. Y. Mullins" (Th.D. diss., Southwestern Baptist Theological Seminary, 1960).

[18]Garrett, "Sources of Authority in Baptist Thought," pp. 41-49.

[19]James Leo Garrett, Jr., "Doctrinal Authority, 1925-1975: A Study in Four Representative Baptist Journals," *Foundations* 22 (January-March 1979): 3-12.

[20]Hinson, supra, p. 148.

personal regeneration/conversion as necessary for salvation without regarding these two as antithetical. In continental Europe, Johann Gerhard Oncken (1800-1884) both advocated religious freedom for persecuted Baptists and served effectively as gospel preacher and founder of churches. English Baptists produced both Charles Haddon Spurgeon (1834-1892), the doctrinal preacher and pastor-evangelist, and John Clifford (1836-1923), the bold champion of the cause of the free churches. In Latin America, Baptists such as Pablo Besson (1845-1932) and Santiago Canclini (1900-1977) have been bold advocates of religious freedom, and Baptists such as Rubens Lopes (1914-1979) and David Gomes (1919-   ) have been evangelical crusaders. Among Southern Baptists, George Washington Truett (1867-1944) modeled the full complementarity of pastor-evangelist and articulate spokesman for religious freedom and the separation of church and state and even exercised the latter function on the steps of the United States Capitol. Baptist history does not present religious freedom and the evangelical as antitheses; rather they are fully complementary.

Furthermore, for one to question whether Southern Baptists are Evangelical Christians would have seemed strange indeed to Southern Baptist leaders of preceding generations. Franklin Howard Kerfoot (1847-1901), pastor of the Eutaw Place Baptist Church, Baltimore, Maryland, and professor of systematic theology, Southern Baptist Theological Seminary, clearly differentiated "the leading tenets which we [Baptists] hold, in common with all evangelical denominations" from "those which constitute our distinctive principles as Baptists."[21] E. Y. Mullins, in the very paragraph in which he defined his concept of soul competency, declared:

> I am not here stating the Baptist creed. On many vital matters of doctrine, such as the atonement, the person of Christ, and others Baptists are in substantial agreement with the evangelical world in general.[22]

---

[21]Kerfoot, "What We Believe according to the Scriptures," in B. W. Spilman, L. P. Leavell, and P. E. Burroughs, *The New Convention Normal Manual for Sunday School Workers* (Nashville: Sunday School Board, Southern Baptist Convention, 1913), pp. 306-12, esp. p. 306. Kerfoot's material also appeared in the 1918 edition of this same volume. It had not been included in B. W. Spilman, L. P. Leavell, and Hight C Moore, *Convention Normal Manual for Sunday-School Workers* (Nashville: Sunday School Board, Southern Baptist Convention, 1909), and it would not later appear in B. W. Spilman, L. P. Leavell, P. E. Burroughs, and G. S. Dobbins, *The Sunday School Manual* (Nashville: Sunday School Board of the Southern Baptist Convention, 1923).

[22]*The Axioms of Religion*, p. 53.

Proper attention should also be given to the common practice among non-Southern Baptist authors today, besides Richard Quebedeaux, of reckoning Southern Baptists among the Evangelicals in the United States. Dean M. Kelley, director for civil and religious liberty, National Council of the Churches of Christ in the U. S. A., in his study of the growth of "conservative churches" considered the Southern Baptist Convention as one of those denominations that was "conservative" and "growing."[23] Robert E. Webber, associate professor of theology, Wheaton College, Wheaton, Illinois, and coeditor of *The Orthodox Evangelicals*, in his fourteen-fold classification of Evangelicals in the United States has classified Southern Baptists under "Main-line Evangelicalism." Webber includes Southern Baptists among the "other groups whose heritage was not rooted in the fundamentalist-modernist controversy, but whose sympathies were with a more conservative, historic, or orthodox Christian persuasion [and which] continued to model a position *in the middle*, between liberals and fundamentalists."[24] Ed Dobson, dean of student affairs and director of pastoral training, and Ed Hindson, professor and chairman of the division of religion, Liberty Baptist College, Lynchburg, Virginia, in a volume edited by Jerry Falwell, pastor, Thomas Road Baptist Church, Lynchburg, and designed to refute both the far-right Fundamentalist critics of Falwell's ministry and the representatives of "drifting Evangelicalism," have written in commendation of the Baptist Faith and Message Fellowship and of the recent inerrancy movement within the Southern Baptist Convention as if wistfully to want to claim Southern Baptists for Fundamentalism.[25] George W. Dollar, chairman of the department of church history, Bob Jones University, Greenville, South Carolina, and an ex-Southern Baptist who helped to found the Southwide Baptist Fellowship in 1956, in his history of Fundamentalism that represents the perspective of militant, right-wing Fundamentalism, has excluded Southern Baptists from the category of Fundamentalism, has espoused J. Frank Norris's criticisms of Southern Baptists, and has identified Southern Baptists as a slow movement "toward outright Liber-

---

[23] *Why Conservative Churches Are Growing: A Study in Sociology of Religion* (New York: Harper & Row, 1972), pp. 21-22, 26, 30, 88-90, 131.

[24] *Common Roots: A Call to Evangelical Maturity* (Grand Rapids: Zondervan Publishing House, 1978), pp. 32, 29.

[25] Jerry Falwell, ed., with Ed Dodson and Ed Hindson, *The Fundamentalist Phenomenon: The Resurgence of Conservative Christianity* (Garden City, N. Y.: Doubleday & Company, Inc., 1981), pp. 138-39. The editor and authors seem to be unaware that "Fundamentalist" and "Conservative" are not totally synonymous terms.

alism," a "downward path," and a denomination that harbors "heretics" and "unbiblical teachings" and supports "the apostasy."[26] The Princeton Religion Research Center has identified Southern Baptists as one of "the Evangelical churches."[27] Samuel S. Hill, Jr., professor of religion, University of Florida, Gainesville, and a former Southern Baptist who joined the Episcopal Church in 1973, has identified Southern Baptists as the leading example of "conversion-oriented" Evangelical Protestants.[28]

Both the thought and terminology of Baptist leaders of the past and the classification of Southern Baptists by contemporary non-Southern Baptist authors seem to warrant the conclusion that Southern Baptists are not incorrectly identified as Evangelicals and that their evangelical characteristics are in no sense antithetical to their espousal of religious freedom for all persons vis-à-vis the civil state.

Why It Matters That Southern Baptists Acknowledge That They Are Evangelicals

The present author wishes to rest his case that Southern Baptists are indeed Evangelicals with his preceding chapters and his fourfold reply to Professor Hinson.

He wishes to acknowledge, however, that it may indeed prove to be necessary to differentiate more clearly the historic and more comprehensive usage of the term "Evangelical" from the more restricted usage of the term that has been associated with American Fundamentalism. Particularly may that differentiation prove to be essential for Southern Baptists. But he would insist that adjectival differentiations among Evangelicals are always more accurate and more viable than and hence preferable to the limitation of the usage of "Evangelical" to any restricted sense. That means that it is better to reckon that there are varieties of Evangelicals than to insist that there can be only one type.

Finally, he wishes to attempt to explain why the issue under discussion is so vital for Southern Baptists. The issue is not merely an academic one as if its consequences would never move outside the walls of Southern Baptist theological seminaries, universities, and colleges. It affects more

---

[26]*A History of Fundamentalism in America* (Greenville, S.C.: Bob Jones University Press, 1973), esp. pp. 122-34, 87, 157, 182, 218, 274.

[27]*Emerging Trends* 2 (January 1980): 3.

[28]"The Shape and Shapes of Popular Southern Piety," in Harrell, ed., *Varieties of Southern Evangelicalism*, p. 101.

than 34,000 churches, the denominational agencies, and the people called Southern Baptists.[29]

The question as to whether Southern Baptists are Evangelicals is not solely pertinent for possible relationships with other Christians or with other churches that regard themselves and are reckoned to be Evangelicals. The question does bear upon such relationships, whether actual or potential, but the issue is more than an ecumenical or interdenominational one. The issue at stake affects the self-understanding of Southern Baptists and the ways in which they seek to conduct their mission and ministry in today's world.

Will Southern Baptists break out of their cultural or regional or class or racial captivity to model an authentic (that is, biblical) and aggressive (that is, evangelistic) form of Christianity at the end of the twentieth century? Will Southern Baptist churches that have vast resources in buildings, church staffs, and trained and increasingly affluent members be willing and able to minister to the hurts and frustrations of the broken, the infirm, the lonely, the poor, the refugee, the immigrant, the factory worker, the egghead, and the up-and-out, and point these to Jesus Christ? Will older Southern Baptist churches, replete with tradition but located amid changed socioeconomic and ethnic patterns, come to new life and find and follow new forms of ministry that are consonant with the abiding gospel? Will Southern Baptists cherish and hold to the Bible and the gospel or be ensnared by the acclaim of the cultic, the tinkle of prosperity, the lure of the liturgical, or the danger of dialogue? Will the Southern Baptist preacher and the Southern Baptist church member rediscover the authority of the Bible, the Christocentrism of the gospel, and the coessentiality of witness by word and witness by life? Will Southern Baptists be in reality conformed to the present age or be transformed as pilgrim people on their way to the City of God? Will a few million Southern Baptists live for themselves and for their ease and comfort or as responsible stewards for the billions of the earth for whom Jesus died and rose again? Will Bold Mission Thrust be only a denominational slogan, rich in rhetoric and profusely promoted, or also our way of

---

[29]The author agrees thoroughly with Professor Hinson that effective teaching of and training in the Baptist heritage is urgently needed today in most Southern Baptist churches.

describing the "mighty work and a wonder" which God—Father, Son, and Holy Spirit—has accomplished among us and through us?

The answers to these urgent questions cannot be divorced from the self-identity of Southern Baptists. Who we understand ourselves to be directly affects how we proclaim, how we live, and how we serve. To make assertions about self-identity means, among other things, that one must consider whether Southern Baptists are Evangelicals. The present writer believes that an affirmative answer to the latter question will significantly aid Southern Baptists in making the right responses to the several questions posed above.

A Response
to Professor Garrett

by E. Glenn Hinson

Dr. Garrett and I have approached the question of the relationship between Southern Baptists and Evangelicals from different directions and thus come out with different answers, though we may not be as far apart as he supposes in his third chapter. He began with the question: "Who are the Evangelicals?" and proceeded, after answering to his satisfaction, to bring in the added question: "Are Southern Baptists Evangelicals?" My concern is quite different. It has to do, above all, with the identity of Baptists, or, more precisely, the nature of the Baptist tradition and whether that tradition is going to survive in the Southern Baptist Convention. Thus I began with the questions: "Who are the Baptists? What is the essence of the Baptist tradition?" My effort to answer these questions led me to the conclusion that this tradition has two strains, evangelical and voluntarist, which must be held in tension if we are to remain true to it. My concern with Evangelicalism is only tangential to my concern for the survival of the Baptist tradition. Thus I merely point to the danger the influence of those who call themselves Evangelicals poses in terms of creating confusion about Baptist identity.

Here, unfortunately, I seem not to have made my major point clearly enough, for Dr. Garrett has misunderstood it, categorizing me among those who say we are *not* Evangelicals. What I am trying to say is: We are *other than* Evangelicals. We have an identity and history interconnected with but also quite distinct from that of many groups who claim the label of Evangelical and at points set clearly over against theirs. Let me try to explain with an analogy. Southern Baptists are also Americans (for the most part if not completely). We are citizens of the United States. We reflect its culture. We participate in its social and political life. Nevertheless, we are *other than* Americans. We have an identity and history connected with but also quite different from the nation's history. And, if we are to be faithful to our distinct heritage as Christians and Baptists, we must not let Baptist identity be confused by Americanism, though, alas, that happens often enough.

Whether or to what extent Baptists belong under the evangelical umbrella depends on how we define the term. If one divides American denominations into three groups—Catholic, Mainline, and Evangelical—as is now popular, Southern Baptists probably fit best in the evangelical category, but they could also be classified as mainline, or possibly even Catholic, in some respects. Dr. Garrett, following Richard Quebedeaux, defines evangelical in such a comprehensive way, of course, that no one could disagree when he argues that Southern Baptists "parallel" the stereotype. Both groups obviously affirm "(1) the complete reliability and final authority of Scripture in matters of faith and practice; (2) the necessity of a *personal* faith in Jesus Christ as Savior from sin and consequent commitment to him as Lord; and (3) the urgency of seeking actively the conversion of sinners to Christ."

When we have defined them in this way, however, how much have we said? We have told virtually nothing about the character of either. Certainly we have not gotten to the essence of either entity. This amounts to about the same thing as hanging the word "humanity" on all the individual human beings or tribes or nations in the world. We know the word applies because it is so general it covers all other possible definitions. But what does it "de-limit"? What does it say specifically?

Dr. Garrett's first chapter seems to me to prove my point here. There are evangelicals and Evangelicals. In Europe, from the Reformation on, the term has designated non-Catholics but especially Lutherans. In England, please note, Puritans and Non-conformists (from whom we as Baptists spring) did not identify themselves usually with this term; instead, it has been applied chiefly to a wing of the Church of England. In Latin America it designates Protestants in general. In the United States it has been applied to a number of denominational bodies, only two of which are Baptist and they very small. It has been used principally by latter-day fundamentalists as a way of purging the bad taste which the fundamentalist movement left in the minds of many because of its divisiveness. Much less accurately, as Dr. Garrett points out, it has labeled Pentecostalists, Neo-Pentecostalists, and the Jesus Movement.

Let no one overlook the fact that I am concerned primarily about the effect a confusion of our identity with the chief claimants of the term, Fundamentalists and their descendants, will have on the Baptist tradition within the Southern Baptist Convention. It is very clear that some Southern Baptists think "Baptist" and "Fundamentalist" are synonymous. I am making every effort to show that they are not. This is not to say that some Baptists may not be Fundamentalists or Evangelicals. Many have been and are. The Baptist tradition, however, is not essentially fundamentalist, and being a Baptist is not the same thing as being a Fundamentalist. Indeed, if I have construed it rightly, the *spirit* of the Baptist tradition stands in direct antithesis to the fundamentalist mentality, that is, that another can be right or Christian only if he or she accepts the fundamentalist credo.

If the problem is Fundamentalism, then why am I concerned to differentiate Baptists from Evangelicals? Mainly because in popular usage the word Evangelical is normally understood to mean the same thing as Fundamentalist, and popular usage is very determinative. I am quite skeptical as to whether the earlier and more general usage of the term can be recovered now, for Fundamentalists have worked forty years to whitewash their movement with it. Even if this were not true, the word is too general and amorphous to supply much help in our effort to define who we are as Southern Baptists. Evangelicalism is not a movement, organization, or theological system but, as several have insisted, a "mood." It reminds me of Gnosticism in the early centuries of Church history. Gnosticism became a movement only as it attached itself to Judaism, Christianity, or other religions, but it was not itself a movement. By attaching itself to these faiths, however, it succeeded in hopping on the back of believers and cupping its hands over their eyes, thus causing them to run off the road. That is what I fear here.

I'm not sure what Dr. Garrett's purpose is in trying to identify Southern Baptists with Evangelicals. Does he expect to unite us more closely with them in some common endeavor? If so, what? Missions and evangelism? Defending the Bible? If the second, does he realize what the consequences of this may be as the divisiveness of evangelical preoccupation with "orthodoxy" begins to do its work? This is particularly risky if Evangelicalism turns out to be warmed-over Fundamentalism, which would bring its own battles into our household, as Harold Lindsell has succeeded in doing.

The "three areas of doctrinal emphasis or agreement among Evangelicals" which Dr. Garrett fixes on in his second chapter sound remarkably like the traditional "fundamentals," give or take a few items: "(1) the nature and necessity of justification or regeneration or salvation: (2) the nature and supreme authority of the Bible; and (3) the deity of Jesus Christ together with certain events of His 'holy history,' namely, virginal conception, atoning death, bodily resurrection, and second coming." In and of themselves these particular views might not be divisive, but insistence on a single way of viewing them could be, and that is exactly the danger. When Dr. Garrett discusses each of these three emphases or areas further, he makes this point for me. Southern Baptists surely do not need a reminder that Fundamentalists will try and are trying to impose the inerrantist view of scriptures upon all and sundry. Biblical authority is not enough. It is either their view of this or none at all.

Despite this clear and present danger, Dr. Garrett presses ahead with his effort to identify Southern Baptists with Evangelicals. His effort, however, results at best in a demonstration of certain parallels but by no means a matching of types. The characteristics he outlines in describing Southern Baptists show little correspondence to the evangelical stereotype sketched earlier. According to his interpretation, Southern Baptists are (1) "Calvinist rather than Arminian in theology" but "very moderately Calvinist"; (2) "missionary and not anti-missionary"; (3) "denominational, but not Landmarkist"; (4) "conservative rather than liberal in theology"; (5) "cooperative as denominationalists, but not ecumenical"; and (6) "advocates of the primacy of a historical method instead of a symbolic method in interpreting the Bible."

When he sorts out "parallels" between Southern Baptists and Evangelicals, Dr. Garrett ends up with a limited selection: evangelistic and missionary commitment, conservative theology, and a denominationalism "parallel to some, but by no means all, contemporary Evangelical Protestants." On the basis of these three characteristics one could make an equally convincing case that Southern Baptists are Roman Catholics!

The major question here, however, is whether Dr. Garrett has given an accurate stereotype of Southern Baptists. In depicting us he has left out features which most people—Baptist as well as non-Baptist—would cite as distinctively Baptist— believers' baptism, religious liberty, and separation of church and state. I hope he has done so only because he wants to highlight correspondences with Evangelicals. For if he has given an accurate profile of the Southern Baptist ethos, then he confirms my worst fears. Southern Baptists are being engulfed in a tide which is threatening to wipe away the very essence of the Baptist tradition. Being the "established" church of the South, they have begun to repress their memories as Non-conformists. If they can succeed in completing their evangelistic dreams, they are ready to become evangelicals pure and simple or, more accurately stated, they are ready to become the "catholic church" for the South. Surely a person who edited the *Journal of Church and State* as Dr. Garrett did for several years would not consider his stereotype a properly balanced one.

At this juncture let me reply to his criticisms of my original paper, "Baptists and Evangelicals: What Is the Difference?" Regarding (1) the common roots of Baptists and Evangelicals in Puritanism, I would again remind Dr. Garrett that I did not say we are *not* related. I said, rather, that "we come from different wombs." We may be cousins to some Evangelicals, but we are not blood brothers and sisters. We had our own birth. Consequently we have genes not found in the evangelical mainstream. And we had better know what these are.

As to (2) the antithesis I have posited between the Baptist understanding of the authority of the Bible and the role of confessions of faith and the Baptist commitment to religious freedom, I do not think I have read our history wrongly. It is time for us again to recognize the strength of the voluntarist strain in our heritage. Our forbears were radical in this, as they had reason to be. The evidence I have given could be supplemented from many other sources.

Concerning (3) the term "voluntarism," I believe my choice of words was apt. The issue we are dealing with is ultimately one of obedience of the will, whether that is to be obtained through voluntary means or through coercion of some sort. Though Baptists would also identify with "voluntaryism," they would do so because of their voluntarism. For our forbears the main concern was freedom to obey God rather than human beings.

As regards (4) Bernard Ramm, I do not object to him thinking of himself as an "Evangelical" as well as a Baptist. One of the chief features of our Baptist heritage has been our willingness to leave room for diversity. This does not mean, however, that every Baptist is an Evangelical nor that Baptists corporately would be identified with Evangelicals. Ramm is one who, I judge, prefers to think of himself as an Evangelical rather than a Baptist.

Regarding (5) Tom Paine's *The Age of Reason*, I hope Baptists did resist it as strongly as they resisted enforcers of conformity. My major point was that they found some of the elements of the Enlightenment which Evangelicals claim to reject quite amenable to their own quest— above all, religious liberty.

Finally, concerning (6) E. Y. Mullins's emphasis upon religious experience, I think it was a response to the search Baptists engaged in both prior to and subsequent to Mullins to understand the American "awakenings." Mullins helped Baptists free themselves from the stranglehold of hyper-Calvinism and to get on with their mission.

In the final analysis, then, I am among those Southern Baptists who prefer to preserve a sense of identity *over against* Evangelicalism. I am quite willing to admit that we may stand under the evangelical umbrella used to categorize one of three blocks of Christians in America, but I wonder whether we are any closer than the periphery even here. We are closest to being accurately typed as "evangelicals" when the term is used to designate those who emphasize personal conversion. We are farthest from them when the term is applied to those who stress "orthodoxy." As Dr. Garrett's work illustrates well, however, Evangelicals are a very diverse lot, just as Baptists are. So long as Fundamentalists have a corner on the term, identification of Southern Baptists with Evangelicals will add to the great difficulty we now confront in defining who we are.

The evangelical influence is, of course, not the only factor contributing to an identity crisis. Rapid social change, growth of the Southern Baptist Convention, the electronic churches, and other factors are causing confusion. Now is the time for Southern Baptists to get in touch with their own deepest roots. If they don't, the next generation may not remember those features which stand at the center of the Baptist tradition.

Breathe there Baptists with memories of their heritage so dead who never to themselves have said, "We will obey God before human beings"? Who never to themselves have said, "God alone is Lord of the conscience"? Who never to themselves have said, "The most paganish or even antichristian consciences are only to be fought against with that sword which is only, in soul matters, able to conquer: to wit, the sword of God's Spirit, the word of God"? Who never to themselves have said, "To be authentic and responsible, faith must be free!"? Sad to say, there are some. But may it not be that there is none either for our generation or the next or the next or the next.

A Concluding Statement

Baptists and "Evangelicals"
—an Open Question?

by James E. Tull

In this concluding chapter I shall not attempt to summarize in detail the discussions of the two loyal Baptists and fine scholars who have labored to illuminate issues which are pertinent to our denominational health and mission. Dr. Garrett has given a synopsis of his three chapters which may be found on pages 125-27. Dr. Hinson does not give a formal summary of his discussion, but I think that the reader can grasp the gist of his argument by reading the introduction to his first chapter, pages 131-33, the introduction to his second chapter, pages 147-48, and the introduction to his third chapter, pages 165-66.

An exchange of the scope and richness of this dialogue is difficult to summarize without leaving out much of the substantive argument found in the larger text. If an admonition to the reader may be permitted me, it is simply this: *read attentively the whole text of the dicussion.* My aim will be to help the reader gain a synoptic view of the subject as presented by the two authors, while avoiding, I hope, undue repetition and gratuitous editorializing.

The points of debate between the two principals have been well stated by them in their rejoinders to each other. I shall interject comment concerning these points sparingly, and then only when I think that some clarification is needed, and/or that some comment is fitting. My failure to speak upon some of even the most important subjects of contention between them should not be construed by the reader as a failure on my part, necessarily, to appreciate the sententiousness of their exchanges, but simply as a sign of respect for their freedom to have their own say. Each one of these articulate men has made an informed and rather formidable statement of his own position. I am convinced that the discerning reader will be aided by this joint discussion in his own efforts to think through vital issues which confront Southern Baptists at this stage of our history.

In his reply to Dr. Garrett, Dr. Hinson has made a helpful explanation of the different approaches which he and Dr. Garrett have followed. I quote a part of his first paragraph.

> Dr. Garrett and I have approached the question of the relation-ship between Southern Baptists and Evangelicals from differ-ent directions and thus come out with different answers.... He began with the question: "Who are the Evangelicals?" and proceeded, after answering to his own satisfaction, to bring in the added question, "Are Southern Baptists Evangelicals?" My concern is quite different. It has to do, above all, with the identity of Baptists, or more precisely, the nature of the Baptist tradition and whether that tradition is going to survive in the Southern Baptist Convention. Thus I began with the question, "Who are the Baptists? What is the essence of the Baptist tradition?"[1]

As Dr. Hinson indicates, Dr. Garrett's initial effort is to characterize Evangelicalism. In his first chapter, he has written a scholarly inquiry concerning the wide variety of usages that the term "evangelical" has received in history. He addresses this question by showing the usages of the term as it has been applied to church bodies in Continental Europe, the British Isles, Latin America, and the United States.

Dr. Garrett's first chapter is a wide-ranging investigation, upon the findings of which he builds his main argument. This argument is that Evangelicalism is a term which historically covers varied shades of meaning, and is applicable to many ecclesiastical bodies. Dr. Garrett holds to this thesis throughout his discourse, refusing to concede that the term should be applied to only one group or to one point of view. "It is better,"

---

[1] Above, p. 205.

he says, "to reckon that there are varieties of Evangelicals than to insist that there can be only one type."[2]

Making allowances for wide diversities in evangelical ranks, Garrett introduces a "threefold test" by which Evangelicals may be identified. This "test" he derives from Richard Quebedeaux, and describes it, with some reservation, as a "useful working hypothesis" for recognizing Evangelicals in the United States today. These tests are:

> (1) the complete reliability and final authority of Scripture in matters of faith and practice; (2) the necessity of a *personal* faith in Jesus Christ as Savior from sin and consequent commitment to Him as Lord; and (3) the urgency of seeking actively the conversion of sinners to Christ.[3]

In chapter 1, as Dr. Garrett states, he has followed "the quest for the varied uses of the term 'Evangelical'." In his second chapter, he proposes to inquire "whether those called 'Evangelicals' have had and do now have any common beliefs and common practices that differentiate them from other Christians or at least clearly characterize them."[4] Dr. Garrett's discussion in this chapter focuses principally upon the theological, ethical, and evangelistic factors in evangelical life.

His task here is not an easy one, for he studiously avoids any artificial harmonization of the beliefs and practices of widely differing evangelical groups. He probes differences and makes comparisons, though again one of his principal aims is to show underlying similarities and kinships.

After projecting by means of an extensive chart a profile of many groups of Evangelicals with respect to their doctrinal beliefs, he summarizes the findings of his study as follows:

> An examination of the chart makes evident that there have been three areas of doctrinal emphasis or agreement among Evangelicals: (1) the nature and necessity of justification or regeneration or salvation; (2) the nature and supreme authority of the Bible; and (3) the deity of Jesus Christ together with certain events of his "holy history," namely, virginal conception, atoning death, bodily resurrection, and second coming. . . .

---

[2]Above, p. 206.

[3]Above, p. 61. Cited from Quedebeaux, *The Young Evangelicals,* pp. 3-4. See Hinson's criticism of these tests, p. 210 in his reply to Garrett.

[4]Above, p. 65.

Other doctrines such as entire sanctification, baptism of the Holy Spirit as evidenced by charisms, the secondary authority of confessions of faith, dual eternal destiny (heaven and hell), the obligation of witnessing and missions, and sacraments as means of grace appear on the chart but may not have been clearly and specifically affirmed by a majority of Evangelicals. The doctrine of the millennium, including the major schools (historic premillennialism, amillennialism, postmillennialism, and dispensational premillennialism), has not been consistently included on the chart because of the difficulty in securing accurate information for all groups of Evangelicals or because of the lack in some cases of an explicit, published affirmation. The obligation of witnessing and missions, commonly practiced by most Evangelicals, may not appear more frequently on the chart because it may have been regarded as something practiced rather than as something believed.[5]

Dr. Garrett believes that there is no conflict among Evangelicals concerning the supreme authority of the Bible, and he thinks that various theories of the mode of biblical inspiration are not at present a topic of dispute among them. There is, however, a sharp controversy over the question of the inerrancy of the Scriptures. This controversy proceeds on two levels. The first concerns whether the Bible is without error not only in matters pertaining to doctrine and ethics, but also in "historical, geographical, and scientific matters."[6] The second is whether the question of infallibility pertains only to matters of doctrine and ethics.[7] This controversy, Garrett notes,

threatens to divide Evangelicals in the United States at precisely that time in their history when they have begun to be conscious of their increasing numbers, their genuine diversity, and their potential influence upon American life and society.[8]

Dr. Garrett's discussion of the Person and Work of Christ, as held by Evangelicals, I believe needs no additional comment here.[9] Concerning

---

[5] Above, pp. 65-67. See Hinson's criticism, p. 212 in his reply to Garrett.

[6] Above, p. 68.

[7] Above, p. 68.

[8] Above, p. 71. See Garrett's acute critique of the "inerrancy" question, above, pp. 68-71.

[9] See this discussion above, p. 71.

evangelical ethics, Garrett observes a difference between more conservative and less conservative Evangelicals. Stricter Evangelicals have frowned upon the use of alcoholic beverages, tobacco, gambling, movies, dancing, the use of narcotics, rock music, and the wearing of long hair by men. Lutheran and Reformed Evangelicals, however, advocate moderation rather than abstinence in the use of alcohol, and condone some forms of gambling. Many Southern Baptists condone the smoking of tobacco (and, one might add, support its production!). The prevailing use of television for entertainment has softened much evangelical opposition to offensive plays and movies. The objection to rock music has been considerably modified by the emergence of Christian rock.[10]

With regard to evangelical social ethics, Dr. Garrett notes that the social ethic of Fundamentalism has been retrograde when compared with that of many Evangelicals of the nineteenth century. On the other hand, he says, many Evangelicals,

> deploring Fundamentalism's lack of a social ethic, have become increasingly concerned and active regarding racism, militarism, poverty, hunger, materialism, sexism, nationalism, cultural captivity, and other great social issues. Evangelicals are less united in confronting such specific issues as homosexuality, abortion, women's liberation, and women's ordination.[11]

On the subject of the evangelical support of evangelism and missions, Garrett observes the increasing leadership of Evangelicals in overseas missions, local evangelistic work, campus ministries, evangelistic and mission conferences, and the impressive impact they are making in the field of Christian education. He concludes his review with the following statement:

> Evangelical Christians in the United States, if unspoiled by their popularity and cultural accomodation during the 1970s and unrent by antagonisms and schisms over secondary issues, have with their common doctrinal affirmations, expanding ethical concerns, and unparallelled technology in communica-

---

[10]Above, p. 72.

[11]Above, p. 79.

tions, a significant evangelistic and missionary opportunity at the beginning of the 1980s.[12]

In his third chapter, entitled "Are Southern Baptists Evangelicals?," Dr. Garrett attempts to show that Southern Baptists fit into the pattern of Evangelicalism. It should go without saying that he rejects the idea that Southern Baptists agree with all other Evangelicals on every item of faith and practice. Nor does he deny that there is considerable diversity among Southern Baptists themselves. In an effort to delineate Southern Baptist character, he conducts a rather extensive historical review of Southern Baptist theological controversies. This review, Dr. Garrett says, "is an interpretation of the major Southern Baptist controversies and their consequences which will contribute to the answer to the question, 'Are Southern Baptists Evangelicals?' "[13]

In his very informative analysis, Dr. Garrett discusses the following topics: Southern Baptists have been "Calvinist rather than Arminian, but very moderately Calvinist"; "missionary, not antimissionary"; "denominational, but not Landmarkist"; "conservative rather than liberal in theology"; "cooperative as denominationalists, but not ecumenical"; "advocates of the primacy of a historical method instead of a symbolic method in interpreting the Bible."[14]

Since Dr. Garrett's immediate purpose in the historical review mentioned above is to show that Southern Baptists are Evangelicals, and to show what kind of Evangelicals they are, he does not undertake to expound the traditionally held distinctive features of Baptists, such as the Baptist insistence upon a regenerate church membership, believers' baptism, religious liberty, the self-government of the local church under God, and the like. In his reply to Dr. Garrett Dr. Hinson takes keen notice of these omissions.[15]

In his discussion of Southern Baptist theological conservatism on page 104, Dr. Garrett lists what he considers to have been the main features of the Southern Baptist theological outlook in the 1920s. I cite this passage below because I think it still indicates most of the main theological tenets espoused by the conservative wing of the Southern

---

[12]Above, p. 85.

[13]Above, p. 117.

[14]Above, pp. 89-117.

[15]Above, pp. 212-13.

Baptist Convention; also because it may be that these points characterize today many of the theological positions of a great segment of the family of American Evangelicals. Whether Dr. Garrett intended this juxtaposition I of course cannot say.

> Southern Baptists believed, preached, and taught the gospel of Jesus Christ as found in the inspired Scriptures of the Old and New Testaments. God the Father is transcendent as well as immanent; Jesus the Son is fully divine as well as human; and the Holy Spirit is divine yet indwells the believer. Human beings are both unique creatures of God and sinners in rebellion against God. Through the atoning death and triumphant resurrection of Jesus the one way of forgiveness and reconciliation has been provided by a gracious God, who accepts repentant believers, but not on the basis of their human achievements. God, who made anew believers, will continue to make them like Himself within the community of believers and will bring them to the heavenly consummation through the coming again of Jesus and the resurrection from the dead. The sharing of this gospel with all humanity in all the nations Southern Baptists regarded as the mandate of Jesus Christ, and to this task they were increasingly committed.[16]

Near the end of his third and last chapter, Dr. Garrett asks, "Can one accurately and properly affirm today that Southern Baptists are Evangelicals?"[17] He replies that he is convinced that the evidence he has gathered and shared with his readers warrants an affirmative answer. Southern Baptists, he says, are "denominational Evangelicals." "They belong to and exemplify the great heritage of Scriptural authority, Christocentric doctrine, gospel proclamation, experience of grace, and evangelistic endeavor which is Evangelicalism."[18]

Yet why is it important, in Dr. Garrett's opinion, that Southern Baptists identify themselves as Evangelicals? What difference does it make? We shall reserve an attempt to answer this question until, at the conclusion of this chapter, we shall make a brief comparison of the views of our two authors.

---

[16]Above, p. 104.

[17]Above, p. 126.

[18]Above, p. 126.

In setting forth some of Dr. Hinson's principal constructive arguments, I shall not follow his thought chapter by chapter, as I sought to do with Dr. Garrett. In order to look at some of his main ideas, which recur in different contexts in his several chapters, I shall attempt to follow a thematic approach.

While Dr. Garrett desires to show that Baptists are Evangelicals, the approach of Dr. Hinson is somewhat more complex. Hinson argues that there is an evangelical element in Baptist life, but that there is also a part of this life which is "other than" evangelical. The Baptist personality, he says, is made up of two dominant strains, the "evangelical" strain and the "voluntarist" strain. These two facets of Baptist history and life, he says, "have stood in tension with one another and frequently done battle."[19] From the evangelical side, he says,

> comes an intense commitment to the Great Commission, from the voluntarist a vigilance on behalf of religious liberty and the separation of church and state. If the two are not held in balance, and integrated in some way, our personality may split. If, for example, the evangelical note crowds out the voluntarist, "zeal for souls" may lead to total disregard for individual and corporate liberty to the point of employing physical or psychological coercion. . . . On the other hand, if voluntarism is carried to an extreme, it may generate indifference toward the divine claim upon human life and our responsibility for announcing that claim. How have Baptists, especially Southern Baptists, brought these together? How can we integrate them today?"[20]

His chief thesis, Dr. Hinson says, "will be that a balance between voluntarist and evangelical strains must be maintained if we are to remain true to our vocation as Baptists." In his second chapter Dr. Hinson undertakes to illustrate, in considerable detail, with reference to a number of periods in Baptist history, how and why the voluntarist-evangelical balance has been disrupted, often with serious damage to the Baptist cause.[21] At the present time, Dr. Hinson believes, it is the voluntarist side that is subject to the greatest jeopardy in Southern

---

[19]Above, p. 147.

[20]Above, pp. 147-48.

[21]Above, pp. 147-63.

Baptist life. The peril of this time, he thinks, is emanating from the evangelical quarter.[22] The crisis which Dr. Hinson perceives as gripping the Southern Baptist Convention now obviously stems from a militant fundamentalist contingent in the convention, which has operated during recent years with considerable success.

In the reading of Dr. Hinson's material, one discovers, I believe, that he uses the term "evangelical" in two senses. When he speaks in terms of maintaining an evangelical-voluntarist balance, he appears to be using the word "evangelical" in its wider, more historical sense, made familiar to us in Dr. Garrett's discussion. In this sense he claims that Baptists have been evangelicals, although even here he believes that Baptists belong on the evangelical "periphery."

The second sense in which he uses the term refers directly to Fundamentalists and their "descendants." When he refers to Evangelicals in the latter usage, he is concerned to differentiate Baptists sharply from this kind of Evangelicals. He admits that the Southern Baptist Convention has a large fundamentalist membership, but he affirms that Fundamentalism itself is an alien element in the Southern Baptist body. It is alien because of its heritage from medieval Scholasticism and its more recent roots in the Princeton-dispensationalist theology, its espousal of an orthodoxy which seeks to force its adherents into the same mold, and its consequent denial of religious freedom.

When Hinson seeks to identify the evangelical strain in the Southern Baptist tradition, he refers primarily, perhaps almost exclusively, to the denomination's historic, intense preoccupation with evangelism and missions. When he says that Baptists have been on the "periphery" of Evangelicalism, he differentiates and distinguishes Baptists from the evangelical penchant for "orthodoxy." Baptists and Evangelicals, he claims, sprang from "different wombs."

In declaring that Baptists dissent from evangelical "orthodoxy," and that Evangelicals and Baptists come from different "wombs," it appears that Hinson means to contrast the Fundamentalist heritage with the Baptist heritage. In this connection, Hinson gives us an illuminating passage on pages 166-67, which I quote below.

> Baptists and Evangelicals: What is the difference? Both of
> us go back to the Protestant Reformers. Both of us commit

---

[22]Above, p. 148.

ourselves to the Scriptures. Both of us have inherited a zeal for evangelical conversion. But make no mistake about it, we come from different wombs. Evangelicals are the descendants of the late sixteenth and early seventeenth century Scholastics. They are the children of English and American Millennialists and Fundamentalists of the late nineteenth and early twentieth centuries. As such, they let nothing stand above what they consider the objective Word of God found in the Scriptures.

Baptists, by contrast, are the descendants of the persecuted and harassed dissenters of the seventeenth century who came forth from the womb crying for liberty. They are the children of refugees who fled from the European continent to these shores to found here a society in which there would be no restriction of conscience, no stifling of freedom to propagate their faith, no circumscribing of faith or practice, and no religious test for public office. As such, they have insisted that faith is free and voluntary if it is to be genuine and responsible faith, that there is no objective word apart from uncoerced human response.

Again on page 166, Hinson expounds his view of the differences between Evangelicals and Baptists. Unlike Evangelicals, he says, Baptists reject the binding quality of the creedal statements of the Reformation and the principal works of seventeenth century Scholasticism. Instead, they have declared that the Scriptures alone are their only rule of faith and practice. While Evangelicals were rooted in "the theological continuity of Protestant orthodoxy," "the passion to be biblical," and "the goal of precision in theology," "Baptists were extracting from it a suspicion of orthodoxy, a penchant for dissent and nonconformity, and a passion for voluntarism in religion."

Hinson speaks of "orthodoxy" virtually always in disparaging terms. The orthodoxy with which he contends is a composite of Protestant Scholasticism, the Princeton theology of Charles Hodge and his successors, of Darbyite Dispensationalism, and consequently of the doctrine and spirit of Fundamentalism and its progeny. Much of the theology of this orthodoxy he does not agree with, but his main quarrel is with orthodoxy's association with creedalism, conformism, and coercion. He feels that orthodoxy's adherence to the "objective Word" of God is a threat to the freedom for which Baptists have stood, sometimes virtually alone.

To understand what Dr. Hinson means by the "objective Word" we must underscore the word "*objective*." It must be acknowledged that Hinson's term here is likely to convey an ambiguous impression. On the one hand he speaks of "the Scriptures alone" as the rule of faith and practice for our Baptist fathers.[23] In the Baptist tradition, he says, the Scriptures occupy a position of "centrality." The Bible is a "primary source" of Christian authority.[24] Secondary sources depend upon this primary source, and do not add anything essential to it.[25]

On the other hand, Baptists also have emphasized heavily the factor of Christian experience. One reason Baptists considered the Enlightenment as in some respects a friend during the colonial and early national period, Hinson believes, is that they appreciated the Enlightenment emphasis upon "experience in religion." Although the Evangelicals reckoned the great theologian Friedrich Schleiermacher (1768-1834) to be an enemy of orthodoxy, "Baptists could warmly respond to his emphasis upon "feeling" and his accentuation of "soul competency."[26]

On this point Dr. Garrett questions whether Dr. Hinson exalts the authority of Scripture over experience or of experience over Scripture. Dr. Garrett appears to believe that Dr. Hinson elevates experiential above biblical authority.[27]

As Dr. Garrett observes, Hinson acknowledges that Baptists historically have held to the principle of *sola Scriptura* (meaning that the Bible alone is our authority in religious matters). However, Hinson, with seeming inconsistency, later asserts the stand of Baptists to be identified with "that version of Christianity which places the priority of voluntary and uncoerced faith or response to the Word and Act of God over any supposed 'objective Word and Act of God'."[28]

Did Dr. Hinson here intend to oppose the authority of Scripture to the authority of Christian experience, affirming the latter to rank above

---

[23] Above, p. 139.

[24] Above, p. 140.

[25] Cf. above, p. 140.

[26] Above, p. 178.

[27] Above, pp. 202-203.

[28] Above, p. 173.

the former? Or did he mean that the "objective Word" is to be set over against what we might call the "appropriated, experienced Word," the Word of God taken to oneself as bread of life and lived through in experience? Perhaps the issue here is not whether experience ranks higher than Scripture, but whether Scripture has achieved its purpose without being received and believed, with heart as well as mind, and lived through.

Hinson would appear to mean by the term "objective Word" a Word which is made to be a heteronomous law, an outside, external creed imposed upon a person or persons, a rule to which assent is forced and to which persons must subscribe in accordance with an interpretation from which the interpreter permits no deviation.

Hinson evidently fears that a coercive bent has characterized many groups of Evangelicals, who seek to impose their own interpretations of Scripture upon others.[29] That this accords with his meaning is brought to light on page 182 of Dr. Hinson's discussion.

> For Evangelicals the Word has such an objective character that human beings can impose it by force, if necessary, on other human beings. For Baptists this cannot be so. Nothing handled by human beings can have such an objective character that we, fallible human beings, can presume to impose it on others. To be valid, our response must be voluntary. It can never be coerced. The Word itself will win us. But it will never coerce.

More specifically, Dr. Hinson fears the predilection of many Southern Baptists for forcing their own interpretations of Scripture upon the denomination. Most particularly, perhaps, he has in mind the militant Fundamentalists in the denomination who, like Dr. Harold Lindsell, would attempt to force Southern Baptists to subscribe to their theory of biblical "inerrancy."

Dr. Garrett's criticism on the relationship of Scripture to experience, however, helps to clarify an important issue. "Baptists," Dr. Garrett says, "both those who have affirmed *suprema Scriptura*, and those who have declared for *sola Scriptura*, have consistently placed the authority of the Bible above that of faith or religious experience."[30] Garrett adds: "Scrip-

---

[29]Cf. above, p. 182.

[30]Above, p. 203.

ture is not to be tested by experience, though it may indeed be confirmed in experience. Baptists therefore share some common ground with other Christians who hold the Scriptures in such an exalted place of authority."[31]

Although we have referred to Dr. Hinson's belief in "voluntarism" as the second facet of the "Baptist personality," perhaps we need to give it a more specific notice. Dr. Hinson appears to use the term "voluntarism" in two senses. In the first place, he means by the term, not that a person initiates his own salvation, but that the person is free to respond to God's overtures of grace. So voluntarism in this sense is what Hinson calls "the spontaneous assent of the human will to God."[32]

The second sense in which Hinson uses the term "voluntarism" he associates with religious liberty, which is correlated with the separation of church and state. While these two uses are intimately related, they are not necessarily identical. Hinson in his discussion here gives a preponderant attention to the first sense rather than to the second.

The model which Hinson claims for his understanding of voluntarism in the sense of a free, personal faith-response to God's grace is E. Y. Mullins's concept of the competency of the individual soul, under God.[33] Dr. Garrett challenges the supposition that Mullins meant the same thing that Hinson means—a challenge which we shall note without discussion here.[34] Garrett also asks whether Hinson means by voluntarism "the primacy of the will over the intellect (the philosophical usage) or the capability of human persons freely to initiate their appropriation of God's saving grace in Christ (the theological usage)."[35]

Garrett asks also whether by voluntarism Hinson really means "voluntaryism." Quoting Franklin Littell, Garrett describes voluntaryism as "the positive side of opposition to state interference in the affairs of the Church."[36] It refers also to the financial self-support of churches by their members without the help or interference of the government. This

---

[31]Above, p. 203.

[32]Above, p. 188.

[33]Above, pp. 136-38.

[34]Above, p. 196.

[35]Above, p. 197-98.

[36]Above, p. 227.

understanding of "voluntaryism" would characterize the kind of religious liberty which involves the separation of church and state.

Dr. Garrett sees voluntarism in the sense of an unconstrained human faith decision, however, as a more complex problem in its application to Baptist history.[37] It involves, he thinks, a judgment about the ancient debate in Christian circles between the advocates of free will and the advocates of divine sovereignty. Augustine argued against Pelagius that God's grace is irresistible and prevenient, a position which entailed the conclusion that God's action is required to enable the human will to accept his grace, and that this grace is irresistible to persons to whom God chooses to grant it.

A similar position was held by Luther and Calvin, and it was from the Calvinists particularly that the debate entered the early Baptist community. Calvinistic Baptists championed predestination, and General Baptists advocated free will. So deeply did the doctrine of particular election (God chooses some persons, not others, for salvation) and limited atonement (Christ died only for the elect) enter Baptist life that for many years a large part of the Baptist family in England and America during the eighteenth century became rigidly double-predestinarian. Voluntarism in the sense of free will, then, in the convictions of these Calvinistic Baptists, could hardly be assumed to be a dominant factor in the Baptist personality.

The above seems to be the argument which Dr. Garrett is making with respect to Dr. Hinson's case for voluntarism. Garrett does not propose to settle this ancient debate, but he does chide Dr. Hinson for not bringing it into the orbit of his discussion, and for apparently assuming that voluntarism has always been an indigenous factor in Baptist life.

Dr. Garrett concedes that both Particular (Calvinist) and General (Arminian) Baptists have traditionally championed religious liberty— that is, the right of the church to be free from the interference of the state in religious matters, and the right of the human soul to deal personally with God without the coercion of state, of church, or of any other institution or individual.[38] On the other hand, Dr. Hinson declares that Baptists have been both voluntarists and voluntaryists. "Though Baptists," he says, "would also identify with 'voluntaryism,' they would do so

---

[37]Cf. above, pp. 196-99.

[38]Cf. above, p. 228.

because of their voluntarism. For our forebears the main concern was freedom to obey God rather than human beings."[39]

In concluding this chapter, it would seem to me to be of particular interest to determine why each of our authors takes the particular position which he has taken in this exchange. Dr. Garrett is avowedly desirous of including Southern Baptists in the ranks of Evangelicals. It appears that he emphasizes that Baptists are Evangelicals, first, because he thinks that the facts dictate this assignation; secondly, because he wants Baptists to identify with the best side of a great heritage which in a broad but accurate sense, he feels, can and should be called the "evangelical" heritage. Perhaps the best statement which he makes on the question of "why" is found in an eloquent passage near the close of his reply to Dr. Hinson.

Dr. Garrett specifies that it may be necessary to differentiate the "historic and more comprehensive usage" of the term 'Evangelical' from the usage which Fundamentalists have made of it, and that this differentiation may be particularly necessary for Southern Baptists. The issue which is at stake, however, concerns the self-understanding of Baptists, and the response which they make to the challenge of their mission and ministry in the world today.[40] Dr. Garrett's understanding as to why Southern Baptists should recognize themselves as Evangelicals is worth quoting in its totality.

> Will Southern Baptists break out of their cultural or regional or class or racial captivity to model an authentic (that is, biblical) and aggressive (that is, evangelistic) form of Christianity at the end of the twentieth century? Will Southern Baptist churches that have vast resources in buildings, church staffs, and trained and increasingly affluent members be willing and able to minister to the hurts and frustrations of the broken, the infirm, the lonely, the poor, the refugee, the immigrant, the factory worker, the egghead, and the up-and-out, and point these to Jesus Christ? Will older Southern Baptist churches, replete with tradition but located amid changed socioeconomic and ethnic patterns, come to new life and follow new forms of ministry that are consonant with the abiding gospel? Will Southern Baptists cherish and hold to the Bible and the gospel or be ensnared by the acclaim of the cultic,

---

[39]Above, p. 213.

[40]Above, p. 206.

the tinkle of prosperity, the lure of the liturgical, or the danger of dialogue? Will the Southern Baptist preacher and the Southern Baptist church member rediscover the authority of the Bible, the Chrisocentrism of the gospel, and the coessentiality of witness by word and witness by life? Will Southern Baptists be in reality conformed to the present age or be transformed as pilgrim people on their way to the City of God? Will a few million Southern Baptists live for themselves and for their ease and comfort or as responsible stewards for the billions of the earth for whom Jesus died and rose again? Will Bold Mission Thrust be only a denominational slogan, rich in rhetoric and profusely promoted, or also our way of describing the "mighty work and a wonder" which God—Father, Son, and Holy Spirit—has accomplished among us and through us?[41]

Who we understand ourselves to be, Dr. Garrett declares, affects how we live, how we minister, and how we proclaim the gospel. For Southern Baptists to take their place self-consciously in the best traditions of Evangelicalism, Dr. Garrett feels, will greatly help them to make the right responses to the questions he has asked in the passage quoted above.

To ask why Dr. Hinson makes his particular stand relative to Baptist self-identification may seem superfluous at this point, because he asserts his central position clearly, repeatedly, and with emphatic feeling. There are many outside dangers which threaten our world, the world Christian community, and the Baptist fellowship. All of this Dr. Hinson certainly recognizes. In his contribution to this book, however, Dr. Hinson's overriding concern relates to the threat to Southern Baptists which arises in the Baptist fellowship itself. It is a threat to the freedom which Baptists have cherished throughout their history, a threat posed by militant Fundamentalists inside the Baptist community who wish to seize the reins of power within the Southern Baptist Convention, impose their own interpretations upon the Southern Baptist larger community, especially upon its agencies and institutions, most especially upon its institutions of higher education, and to shape the whole program of Southern Baptists into the mold of fundamentalist conformism. Hinson's message is a call to Southern Baptists to man the ramparts of freedom, to allow

---

[41]Above, pp. 207-208.

latitude for a wholesome diversity within the framework of genuine Christian dedication, while at the same time cherishing and practicing the distinguishing principles which make us Baptists.

On pages 131 and 132 of his discussion we touch the nerve of his principal concern. Dr. Hinson says,

> the current crisis has been triggered by the effort of some to equate the term "Baptist," particularly "Southern Baptist," with "Fundamentalist" or "Evangelical." Belief in biblical inerrancy, according to this group, is the chief test point. . . . It [the crisis] has less to do with defense of the Bible than with the effort of certain persons to set themselves up as the inerrant and infallible interpreters of the Bible and guides to Baptist orthodoxy. . . . Fundamentalism is a mentality which says, "I am right and only those who agree with me can be right or Christian or Baptist!" Where such an attitude prevails, we have little hope of discovering who we are as Southern Baptists.

Whether you agree with one of our writers in this book or the other, or neither, it seems to me that one cannot read this joint discussion without realizing that he or she has received a probing, instructive lesson in Baptist history and the Baptist heritage. The work is searching and provocative. Neither writer, of course, has said the last word on the subjects discussed. The "debate" does not close the discussion or settle an argument. It helps to open an area for continued exploration. It is a salutary invitation to Southern Baptists to consider more deeply issues which are vital to their character, their heritage, their mission, and their freedom. It would be healthy for the denomination if its subject matter were debated incisively and open-mindedly. But, more importantly, we may hope that it will help to focus the minds of thoughtful Southern Baptists upon some of the most demanding issues of our denominational life. The book is sent forth upon its career with the hope and prayer that we may think together about our faith, that we may work together in a climate of brotherliness which, without concealing our differences or minimizing their importance, will allow us to debate them with mature understanding and sagacious vision, so that in the overarching fellowship of Christ we may appreciate keenly the precious heritage which we have in being Baptists.

Selected Bibliography

Bloesch, Donald G. *The Evangelical Renaissance*. Grand Rapids: William B. Eerdmans Publishing Company, 1973.

An assessment of the "new evangelicalism" and a setting forth of the hypothesis that Fundamentalism represented "a union of scholastic orthodoxy" and "latter-day Pietism" of "both premillennial and perfectionistic strands."

Dollar, George W. *A History of Fundamentalism in America*. Greenville, SC: Bob Jones University Press, 1973.

A study written from the perspective of militant, hostile Fundamentalism which reflects antipathy toward the Southern Baptist Convention, its churches and its people.

Falwell, Jerry, editor, with Ed Dodson and Ed Hindson. *The Fundamentalist Phenomenon: The Resurgence of Conservative Christianity*. Garden City, NY: Doubleday and Company, Inc., 1981.

A book that mixes church history with the advocacy of the positions being advanced by Moral Majority, Inc., and is designed to answer Falwell's critics, both from exclusivistic or "reactionary Fundamentalism" and from "drifting Evangelicalism."

Garrett, James Leo, Jr., editor. *Baptist Relations with Other Christians*. Valley Forge, PA: Judson Press, 1974.

Reports by seventeen authors as to how present-day Baptists throughout the world do or do not relate to other Christians, either in conciliar ecumenism or in evangelical ecumenism.

Harrell, David Edwin, Jr., editor. *Varieties of Southern Evangelicalism*. Macon, GA: Mercer University Press, 1981.

Six essays, of which those by Martin E. Marty and Samuel S. Hill, Jr., are most relevant to the subject of this book.

Hinson, E. Glenn. "Southern Baptists: A Concern for Experiential Conversion," in Martin E. Marty, editor, *Where the Spirit Leads: American Denominations Today*. Atlanta: John Knox Press, 1980. Pp. 137-48.

An interpretation of diverse Southern Baptists which finds the denominational *raison d'être* to be the Great Commission and their supreme task to be missions and evangelism.

Hutcheson, Richard G., Jr. *Mainline Churches and the Evangelicals: A Challenging Crisis?* Atlanta: John Knox Press, 1981.

A thoughtful analysis of the growth of Evangelicalism within mainline denominations and its implications for church programs.

Kelley, Dean M. *Why Conservative Churches Are Growing: A Study in Sociology of Religion*. New York: Harper and Row, 1972.

A study of the numerical expansion of conservative churches in the United States and the lack of the same among mainline Protestant churches, written by the director for civil and religious liberty of the National Council of Churches.

Lindsell, Harold. *The Battle for the Bible.* Grand Rapids: Zondervan Publishing House, 1976.

——————. *The Bible in the Balance.* Grand Rapids: Zondervan Publishing House, 1979.

These volumes deal with the contemporary issue of biblical inerrancy; each contains a chapter on the Southern Baptist Convention.

Lumpkin, William L. *Baptist Foundations in the South.* Nashville: Broadman Press, 1961.

An illuminating contribution to the study of the character of Baptists in the South.

Marsden, George M. *Fundamentalism and American Culture: The Shaping of Twentieth Century Evangelicalism, 1870-1925.* New York: Oxford University, 1980.

A classic on the origins and development of "Evangelicalism" in the United States.

Marty, Martin E. *The Public Church: Mainline—Evangelical—Catholic.* New York: Crossroad, 1981.

A depiction of American church life by a leading observer of American religious life.

Mullins, E. Y. *The Axioms of Religion: A New Interpretation of the Baptist Faith.* Philadelphia: Griffith and Rowland Press, 1908.

The influential effort of a past president of Southern Baptist Theological Seminary to establish the chief features of the Baptist tradition.

Quebedeaux, Richard. *The Worldly Evangelicals.* New York: Harper and Row, 1978.

A sequel to the author's *The Young Evangelicals* (1974), this volume somewhat comprehensively describes contemporary Evangelicals of the right, center, and left, and places the Southern Baptist Convention among the Evangelical denominations of the right and center.

Ramm, Bernard. *The Evangelical Heritage.* Waco, TX: Word Books, 1973.

A carefully constructed historical study of the development of Evangelicalism from the Protestant Reformation to the present.

Shurden, Walter B. *Not a Silent People: Controversies That Have Shaped Southern Baptists.* Nashville: Broadman Press, 1972.

A brief and popular, yet insightful treatment.

Wells, David F. and John D. Woodbridge, editors. *The Evangelicals: What They Believe, Who They Are, Where They Are Changing.* Revised edition. Grand Rapids: Baker Book House, 1977.

Thirteen carefully documented essays; the one by Robert D. Linder treats the role of Southern Baptists in the reawakening of "the evangelical social conscience."

Index of Persons

MP ARE SOUTHERN BAPTISTS "EVANGELICALS"?

Composition was by Omni Composition Services, Macon, Georgia
    designed by Margaret Brown
        the text was typeset in Garamond and Korinna on an Addressograph
            Multigraph Comp/Set phototypesetter 5404, and paginated
            on an A/M Comp/Set 4510.

Production specifications:
    text paper—60 pound Warren's Olde Style
    endpapers—Multicolor Antique, Thistle
    cover (on .088 boards)—Holliston Roxite B 51548
    jacket—100 pound offset enamel, printed two colors, PMS 300
        blue and PMS 343 green, and varnished

Printing (offset lithography) by Omnipress, Inc., Macon, Georgia
Binding by John H. Dekker and Sons, Inc., Grand Rapids, Michigan